Shari'a Compliant Equity Investments

Rizwan Malik

Shari'a Compliant Equity Investments

The Development and Benefits of Shari'a Screening Methodologies

palgrave
macmillan

Rizwan Malik
Head of Islamic Finance Centre
Bahrain Institute of Banking
and Finance
Manama, Bahrain

ISBN 978-3-031-70821-3 ISBN 978-3-031-70822-0 (eBook)
https://doi.org/10.1007/978-3-031-70822-0

This Palgrave Macmillan imprint is published by the registered company Springer Nature Switzerland AG
The registered company address is: Gewerbestrasse 11, 6330 Cham, Switzerland

To my beloved parents, in particular my dad (Abu ji).

Without him, who am I!!

Foreword

The Islamic banking and finance industry has developed significantly over the last four decades, reaching a size of more than USD 4.5 trillion. Today, there are over 2,000 institutions operating in no less than 75 countries around the world offering Islamic banking and finance services. The banking sector has developed and grown faster than the capital markets and other sectors, with more than 75 per cent of the Islamic finance assets held in the Islamic banking sector. This development of the sector is a recent phenomenon, as Islamic banking and finance was once of insignificant size, with most activities witnessed in the Gulf Cooperation Council (GCC) and the Far East.

The advent of the internet has transformed the global economy, making it increasingly interconnected. This has led to a significant growth in the demand for financial products and services that align with Islamic principles. This trend was driven not only by the rising affluence of Muslim consumers, but also a broader societal shift towards more ethical and sustainable investing. One such demand was the need to invest in the stock market in line with Shari'a principles and rules.

As a Shari'a scholar, I had the privilege of engaging in extensive discussions with various stakeholders, particularly the tech-savvy younger generation, to deeply understand this challenge. To address this need, a select group of Shari'a scholars, of which I was a part, collaborated with the Dow Jones Islamic Market Index (DJIMI) to develop the first comprehensive Shari'a screening methodology. This provided clear guidance to ensure Shari'a sensitive investors could participate in the stock market without engaging in prohibited activities, while generating returns in accordance with Islamic principles.

The development of the DJIMI was a pioneering endeavour that has since paved the way for the growth of Islamic finance and investment products globally. As one of the Shari'a scholars involved in this initiative, I am proud to have contributed to this important milestone in the evolution of the industry.

Since then, Shari'a-compliant equity investments have emerged as a key component of the Islamic finance ecosystem. Many index providers, fund managers, banks, and infrastructure organisations have issued different screening methodologies. By applying rigorous screening criteria to identify suitable stocks and funds, these investment strategies provide Muslim investors with a way to deploy their capital in a manner that is faithful to their religious and moral values, while also offering attractive risk-return profiles that can appeal to a wider audience of socially conscious investors.

However, navigating the complexities of Shari'a-compliant equities is no easy feat. The criteria for determining Shari'a compliance are multifaceted, encompassing not just the core business activities of a company, but also its financial structures, ownership, and management practices. Keeping abreast of the evolving landscape of Shari'a-compliant investing, including the latest fatwas, industry standards, and investment products, requires a deep understanding of Islamic jurisprudence as well as financial acumen.

This book aims to serve as an invaluable resource in this regard. The authors have drawn upon their extensive experience in Islamic finance to create a comprehensive and accessible guide to Shari'a-compliant equity investing. They delve into the theological underpinnings of Islamic investing, explaining the key principles and prohibitions that frame this approach. Importantly, they then translate these theoretical concepts into practical investment strategies, offering detailed frameworks for stock selection, portfolio construction, and risk management.

Particularly noteworthy are the real-world case studies and insights from industry experts and scholars that are woven throughout the book. These provide readers with a window into how Shari'a-compliant equity investing is being implemented on the ground, surfacing the challenges, innovations, and best practices that are shaping this rapidly evolving field.

This book is of particular interest to stakeholders who have highlighted the shortcomings of existing screening methodologies and the need for enhanced screening methodologies. In the light of the various developments in the Islamic banking and finance industry and the enhanced availability of Islamic financing and investment opportunities, the book, with the help of various scholars and practitioners, aims to understand and advocate for various enhancements that can be integrated within the existing screening methodologies. Additionally, the book also tests the practicality of some of the suggested enhancements and provides policy recommendations.

Whether you are a Muslim investor seeking to align your portfolio with your faith, a finance professional looking to serve the burgeoning Islamic wealth management market, or simply someone interested in the intersection of ethics and investing, this book is an essential read. It equips you with the knowledge and tools needed to make informed decisions and capitalise on the tremendous growth potential of Shari'a-compliant equities.

In doing so, it advances the cause of ethical and socially responsible finance—an imperative not just for the Muslim community, but for all who wish to build a more sustainable global financial system. I have no doubt that this book will make a valuable contribution to this important endeavour.

Kingdom of Bahrain — Sheikh Nedham Yaquby

Preface

From a theoretical perspective, Islamic banking and finance is different from conventional banking and finance because interest (*riba*) is prohibited in Islam. The unique features of Islamic banking and finance is its profit-and-loss sharing (PLS) paradigm coupled with emphasis on risk sharing and ethical investments. As such, the equity stock market mechanism follows this unique PLS paradigm without the involvement of *riba*, gharar and maysir, allowing *Shari'a* sensitive investors' access to the stock market. But the problem is to identify the *Shari'a*-compliant equity stocks (that are both *Shari'a* compliant in the capital structure and the underlying business) within the equity stock market. In order to assist the *Shari'a* sensitive investors, the Dow Jones Islamic Market Index (DJIMI) for the first time in history issued the first *Shari'a* screening methodology in 1999 that facilitated access to the stock market. Subsequently, a number of other *Shari'a* screening methodologies were developed by other index providers, banks and regulators; all of them are derivatives of the DJIMI. The rules used in the screening process have not originated from the Holy Quran or the traditions of the Prophet Muhammad *(PBUH)*, and accordingly are not considered absolute rules. These screening methodologies have been criticised in the literature for being imprecise, inconsistent, lacking credibility and on the use of *Shari'a* screening thresholds restricting the *Shari'a* non-compliant activities.

The book is designed to address two main areas: to examine the historical developments of *Shari'a* screening methodologies to date and to investigate how the existing *Shari'a* screening methodologies can be enhanced for the benefit of the Islamic banking and finance (IBF) industry. A qualitative analysis and a statistical technique of exploratory factor analysis (EFA) are carried out in to achieve the objectives of this book.

It is anticipated that via this book the readers would be able to understand the 360 degrees of *Shari'a*-compliant equity investments and would comprehend the reforms required in this regard.

Manama, Bahrain Rizwan Malik

Acknowledgments

First and foremost, I thank Allah SWT for His countless blessings, including the opportunity to bring this book to fruition. I am deeply thankful to my parents, brothers and sisters, and in-laws; your constant belief in my abilities and enduring support have been invaluable. To my wife and kids, your unwavering love and encouragement have been my greatest motivation.

I am especially grateful to my mentor, Prof. Dr. Humayon Dar, whose guidance and wisdom have profoundly shaped my understanding of the field. I would also like to thank Dr. Aishath Muneeza, Dr. Mohamed Nurullah, Dr. Mehmet Asutay, Sh. Kamran Sherwani, Sh. Khalid Al Yahmadi and many others, for their support, encouragement, and insights that enriched this work.

A special thanks to Rahman, Rizwan, Baaj, and Bushra, whose camaraderie and encouragement have been a source of strength. I am grateful to my team at the Islamic Finance Centre at BIBF for their support and resources.

I would also like to acknowledge my colleagues at AAOIFI, ASAAS, and Cambridge IFA for their collaboration and friendships. My sincere thanks go to Dr. Ahmad Al Shaikh, CEO of BIBF for his guidance and support.

To all who have contributed in any way, thank you for being part of this journey. Your support has made this book possible.

PRAISE FOR *SHARI'A COMPLIANT EQUITY INVESTMENTS*

"I found this book on Shari'a-compliant equities to be an invaluable resource for both beginners and seasoned investors. The author expertly demystifies the principles of Shari'ah finance and equity investments providing clear guidelines and practical examples that make it easy to understand. The insights into the sector not only aim to broaden the perspective but also empower to make informed decisions that align with the underlying values driven by Shari'a. Highly recommended for anyone looking to navigate the world of Shari'ah-compliant investments!"

—Adnan Ahmed Yousif, *Chairman, Bahrain Association of Banks and Former President and CEO of Al Baraka Banking Group*

"I am pleased to endorse this insightful book on Islamic equity investments. Having had the privilege of working closely with Dr. Rizwan Malik, I can attest to his dedication and passion for advancing knowledge in this vital field. This work not only provides a thorough analysis of Shari'ah-compliant equity markets but also reflects his commitment to excellence.

At BIBF, I have witnessed firsthand the impact of his research and contributions to Islamic finance. This book serves as a valuable resource for both academics and practitioners, offering practical insights that can drive the industry forward. I wholeheartedly support Dr. Rizwan Malik's endeavors and highly recommend this book to anyone interested in understanding the complexities of Islamic equity investments."

—Dr. Ahmad Al Shaikh, *CEO, Bahrain Institute of Banking and Finance (BIBF)*

"This comprehensive book is a remarkable contribution to the field of Islamic finance, particularly in the area of equity investment. The author's thorough exploration of both the theoretical and applied aspects of this topic sets this work apart from many others that tend to focus solely on the theoretical foundations. The in-depth examination of the historical evolution of Shari'a-compliant screening methodologies provides readers with a valuable contextual understanding, enabling them to appreciate the significant efforts and ijtihadic views that have shaped the development of this crucial aspect of Islamic investing. Furthermore, the author's incorporation of qualitative analysis and statistical techniques, such as exploratory factor analysis, adds a layer of analytical rigor and practical relevance to the book. This work is a must-read for anyone seeking a comprehensive and insightful understanding of the art of investing in Shari'a-compliant equities."

—Sh. Dr. Mohamed A. Elgari, *Renowned Shari'ah Scholar*

"Investment in equities is one of the important elements in Islamic finance. Much research and articles have been conducted in this area and this book is one of the unique pieces that investigate this topic in a comprehensive matter. Many writings focus more on the theoretical aspects of equity investment and neglect the most important aspects that is the applied aspects. From my reading of this book, I found out that it has comprehensively covered the theoretical and applied aspects related to equity investment particularly the area related to equity screenings. The historical evolution of Shari'a compliant was also discussed and readers can obtained interesting insights on how the evolution processes in the development of comprehensive screening methodologies and the efforts that were put in by the Shari'a scholars and practitioners in come up with interesting ijtihadic views to allow the investment in equities. What is also interesting in this book is that it has deployed the qualitative analysis and statistical technique of exploratory factor analysis (EFA) in order to achieve the objectives of this book. Finally, I would like to congratulate the author for this wonderful work and this book is a must-read for those who would like to understand the art of investing in Shari'ah compliant equities."

—Datuk Sh Dr Akram Laldin, *Shari'ah Advisor*

"It is with great pride that I endorse this exceptional book on Islamic equity investments, authored by my former student and colleague. This work represents a significant contribution to the field, offering a comprehensive analysis of Shari'a-compliant equity markets and the methodologies that govern them. The author's meticulous research and thoughtful insights not only illuminate the complexities of Islamic finance but also provide practical guidance for both practitioners and scholars. I am thrilled to see such a vital resource come to fruition and highly recommend it to anyone interested in the future of Islamic equity investments."

—Prof. Dr. Humayon Dar, *Director General, Cambridge Institute of Islamic Finance*

"When we launched the Dow Jones Islamic Market Index in 1999, it put faith-based negative screening and three financial ratios, thematic investing with more transparency, on the radar of global investors. After a few years, I recognized the limitation of negative screens, as it did not capture the sustainability movement (positive screening), created biases (overweighting) for certain sectors, like Technology, and resulted in very few compliant companies in Muslim-majority countries with stock exchanges.

The PhD from a practitioner and insider of IBF, Dr Rizwan Malik, is timely as it raises these challenging issues as we look ahead to the next 25 years of Shari'ah-compliant equity investing. Islamic investing must be part of the sustainability/ESG mega-trend movement, and, where required, possibly provide leadership. This is an extremely important issue for the conscientious younger generation of Muslims, which dominates demographics in the Muslim world.

The screening 2.0 must continue to align itself with the principles of Shari'a, as interpreted by our scholars, but must be cognizant of keeping Muslim money in Muslim countries, and address capital flight. The exposure to global compliant sustainability companies, to companies listed in Muslim majority countries, including listed Islamic banks and Takaful operators, etc., is a needed disruption to stay relevant. Furthermore, if the performance of 2.0 screening provides, at minimum, market returns over a market cycle, you will see, from non-Muslim world, more/long-term flows into such financial investment schemes off of such Islamic indexes."

—Rushdi Siddiqui, *Founder, Dow Jones Islamic Market Index (DJIMI)*

"This book on Islamic equity investments is a remarkable achievement that reflects both dedication and expertise. As a friend and colleague, I have witnessed the author's commitment to exploring the complexities of Shari'a-compliant equity markets. The thorough research and practical insights presented in this work provide invaluable guidance for both practitioners and scholars. I am excited to see how this book will contribute to the understanding and growth of Islamic finance. I wholeheartedly recommend it to anyone interested in this vital field."

—Sh. Kamran Sherwani, *Head of Internal Shari'ah Control, ADCB Islamic*

"As Islamic finance continues to expand globally, this book stands out as a vital resource for both academics and practitioners. This book offers a deep dive into the critical role of Shari'a screening methodologies, exploring their evolution and how they shape the Islamic banking and finance industry today. With a thoughtful blend of historical analysis, practical insights, and forward-thinking recommendations, it fills a significant gap in the literature. I highly recommend this book for anyone looking to gain a deeper understanding of Shari'a-compliant investments and their future potential."

—Prof. Dr. Aishath Muneeza, *Associate Dean, INCEIF University*

"This book is an important and thorough contribution on an under-researched topic of growing importance. Shari'a-compliant finance has become a systemically important segment of financial services in many economically dynamic emerging markets while serving as an effective driver of stability and socio-economic inclusion. The continuing dynamism of the industry amid rapid economic and technological change is critical for ensuring that capital is allocated ever more efficiently while safeguarding the core advantages of a principles-based financial paradigm."

—Dr. Jarmo Kotilaine, *Economic Advisor, Tamkeen*

Contents

1 Introduction 1
1.1 Background of the Book 2
1.2 Research Aims, Objectives and Research Questions 6
1.3 The Rationale and Significance of the Book 7
1.4 Overview of the Book 8
References 11

2 A Review of Islamic Finance 13
2.1 Financial System 14
2.2 Islamic Finance 15
2.3 Principles of Islamic Finance 15
2.4 Islamic Financial Instruments 20
Brief Overview of the Historical Development of Islamic Banking and Finance 21
Overview of the Global Developments in Islamic Banking and Finance 25
2.5 Size and Growth of Islamic Banking and Finance 29
References 31

3 Islamic Equity Investments 33
3.1 Introduction 33
3.2 Historical Development 34
3.3 Shari'a *Legitimacy of Shares and Joint Stock Companies* 35
Joint-Stock Company and Shari'a 37

Concept of Share 42
3.4 *Trading in Equity Shares* 43
Treatment of Companies Involved in Mixed Businesses 46
3.5 Shari'a *Screening for Equity Investments* 48
Business Screening 49
Financial Screening 53
Purification Requirements 62
3.6 *Issues Within Existing* Shari'a *Screening Methodologies* 63
Imprecision 64
Standardisation 65
Credibility 67
Financial Screening and Tolerance Thresholds 68
Socially Responsible Principles and Shari'a Screening Methodologies 71
3.7 *Research Focus* 75
References 77

4 Methodology and Data 81
4.1 *Introduction* 81
4.2 *Research Design* 81
4.3 *Research Methods* 85
The Qualitative Research Method 85
The Quantitative Research Method 99
4.4 *Concluding Remarks* 117
References 118

5 A Review of the History and Existing Practices of the *Shari'a* Screening 121
5.1 *Introduction* 121
5.2 *Data Analysis* 122
History of Shari'a-Compliant *Screening Methodologies and How and Why They Were Introduced and Rationale Behind the Use of the Screening Thresholds* 122
5.3 *Results Discussion* 162
History of Shari'a-Compliant *Screening Methodologies, How and Why They Were Introduced; and Rationale Behind the Use of the Screening Thresholds* 162
5.4 *Conclusion* 188
References 192

6 **Enhancing the *Shari'a* Screening Methodologies: An Empirical Analysis** 193
6.1 Introduction 193
6.2 Research Analysis 1 194
Nasdaq 100 194
S&P 500 197
FTSE 100 200
6.3 Research Analysis 2 214
Data Analysis 216
Islamic Banking and Finance (IBF) Index 226
Shari'a *Screening and Development in IBF* 232
Proposed New Screening Thresholds 235
6.4 Conclusion 249
References 251

7 **Conclusion** 253
7.1 Introduction 253
7.2 Reflections and Findings of the Book 254
7.3 Policy Recommendations 258
7.4 Conclusion 259
References 260

References 261

Index 271

Acronyms

AAOIFI	Accounting and Auditing Organisation for Islamic Financial Institutions
AUM	Assets under Management
CIBAFI	General Council for Islamic Banks and Financial Institutions
DFU	Deficit Funds Units
DJIMI	Dow Jones Islamic Market Index
EFA	Exploratory Factor Analysis
FTSE	Financial Times Stock Exchange
GCC	Gulf Cooperation Council
IBF	Islamic Banking and Finance
IFSB	Islamic Financial Services Board
IIBR	Islamic Inter Bank Offer Rate
IIFM	International Islamic Financial Market
IIRA	International Islamic Rating Agency
IMF	International Monetary Fund
IPO	Initial Public Offering
ISRA	International Shari'ah Research Academy
LMC	Liquidity Management Centre
MSCI	Morgan Stanley Capital International
OIC	Organisation of the Islamic Conference
OTC	Over the Counter
PSX	Pakistan Stock Exchange
SEC	Securities and Exchange Commission
SFU	Surplus Funds Units
SRI	Socially Responsible Investments
SSB	Shari'a Supervisory Board

List of Figures

Fig. 2.1	A financial system (*Source* Sandhya. Ch. V.L—Indian Financial System)	16
Fig. 2.2	Principles of Islamic finance (*Source* Zamir Iqbal [1997])	19
Fig. 2.3	Types of Islamic financial contracts	23
Fig. 2.4	Size and growth of Islamic banking and finance between 2008 and 2012 (US$billion) (Adapted from GIFR [2023])	30
Fig. 3.1	Growth in Assets Under Management of Islamic Funds (2008–2023) (*Source* IFSB estimates based on data from Refinitiv for 2019–2023, including Iran. Data for the years 2008–18 from bloomberg database as per previous reports (excluding Iran due to data limitations))	35
Fig. 3.2	Islamic Fund Assets by Asset Class (2023) (*Source* IFSB estimates based on data from Refinitiv; Islamic Finance Services Board Stability Report 2024)	36
Fig. 4.1	Conceptual framework (Own compilation)	84
Fig. 4.2	Post-execution activities in the interviews process	94
Fig. 4.3	Research book outcome	117

Fig. 5.1 Historical background of *Shari'a* screening methodologies (*Source* Malik, R., Dar, H. and Muneeza, A. (2024), "Reforms required for Shariah screening of equities using the case study of Dow Jones Islamic market index (DJIMI)", *International Journal of Law and Management*, Vol. ahead-of-print No. ahead-of-print. https://doi.org/10.1108/IJLMA-08-2023-0171) 168
Fig. 5.2 *Shari'a-compliant* screening process (*Source* Malik, R., Dar, H. and Muneeza, A. (2024), "Reforms required for Shariah screening of equities using the case study of Dow Jones Islamic market index (DJIMI)", *International Journal of Law and Management*, Vol. ahead-of-print No. ahead-of-print. https://doi.org/10.1108/IJLMA-08-2023-0171) 170
Fig. 5.3 *Shari'a* Screening Process and issues (*Source* Malik, R., Dar, H. and Muneeza, A. (2024), "Reforms required for Shariah screening of equities using the case study of Dow Jones Islamic market index (DJIMI)", *International Journal of Law and Management*, Vol. ahead-of-print No. ahead-of-print. https://doi.org/10.1108/IJLMA-08-2023-0171) 171
Fig. 5.4 Socially responsible investments and *Shari'a* screening methodologies (*Source* Malik, R., Dar, H. and Muneeza, A. (2024), "Reforms required for Shariah screening of equities using the case study of Dow Jones Islamic market index (DJIMI)", *International Journal of Law and Management*, Vol. ahead-of-print No. ahead-of-print. https://doi.org/10.1108/IJLMA-08-2023-0171) 180
Fig. 5.5 Purification (*Source* Malik, R., Dar, H. and Muneeza, A. (2024), "Reforms required for Shariah screening of equities using the case study of Dow Jones Islamic market index (DJIMI)", *International Journal of Law and Management*, Vol. ahead-of-print No. ahead-of-print. https://doi.org/10.1108/IJLMA-08-2023-0171) 183

Fig. 5.6	Future screening and research (*Source* Malik, R., Dar, H. and Muneeza, A. (2024), "Reforms required for Shariah screening of equities using the case study of Dow Jones Islamic market index (DJIMI)", *International Journal of Law and Management*, Vol. ahead-of-print No. ahead-of-print. https://doi.org/10.1108/IJLMA-08-2023-0171)	186
Fig. 6.1	Islamic finance growth projection (*Source* Islamic Finance Development Indicator Report 2024)	221
Fig. 6.2	Islamic financial assets and No. of IFIs (*Source* Islamic Finance Development Indicator Report 2024)	222
Fig. 6.3	Islamic banking assets and No. of Islamic banks and windows	222
Fig. 6.4	Takaful assets	223
Fig. 6.5	Sukuk outstanding	224
Fig. 6.6	Value of Islamic funds	225
Fig. 6.7	Screen plot—PCA	228
Fig. 6.8	Grouping of variables into four factors	230
Fig. 6.9	Rankings of countries based on IBF index	231

List of Tables

Table 2.1	*Shari'a-compliant* instruments	22
Table 2.2	Overview of the global developments in IBF	26
Table 3.1	*Shari'a-compliant* screening methodologies	59
Table 4.1	IBF index variables and description	106
Table 5.1	List of codes	123
Table 5.2a	Data analysis for interview questions 1	126
Table 5.2b	Focused coding no.1 for interview questions 1	128
Table 5.2c	Focused coding no.2 for research questions 1	129
Table 5.2d	Focused coding no.3 for interview question 1	130
Table 5.2e	Focused coding no.4 for interview question 1	131
Table 5.2f	Focused coding no.5 for interview questions 1	133
Table 5.2g	Focused coding no.6 for interview questions 1	134
Table 5.3a	Data analysis for interview question 2	135
Table 5.3b	Focused coding no. 1 business screening for interview questions 2	138
Table 5.3c	Focused coding no. 2 data analysis of financial screening for interview question 2	140
Table 5.3d	Focused coding no. 3 data analysis liquidity ratio for interview question 2	141
Table 5.3e	Focused coding no.4 data analysis for interest income for interview question 2	142
Table 5.3f	Focused coding no.5 data analysis for standardisation for interview question 2	143
Table 5.3g	Focused coding no. 6 data analysis for market cap to total assets for interview question 2	144

Table 5.3h	Focused coding no. 7 data analysis for enterprise value for interview question 2	144
Table 5.3i	Focused coding no. 8 data analysis for interest expense for interview question 2	145
Table 5.3j	Focused coding no.9 data analysis for debt culture for interview question 2	145
Table 5.3k	Focused coding no.10 data analysis for Source of Funds for interview question 2	146
Table 5.3l	Focused coding no. 11 data analysis for the feasibility of SOF for interview question 2	146
Table 5.3m	Focused coding no. 12 data analysis for window dressing for interview question 2	147
Table 5.4a	Data analysis for interview question 3	148
Table 5.4b	Focused code 1 Tayeb and Preferred for interview question 3	149
Table 5.4c	Focused code 2 different levels of SRI for interview question 3	149
Table 5.4d	Focused code 3 not required by *Shari'a* for interview question 3	149
Table 5.4e	Focused code 4 whose responsibility for interview question 3	150
Table 5.4f	Focused code 5 market needs and investor demands for interview question 3	150
Table 5.4g	Focused code 6 different SRI principles for different countries for interview question 3	151
Table 5.4h	Focused code 7 Muslims are concerned about SRI principles for interview question 3	151
Table 5.4i	Focused code 8 not wise for all stocks for interview question 3	152
Table 5.4j	Focused code 9 investment opportunities for interview question 3	152
Table 5.4k	Focused code 10 increase in AUM for interview question 3	153
Table 5.5a	Data analysis for interview question 4	154
Table 5.5b	Focused code 1 capital gains for interview question 4	154
Table 5.5c	Focused code 2 dividend purification for interview question 4	154
Table 5.5d	Focused code 3 purification does not make sense for interview question 4	155
Table 5.5e	Focused code 4 preferred model for interview question 4	155
Table 5.6a	Data analysis for interview question 5	156

Table 5.6b	Focused code 1 business screening changes for interview question 5	157
Table 5.6c	Focused code 2 changes to financial screening—33% for interview question 5	158
Table 5.6d	Focused code 3 interest expense for interview question 5	158
Table 5.6e	Focused code 4 Islamic stock exchange for interview question 5	158
Table 5.6f	Focused code 5 need for revision for interview question 5	159
Table 5.6g	Focused code 6 different criteria for mining and service sector for interview question 5	159
Table 5.6h	Focused code 7 progressive reduction for interview question 5	160
Table 5.6i	Focused code 8 static model to effect model for interview question 5	161
Table 5.6j	Focused code 9 more practical methodology for interview question 5	162
Table 6.1	*Shari'a-compliant* based on both methodologies	196
Table 6.2	Stocks non-compliant based on both methodologies	197
Table 6.3	Stocks non-compliant based on existing methodology but compliant based on interest income and expense	198
Table 6.4	Stocks compliant based on existing methodology but non-compliant based on interest income and expense	198
Table 6.5	Information missing and are *Shari'a* compliant	199
Table 6.6	Information on interest missing and are non-compliant	199
Table 6.7	S&P non-compliant based on both filters	201
Table 6.8	S&P *Shari'a-compliant* based on both filters	204
Table 6.9	S&P information missing and *Shari'a* non-compliant	211
Table 6.10	S&P information missing and *Shari'a* compliant	213
Table 6.11	*Shari'a* non-compliant based on existing methodology but *Shari'a-compliant* based on new	215
Table 6.12	*Shari'a-compliant* based on existing methodology but *Shari'a* non-compliant based on new	217
Table 6.13	FTSE *Shari'a-compliant* based on both filters	217
Table 6.14	FTSE stocks non-compliant based on both filters	218
Table 6.15	FTSE information missing but *Shari'a-compliant*	219
Table 6.16	FTSE information missing and are non-compliant	220
Table 6.17	Non-compliant based on existing but compliant on new	220
Table 6.18	*Shari'a-compliant* based on existing but non-compliant based on new	220
Table 6.19	KMO and Bartlett's test	226
Table 6.20	After extraction four factors with eigenvalues > 1	227

Table 6.21	Rotated component matrix	229
Table 6.22	Index grouping based on the development in the IBF industry	233
Table 6.23	GCC *Shari'a-compliant* stocks based on 25% thresholds	237
Table 6.24	Bahrain *Shari'a-compliant* stocks	238
Table 6.25	Abu Dhabi *Shari'a-compliant* portfolio	239
Table 6.26	Dubai stocks *Shari'a-compliant* based on 25% thresholds	240
Table 6.27	DJIMI- Indonesia *Shari'a-compliant* stocks based on 25% thresholds	242
Table 6.28	Tadawul stocks after *Shari'a* screening based on AAOIFI	243
Table 6.29	*Shari'a-compliant* stocks based on 20% thresholds	246
Table 6.30	Malaysian *Shari'a-compliant* stocks based on 20%	248

CHAPTER 1

Introduction

The book is motivated by the impressive growth of *Shari'a*-compliant equity investments. Equity investment, or rather sharing in the profit and loss, is considered ideal when partaking in Islamic financial transactions. Over the past two decades, the assets under management (AUM) of *Shari'a*-compliant investments have increased significantly. As the growth of the general Islamic banking and finance (IBF) industry continues, and awareness among the public is enhanced, there is a growing demand for the *Shari'a-compliant* investments. The unique feature of the Islamic equity industry, compared to conventional equity investments, is that investments can only be made in assets deemed *Shari'a* compliant. *Shari'a* compliancy for equity investments is achieved through a process of *Shari'a* screening approved by *Shari'a* boards. There are contrasting *Shari'a* screening methodologies implemented by different institutions; all of them are equally *Shari'a* compliant.

This chapter discusses the background of the research in the subsequent section, followed by an outline of research aims and objectives together with research questions in Sect. 1.3. Section 1.4 discusses the rationale and significance of the research book, whilst in Sect. 1.5 discusses the chapter flow of the book.

R. Malik, *Shari'a Compliant Equity Investments*,
https://doi.org/10.1007/978-3-031-70822-0_1

1.1 Background of the Book

Interest in the ethical investment industry, which originated with screening investments based on religious beliefs, has intensified during recent decades due to the increase in demand from investors. The developments in the industry and the enhanced understanding of the investors have caused it to further expand to include religious beliefs, and social, environmental and personal values. The value of socially responsible industry (SRI) in the US has grown to USD 16.6 trillion and globally it has reached USD 35 trillion by 2020 (in five major areas including US, Canda, Japan, Europe and Austrailasia). The Islamic financial services industry is among the fast growing industries, with assets now in excess of US$ 4.9 trillion; it has been growing at more than 10% per annum in the last 15 years. Although a niche and new industry, the total assets value of the IBF industry has witnessed a strong growth recently with a notable increase in demand since the late 1990s, primarily owing to the increase in liquidity due to a notable escalation in oil revenues. As such, countries with considerable Islamic finance activities are also oil-rich countries, and therefore, they converted the revenues raised from strong long-term oil prices towards the IBF sector's development. The demand for IBF has grown further than its traditional markets of Muslim-majority countries and now has assets in more than 75 countries; additionally, more than one thousand institutions provide Islamic financial services. The substantial growth in IBF assets was accompanied by the expansion of the range of IBF products from traditional banking services to more dynamic products including stock market investments (Islamic equities) and sukuk (Islamic bond). Having said this, IBF's predominant growth has evolved from the countries in Gulf Cooperation Council (GCC), Far East (Malaysia and Indonesia) and Pakistan.

Concurrently, it is notable that an important class of investments, *Shari'a-compliant* equity investments, originated from the US with the launch of the Amana fund in 1986. Prior to this, *Shari'a-compliant* investors were not permitted to invest in the stock market as the most conservative view is that *Shari'a* sensitive investors cannot invest in a company that is involved in even a minimal amount of *Shari'a* non-compliant activities,[1] whether directly or indirectly. However, the Amana

[1] In terms of generating revenue from *Shari'a* non-compliant business or having interest involved in the capital structure of the company.

fund was launched based on a methodology that was not publically available at the time and as such only limited people were able to access the stock market. Dow Jones, coupled with the assistance provided by renowned *Shari'a* scholars, launched Dow Jones Islamic Market Index (DJIMI), which was based on a methodology[2] (*Shari'a* screening process) enabling *Shari'a* sensitive investors to access the stock market in 1999. Resultantly, a company is required to undertake a *Shari'a* screening process to qualify as *Shari'a* compliant.

Shari'a screening is a process of identifying whether companies are involved in *Shari'a* non-compliant activities. Screening is a term new to Islamic finance; however, it is very central to recent developments as it will determine what a *Shari'a* sensitive investor is permitted to invest. He further stated that *Shari'a* screening practices were not conducted in the past as most of the investments were in *Shari'a-compliant* ventures as there were very limited joint ventures between Muslim and non-Muslim investors. Islamic jurisprudence (fiqh) would ensure that the transactions undertaken by the joint venture correspond with *Shari'a*. However, the situation has now changed and investors in particular companies may not necessarily know each other as the shares are publically available to purchase and the business of the company may still be streamlined. At the early stages of screening, the aim was to screen the companies to identify if they are in compliance with *Shari'a* principles in absolute terms. The scholars at the time may use different methodologies and *ijtehad*; however, the main aim was to ensure the company is *Shari'a compliant* (Baker, 2011).

Islamic equity investment appears to align with ideal Islamic financial principles.[3] Khatkhatay and Nisar (2007) state that in order for an investment proposal to be considered compliant with *Shari'a* guidelines, it needs to be assessed from two perspectives: the nature of the transaction and the nature of contracting parties. Such assessment can be achieved by contemplating the following aspects:

[2] *Shari'a* screening methodology and *Shari'a* screening filters are used interchangeably but they mean the same for the purpose of this research.

[3] In case of equities the structuring of equities transaction itself appears unobjectionable as equities do not have any assured benefits on the holder. Further the shareholder can even lose all of his capital/investment.

a. Whether there is any *gharar*, *riba*, etc., involved in the structuring of the transactions
b. Nature of the business

Shari'a scholars implement thresholds for business and financial screening on the basis of "hajah" or "essential needs of the society". Furthermore, although *Shari'a* screening is not within the nomenclature of screening, it is particularly vital to conclude the result of screening given the developments in the industry. Khatkhatay and Nisar (2007) additionally stated that equities generally avoid any element of randomness and uncertainty associated with gambling and other games of chance. However, the particular nature of business that a company operates in can pose problems. As holders of equity shares, the shareholders are regarded as part owners in the company and thus responsible for the business of the company going against *Shari'a*. However, as a minority shareholder, an investor is unable to influence the policy decisions of the management with regards to the nature of the business and how they operate. Both of these have the tendency to evolve over time and become *Shari'a compliant* from *Shari'a* repugnant and vice versa. Derigs and Marzban (2008) further suggested that in addition to usual investment requirements, Islamic investors only invest if the investment does not conflict with their religious beliefs. Such investments also fall in the category of SRI or ethical investments. Similarly, Hayat and Malik (2014) stated that Islamic equity funds, as with their conventional ethical funds, are subject to an exclusionary screening criterion to avoid companies whose line of business conflicts with *Shari'a*. McMillen (2013) commented that two sets of tests were established to ensure that the investments of *Shari'a* sensitive investors comply with *Shari'a*. The first test has two parts: (a) if the security in trade is permissible (i.e. it cannot be preferred stocks which are not allowed) and (b) if the core business of the company is impermissible as they are involved in dealings in alcohol, tobacco, pork products, interest-based financial services (including banks and insurance companies), defence and weapons or entertainment (hotels, cinema, pornography, music or gambling). *Shari'a* screening methodologies were introduced to streamline the companies whose main line of business is *Shari'a compliant* but receive some *Shari'a* non-compliant revenue. The screening methodologies control the involvement of these *Shari'a* non-compliant revenue in the investment portfolio.

Since DJIMI, a number of other Islamic indexes have been set up including Nasdaq OMX, Morgan Stanley Capital International (MSCI) and Financial Times Stock Exchange (FTSE) and others. Organisations have also created a family of indexes to target different markets or assets. Each of these indexes has different methodologies, all of them are equally *Shari'a* compliant, yet they instigate a diverse set of *Shari'a-compliant* stocks and portfolios. This universe of stocks is largely dependent on the attached *Shari'a* scholar or board that formulate the criteria to assess *Shari'a* compliance of the stocks. To ensure adherence to the methodologies agreed, *Shari'a* auditors are employed to provide a rigorous analysis of stocks. These auditors could be internal or represent an external consultancy firm. Today, there are a number of *Shari'a* auditors, reflecting a transition from relying on *Shari'a* scholars to assess the *Shari'a* compliance of stocks. There are also a number of information providers that screen stocks according to various methodologies.

The screening process ensures that *Shari'a*-compliant stocks are not involved in excessive risk taking, high levels of borrowing, and exploitation of contracts. A *Shari'a*-compliant portfolio is also less likely to be exposed to liquidity concerns and excessive portfolio risk. Today, the *Shari'a* sensitive investor has more information and access to *Shari'a*-compliant equity investments. The use of computer technology and information systems also facilitates broader and quicker assessment of stocks. Funds allow convenient investments, safe in the knowledge that investor money is being invested in compliant stocks and indexes, and provide more information about the state of the market.

As stated above, the most conservative view does not tolerate even a small amount of *Shari'a* non-compliant activities. Hence, as the IBF industry grows, the aim was to slowly and steadily move towards the most conservative view. Furthermore, there is criticism in the literature on the filters used for screening; these are referred to as imprecise and inconsistent.

To conclude, the author's research is an attempt to enhance the existing practices of *Shari'a* screening methodologies in line with the criticisms in the literature, in both business screening and financial screening. Furthermore, the research considers how the existing *Shari'a* screening methodologies can be enhanced to correspond with the developments in IBF industry.

1.2 Research Aims, Objectives and Research Questions

There are two primary aims of this book. The first is to explore and analyse the views of *Shari'a* scholars on the history and existing practices of *Shari'a* screening methodologies. The second is to contemplate how they can be enhanced to incorporate the current developments in Islamic banking and finance.

The main objectives of the book are:

i. ***Shari'a-compliant* equity investments: A review of the history and existing practices of the *Shari'a* screening**

   An empirical analysis will be conducted based on the semi-structured interviews conducted with *Shari'a* scholars, who developed the first *Shari'a* screening methodology. In doing so, a detailed review will be undertaken regarding the history of *Shari'a* screening methodologies and resultantly how were they introduced. The primary data will also be collected on how the existing methodologies can be developed to tackle the issues highlighted in the literature such as the methodologies being imprecise, inconsistent, unstandardised and lacking credibility. Furthermore, consideration will be given to how the methodologies can be developed to take into account the current developments in IBF industry and ensure that the *Shari'a-compliant* stocks do not violate the socially responsible principles. More importantly, the interviews offer fresh insights, lacking in the existing literature related to *Shari'a-compliant* equity investments.

ii. **Enhancing the *Shari'a* screening process: An empirical analysis**

   There are two parts to this book:

   First, expanding on the interviews of the *Shari'a* scholars and the advancement in the technology and disclosure requirements for listed companies, the research in this part conducts an exploratory research based on the actual prohibited income, interest income and interest expense to analyse if the results of this methodology better serve the purpose of *Shari'a* screening compared to existing *Shari'a* screening methodology.

   Second, the book with the help of statistical techniques of exploratory factor analysis, using Principle Component Analysis (PCA), develops an IBF Index, which quantifies the development of IBF in different countries. Based on the developments in IBF industry, this part of the research proposes the screening thresholds to be different for companies based in different countries, while proposing an ongoing review of the development on a regular basis.

Based on the research aims and objectives, the following research questions have been developed (more details on the semi-structured interview questions are available within the Interview Questions' Section in Chapter 4):

1. What is the history of *Shari'a-compliant* screening methodologies, how and why they were introduced and what is the rationale behind the use of the screening thresholds?
2a. How can the existing *Shari'a* screening methodologies be revised?
2b. Can the thresholds for the *Shari'a* screening methodologies be based on the development in the IBF industry?

1.3 The Rationale and Significance of the Book

Despite the growth of *Shari'a-compliant* investments worldwide and the continuing strong interest in the IBF globally, academic literature on *Shari'a-compliant* equity investments remains limited. In particular, there is scarce literature on the *Shari'a-compliant* screening methodologies as the literature on the performance of *Shari'a-compliant* equity investments is extensive comparatively. Furthermore, the existing academic literature lacks empirical analysis on the rationale behind the development of *Shari'a* screening methodologies conducted with the founding *Shari'a* board as well as IBF experts who possessed a vital role in the introduction of *Shari'a* screening methodologies. We are fortunate enough that all the *Shari'a* scholars and the experts that were part of the founding team of the first *Shari'a* screening methodology are alive and hence it is an excellent opportunity to analyse the true account of introducing the screening methodologies. Simultaneously, we can consider how the existing screening methodologies can be developed to integrate the development in IBF industry and resolve the existing criticisms in the literature.

The findings of the book may add to the body of the literature in understanding the factors considered in developing the *Shari'a* screening methodologies and provide original empirical analysis of the founding *Shari'a* board on how these methodologies can be developed to take into account the development of IBF industry. Furthermore, the research undertakes an exploratory research on different portfolios using secondary data, in line with the criticism in the literature and suggestions from the *Shari'a* scholars. Lastly, the research then creates an IBF index, which quantifies the development in IBF industry in various countries using a statistical technique based on a variety of different variables. The input from *Shari'a* scholars and other experts (primary data), together with the exploratory research on different portfolios (secondary data), enhances the depth of the analysis and offers real-life perspective to the issues at hand. Therefore, this book makes an important contribution to the existing literature by clearly enriching the quality of research on the *Shari'a* screening methodologies and thus paves the way for future research in relation to enhancing the *Shari'a* screening filters.

1.4 Overview of the Book

This book is organised as follows. This chapter, being the introduction chapter, presents the general introduction and background of this book. This is followed by the research aims and objectives, research questions, rationale and the significance of this book. Finally, the chapter provides a chapter-wise overview of the whole book.

A comprehensive analysis of the past studies on *Shari'a-compliant* equity investments and *Shari'a* screening methodologies is discussed in the literature review, which spans two chapters. Chapter 2 provides a detailed discussion on the principles and review of Islamic finance. The chapter commences with a brief overview of how Islamic finance is a part of the global financial system. It then presents a theoretical background of Islamic finance by discussing the underlying principles, different types of instruments and financial contracts used in structuring an Islamic financial transaction. The chapter also provides a detailed overview of the historical developments and trends in IBF industry over the last four decades and introduces the Islamic equity investments and *Shari'a* screening.

Chapter 3 provides a detailed review of the historical developments in *Shari'a-compliant* equity investments. The chapter then provides an extensive analysis of the *Shari'a* stance on joint-stock companies, outlining how they are similar to the *Mudaraba* contract used in Islamic finance whilst also emphasising their differences. It further develops in providing an analysis on the *Shari'a* view of investments and trading in shares, and the Fatwa of International Islamic Fiqh Academy. A detailed analysis is provided on investment in companies involved in both *Shari'a-compliant* and *Shari'a* non-compliant activities and the introduction of *Shari'a-compliant* screening methodologies by different institutions by following DJIMI screening methodology. A comprehensive discussion and analysis is provided on the business screening and the screening filters used in financial screening; the rationale behind the usage of both liabilities side (debt) and assets side (cash and receivables and securities) filters is provided. The chapter then analyses and presents an extensive discussion on the issues facing the *Shari'a* screening methodologies, which provides a solid foundation for conducting this book.

The research methodology and data collection are elaborated on in Chapter 4. The book employed two research methods, namely qualitative analysis and quantitative analysis, which makes the book unique and essentially different from previous studies in the area of *Shari'a-compliant* equity investments. The chapter starts by providing the general research approach of this book and then utilises a detailed discussion on the qualitative and quantitative methods used in the book together with the discussion on analysis techniques used. The qualitative analysis is undertaken with the help of semi-structured interviews with *Shari'a* scholars and other experts, and provides a rationale of the sample section. The chapter then discusses the interviews using coding analysis based on the template analysis method. The section also presents the overall semi-structured interview process from designing the questionnaire till the post-execution stage of transcribing, coding and analysis. The chapter then explains the quantitative research methods employed. Based on the analysis and results of qualitative analysis, the quantitative analysis section is divided into two parts. The first part is based on conducting an exploratory book by selecting different portfolios and screening them based on the proposed filters of interest income to total revenue and interest expense to total expenses, to compare against the existing *Shari'a* screening results. The second part of the quantitative analysis is based on enhancing the *Shari'a* screening filters by proposing them to be more dynamic and based on the growth and development in IBF industry. To quantify the development in IBF industry, an Islamic banking and finance index is created using the statistical technique of exploratory factor analysis, as explained in the chapter.

Chapter 5 presents the results and discussions based on the qualitative analysis. The analysis found that *Shari'a-compliant* screening methodologies were introduced to cover an interim period until the IBF industry is developed. It was implemented following the impressive growth of technology, which eased the stock market investments for potential investors. However, it was difficult to find any company that did not have a trace of *Shari'a* non-compliant activities. As such, the *Shari'a* screening methodologies were introduced based on how much of *Shari'a* non-compliant activities can be tolerated in this interim period until a more developed IBF industry is initiated. The analysis identified several factors that significantly influence *Shari'a-compliant* screening methodologies such as screening stocks based on the interest income and interest expense, and integration of socially responsible investment principles in the screening methodologies. The analysis also proposed a move from the existing static screening methodologies to the one based on the growth and development in the IBF industry. This is to ensure that efforts are made in ensuring a move towards investments in completely *Shari'a-compliant* portfolio with 0 impermissible income.

Chapter 6 expands on the results and analysis of qualitative research. The quantitative analysis in this chapter is divided into two parts: Research Analysis 1 undertakes an exploratory analysis by selecting a number of different portfolios and screening them based on the proposed interest income and interest expense filters and compares it with the results of existing screening methodologies. It was notable that, while the proposed method is the preferred option, the lack of data might not permit its use in practice. The analysis revealed that although we may not be able to completely rely on the results of these filters, the inclusion of these filters will certainly enhance the *Shari'a* credibility of the results. Concurrently, efforts should be made in ensuring that more accurate information is collected on these proposed filters. Research Analysis 2 developed an IBF index using the statistical technique of exploratory factor analysis to rank 41 countries according to their IBF growth and development. In line with the IBF development, the book divided these countries into five groups. The conclusion of the chapter was that the screening thresholds for groups' "leaders" and "advanced countries" can be reduced to 20% and 25%, respectively. Simultaneously, the research concluded that the IBF index needs to be updated on a regular basis to ensure screening thresholds are adjusted in line with the developments in the country and ultimately achieve the objective of zero percent tolerance on *Shari'a* non-compliant activities.

Chapter 7 provides the conclusion of the book. The chapter summarises and concludes the findings of the book, discusses its implications and highlights the limitations as well as recommendations for future studies related to *Shari'a-compliant* equity investments and *Shari'a* screening methodologies.

References

Dergis, U., & Marzban, S. (2008). Review and Analysis of Current Shariah-Compliant Equity Screening Practices. *International Journal of Islamic and Middle Eastern Finance and Management, 1*(4), 285–303.

Hayat, U., & Malik, A. (2014). *Islamic Finance: Ethics, Concepts and Practice.* CFA Institute Research Foundation.

Khatkhatay, M. H., & Nisar, S. (2007). *Shari'a*h Compliant Equity Investments: An Assessment of Current Screening Norms. *Islamic Economic Studies, 15*(1).

McMillen, M. (2013). *Islamic Finance and the Shari'ah.* Riverstone Publishing Group.

CHAPTER 2

A Review of Islamic Finance

Before going deeper into the specific topic of this book, it is essential to consider the overall context of the Islamic banking and finance (IBF) industry. Understanding the broader landscape will underscore the significance of this research's contributions to the development of the IBF sector as a whole.

This chapter begins with a brief overview of the global financial system, highlighting the position of Islamic finance as a niche yet rapidly growing segment within it. The discussion then transitions to the fundamental principles and components that define Islamic finance, providing a comprehensive background on its unique features compared to conventional finance.

Subsequently, the chapter explores the various instruments and contracts utilised in Islamic finance, offering an in-depth analysis of their structure and application. This examination is crucial for appreciating the innovative approaches that Islamic finance brings to the table.

The chapter also charts the historical development of the IBF industry, with a particular focus on the significant advancements made over the past four decades. This historical perspective is vital for understanding the current state of the industry and the ongoing trends shaping its future.

R. Malik, *Shari'a Compliant Equity Investments*,
https://doi.org/10.1007/978-3-031-70822-0_2

By setting this broader context, the chapter aims to provide a solid foundation for the subsequent detailed analysis, highlighting how this research can contribute to the ongoing evolution and maturation of the Islamic banking and finance industry.

2.1 Financial System

A financial system is a diverse set of financial institutions and markets that unites lenders and borrowers; this includes banks, insurance companies, funds and other finance companies. Additionally, its most important purpose is to facilitate the flow of funds between surplus funds units (SFUs) and deficit funds units (DFUs) by creating products and instruments that meet the requirements of both lenders and borrowers. Hence, the main objective of the financial system is to organise a large amount of small savings and use them to channel for productive investments in the economy. This can be implemented through financial markets (stocks exchanges, Over the Counter (OTC) trading, etc.) or in the indirect manner through intermediaries (banks and other financial institutions). The central banks around the world generally conduct monetary policies through financial institutions and the financial system in general. Hence, an effective financial system is crucial for the economic growth of a country (producing goods and services and creating employment) (ISRA, 2012).

The financial system consists of many different types of financial markets and institutions with each having its own objectives and purposes. These can be categorised into debt and equity markets, money and capital markets, primary and secondary markets, and organised and OTC markets (ISRA, 2012). The main role of channelling funds within the economy can be achieved directly or indirectly with the help of financial intermediaries. These financial intermediaries play an important role in the well-functioning of the markets. They act as intermediaries between the SFU and DFU, while on the other hand providing liquidity, risk sharing and other relevant information to market players. This transfer of funds through financial intermediaries is known as indirect finance. The financial intermediaries are classified into deposit taking and non-deposit taking institutions. Deposit taking institutions include institutions that take excess funds from SFUs and facilitate DFUs with these funds by means of loans and securities. These are, for instance, commercial banks, saving institutions and credit unions. The non-deposit taking institutions include those institutions that do not take deposits but generate funds from other sources; these include insurance companies, pension funds, finance companies, mutual funds and investment banks.[1] A financial system is presented in Fig. 2.1.

2.2 Islamic Finance

Islamic finance in the current form is relatively a new phenomenon and only received prominence in the mid-1980s. ISRA (2012) defines Islamic economics and financial system as a system that refers to financial market transactions, operations and services that follow rules and laws collectively known as *Shari'a*. *Shari'a* is often translated as "the path", the "Islamic way" or "Islamic law" that governs all aspects of Muslim societies from economic to social, political and cultural aspects (Hayat & Malik, 2014).

2.3 Principles of Islamic Finance

The primary sources of *Shari'a* are the Holy Quran (religious book of Muslims, and believed to be the word of God) and Sunnah (sayings, actions and tacit approvals of the Prophet Muhammad ﷺ in the form of hadiths)—together these two texts form the basis of *Shari'a*. The secondary sources are Islamic jurisprudence (fiqh—also translated as understanding of *Shari'a*), based on the consensus of scholars (ijma), deductive reasoning (qiyas) and interpretations (ijtihad) of experts. In interpreting the Quran and the traditions of the Prophet Muhammad ﷺ, jurists rely on different tools of reasoning that broadly fall under the umbrella of independent reasoning. Many aspects of Islamic finance are covered by fiqh (jurisprudence) or *fiqh al muamalat* (Islamic commercial jurisprudence). Kamali (2005) states that *fiqh* is the output and the "the methodology of principles of jurisprudence really refers to methods of reasoning such as analogy (qiyas), juristic preference (istihsan), presumption of continuity (istishab) and the rules of interpretation and deduction". Furthermore, there are competing interpretations of Islamic jurisprudence as it involves human endeavour. Usman and Hayat (2014) cited Khalid Zaheer, a *Shari'a* scholar, who states that juristic differences among Muslim scholars is a general rule and not an exception;

[1] Insurance companies and pension funds are known as savings institutions while finance companies, mutual funds and investment banks are known as investment intermediaries.

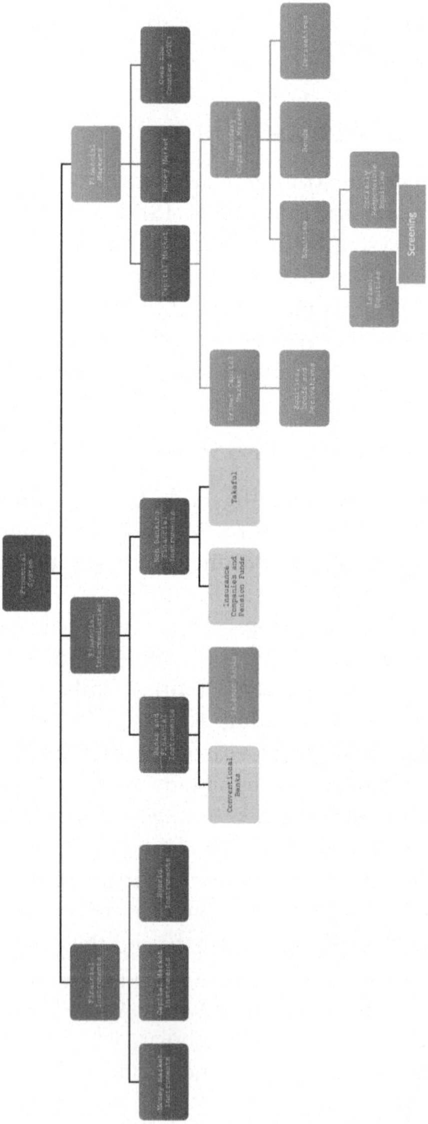

Fig. 2.1 A financial system (*Source* Sandhya. Ch. V.I.—Indian Financial System)

this will be noted by anyone familiar with work done on *Shari'a* in the last 1400 years. This means that there are differences of opinions among the *Shari'a* scholars and in general *Shari'a* compliance references to meeting the technical requirements of Islamic commercial jurisprudence as opined and determined by the *Shari'a* scholar, who also issues a certificate of compliance known as *fatwa*.

As Islamic finance is founded on the absolute prohibition of any payment or receipt of any predetermined guaranteed rate of return, this means the payment and receipt of any type of payment above the principle amount is not allowed. Additionally, Islamic finance is supported by other principles of Islamic doctrine, such as risk sharing, individual rights and duties, property rights and the sanctity of contracts. Islamic finance is not only limited to banking, but also incorporates financial instruments, financial markets, and all other types of financial intermediation (Zaher & Hassan, 2001). All earlier references to the commercial financial system are based on the system that complies with teachings of *Shari'a*. It has the distinctive feature that tries to combine the financial system with the basic principles of Islamic faith. *Shari'a* governs all aspects of human life and hence there is little concept of the economy functioning independent of the religious beliefs (ECB, 2013).

Islam is a complete code of life and, unlike the conventional financial system, *Shari'a* promotes ethical values and hence the Islamic finance is not value neutral (ISRA, 2012). Islam is a fusion of worldly and spiritual aspects of life and is a life style and differs from other religions like Christianity and Judaism due to there being no division between the state and religion itself (Forte & Miglietta, 2007). The values that the Islamic finance promotes are practices that are in the public interest (*Maslahah)* and prevent harm (*Mafasadah*). This means promoting activities that are productive, adding real values, genuine trade and business transactions related to the real sector of the economy, advocating ethical values such as justice, honesty, integrity and a balanced society, promoting brotherhood and co-operation through partnership, equity-based and risk-sharing financial instruments, good governance, transparency and avoiding activities that will or have the potential to damage the public interest. According to Ainley et al. (2007), there are four core principles that make up the financial system based on Shari'a. These are:

Firstly, social justice and prosperity of the whole society; this is evident from the fact that *Shari'a* rulings try to reduce the concentration of wealth in few hands and provide relief for poor.

Secondly, the religion Islam does not prohibit the making of any profit that is in line with *Shari'a;* rather, it encourages people to get into business or trade. It is clearly stated in the Holy Quran (2:275).

Allah has permitted trade and has forbidden interest.

Thirdly, the Islamic economic model is based on risk and profit sharing; interest and *riba* have been forbidden.

Lastly, *Shari'a* provides a comprehensive regulation for contracts. These rules ensure that all decisions that are made are well-informed and avoid any uncertainty or ambiguity.

Similarly, Akram et al. (2011) mentioned that Islamic finance promotes risk sharing,[2] materiality,[3] no exploitation,[4] non-financing of sinful activities,[5] social justice and entrepreneurship. The system further emphasises ethical, moral, social and religious dimensions to enhance equality and fairness for the good of the entire society. The main principles of the Islamic finance are highlighted in Fig. 2.2.

The idea of the financial system in line with Shari'a started to emerge in the twentieth century when the Islamic banking industry commenced in the 1970s with a huge inflow of funds from the oil-rich Gulf States that created institutions offering Islamic banking and finance services. It was seen as an alternative system to capitalist, liberalism and socialist planning (ECB, 2013). Since 1970s, Islamic finance has evolved and has developed a wide range of products and offerings for both Muslim and non-Muslim communities (seeking ethical investments and risk diversification).

The basic principles of an Islamic finance are:

Among the Muslim countries in the world there are three countries (Iran, Sudan and Pakistan) that converted their financial system to be in line with Shari'a. However, since the late 1990s, Pakistan has opted for a dual financial system, allowing both the Islamic and conventional systems

[2] The terms of financial transactions need to reflect a symmetrical risk/return distribution among each participant.

[3] All financial transaction must be directly linked to real underlying economic transaction.

[4] Neither party to the transaction should be exploited.

[5] It cannot be used to produce goods banned by the Holy Quran (e.g. alcohol, pork, gambling, etc.).

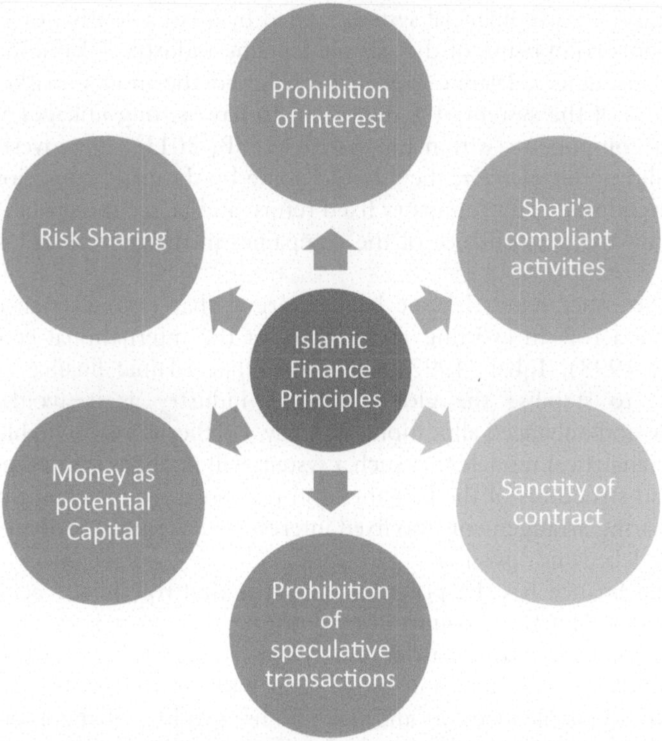

Fig. 2.2 Principles of Islamic finance (*Source* Zamir Iqbal [1997])

to grow side by side[6] (Iqbal & Molyneux, 2005). Islamic finance, as an integral part of the overall Islamic economic system, requires an encouraging environment that conforms to *Shari'a* and enables it to operate effectively and efficiently. Effective risk management practices, regulation of Islamic financial institutions, sound corporate governance (including *Shari'a*), supportive legal framework and robust accounting disclosure and taxation regime collectively instigate such an environment (ECB, 2013).

[6] Although the aim of dual banking system in Pakistan is to allow Islamic banking to develop more so that the concentration of conventional banking is reduced and eventually phased out.

A comprehensive financial system guided by Shari'a consists of a set of components comprising of the Islamic banking industry, takaful industry (Islamic insurance), Islamic capital markets and the money market. For the success of the system, it is important to have strong linkages among different components within the system (IFSB, 2011). For investments to be valid under *Shari'a*, they should abide by the basic condition that there should not be a promissory fixed return and hence the profit should depend on the performance of the companies in the portfolio (Usmani, 2002).

On the other hand, Islamic bankers argue that Islamic finance may even have a role in assisting the stability of the international economy (Dudley, 1998). Iqbal (1997) mentioned that Islamic finance can be expected to stabilise the global financial industry as it avoids debt financing and enhanced allocation efficiency. Furthermore, he highlighted through analytical models that such a system will be more stable since the terms and structures of the liabilities and the assets are matched through profit-sharing arrangements, no fixed interest cost accrues and refinancing through debt is not possible.

Islamic finance has the potential to play a vital role in the economic development of Islamic countries by ensuring that savings are separated from the interest-based financial system and concurrently developing the capital markets. The development of such markets and financial instruments would enable investors and savers to use products that comply with their business needs, social values and religious beliefs (Iqbal, 1997).

2.4 Islamic Financial Instruments

The instruments offered in Islamic markets to satisfy providers and users of funds are different to conventional markets in a number of ways in different transactions including sales, trade financing and investment. They are classified as PLS (profit and loss sharing) or non-PLS (non-profit and loss sharing).

Some of the basic instruments or contracts include:

- *Musharaka* (partnership): It is a partnership contract between two parties where both investor and entrepreneur contribute to the capital of operations.

- *Mudaraba* (partnership): It is another form of partnership, where the investor contributes the capital while the entrepreneur manages it.
- *Murabaha* (cost-plus financing): It is the sale on profit which is mutually agreed.
- *Ijara* (leasing): It is the contract or the legal right against a lawful or a specified return for the effort or work which is proposed to be expended and for the benefits that are proposed to be taken.
- *Salam* (forward sale): It is a sale and purchase transaction whereby the payment is made in cash on spot while the delivery is deferred. More details are provided in Table 2.1.

These instruments are also the basic contracts used to develop further complex products. Figure 2.3 highlights some of the Islamic financial contracts.

Brief Overview of the Historical Development of Islamic Banking and Finance

The origins of seeking guidance for economic transactions from Islamic teaching can be traced back 14 centuries to the Prophet Muhammad era. However, trade and business transactions were common among the people of Arabian Peninsula and Middle East for centuries. Some of these customary traditions and practices followed by the people were not in conflict with Islamic principles while others that did deviate from this moral code were ratified to comply with the Islamic principles and teachings (ISRA, 2012). This paved the way for the formalisation of traditional trade and business practices into the legal system of standardised contracts consistent with *Shari'a*. Islamic methods of finance often drew examples from the Prophet's experiences. There are several sayings about the Prophet ﷺ buying on credit, taking finance and also giving personal property as a security measure. Additionally, it is also reported that the Prophet ﷺ used *Mudaraba* (partnership) contract to trade with Khadija (the Prophet's business partner, later turned wife), which included the Prophet ﷺ travelling to Syria (ISRA, 2012). Furthermore, it is additionally suggested that the people of Arabia practised *Musharaka* (full partnership) widely. Additionally, the Prophet Muhammad ﷺ made it permissible to buy on credit (*bay' al-salam*). Another form of financing *Qard* (benevolent loan) was also encouraged.

Table 2.1 *Shari'a-compliant* instruments

Contract	*Explanation*	*When is it used*
Musharaka (Partnership based)	A partnership contract between two parties when both contribute capital towards the financing of a project. Both parties share profit in agreed proportion while losses are borne in proportion to the capital provided	The financing mode is suitable for working capital financing, fixed asset purchased, project finance, etc
Mudharaba	An agreement between two parties where one party provides capital (known as rab ul maal) while the other who manages is known as mudarib. Profits are shared in accordance with predetermined ratio while losses are borne by rab ul maal	The financing mode is suitable for working capital financing, fixed asset purchased, project finance, etc
Murabaha	Cost plus sales	All purchases
Ijarah	A contract under which a bank purchase and leases out equipment required by its clients for a rental fee. The duration of the lease and rental fees are agreed in advance. Ownership of the equipment remains in the hands of the bank	The instrument is suitable for financing fixed assets such as machinery and motor vehicles
Salam	A contract of sale of good where the price is paid in advance and the goods are delivered in the future	The financing mode is suitable for agricultural financing which requires capital at certain critical stage (e.g. during plantation stage)

(continued)

Table 2.1 (continued)

Contract	*Explanation*	*When is it used*
Istisna	A contract of acquisition of goods by specification or order, where the price is paid in advance, but goods are manufactured and delivered at a later stage	This financing mode is suitable for financing assets which require capital at different stages of construction and tailor made manufacturing
Sarf	It is a sale of money for money such as sale of gold for gold or silver for silver. However, Maliki scholars consider money exchange only if the sale is gold for gold or silver for silver, but gold for silver does not belong to such transaction	This contract is mainly used for currency trading and exchange

Adapted from Dusuki and Abdullah (2014)-edited

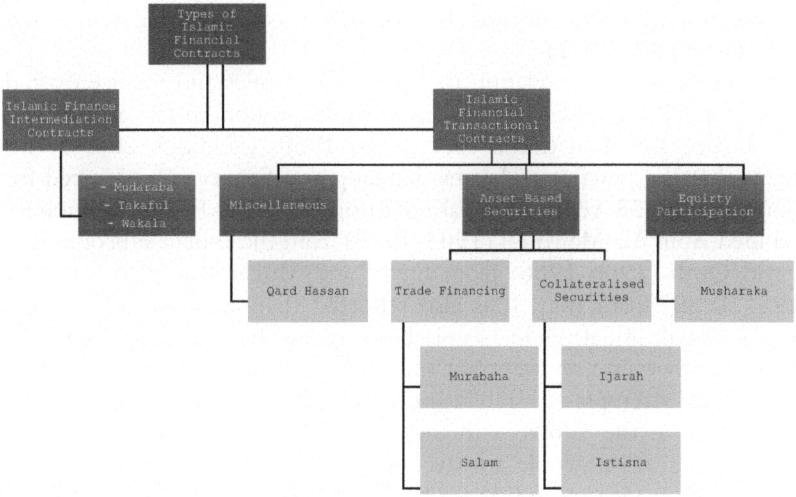

Fig. 2.3 Types of Islamic financial contracts

According to Hayat and Malik (2014), financial decisions continued to be influenced by *Shari'a* without them being referred to as "Islamic economics" or "Islamic finance". Dusuki and Abdullah (2014) state that in the early history of Islam, the prohibition of interest was strictly observed; however, with the declining adherence to religion, together with the influence of West as a result of long period of their colonial domination of Muslim countries, the interest-based financial system created a strong base. After the colonisation period (post-World War II), there was a strong inclination by Muslim countries to follow the teachings of Islam in all aspects of life including political, economic and social decisions.

The growth of modern Islamic banking can be attributed to three factors: first, the petrodollars (oil revenues of 1970s) offered strong incentives for high net worth individuals to invest in a *Shari'a-compliant* manner. Second, devout Muslims would not like to be involved in a financial system that does not comply with the teachings of Islam. The third factor was that as countries received independence post-colonisation and the businesses evolved, the belief grew that the best response for the communities and individuals was to rediscover Islamic values and traditions (ISRA, 2012).

Academic literature relating to Islamic economics and finance existed before the 1940s, while the pioneering works in modern Islamic banking and finance are often traced back to the 1960s (Siddiqui, 2007). This means that the practice of Islamic banking and finance has occurred for approximately 55 years. The earliest proponents of Islamic economics included Abul Ala Mawdudi (1903–1979) from the Indian subcontinent, Sayyid Qutb (1906–1966) from Egypt and Muhammad Baqir Al-Sadr (1931–1980) from Iraq. It is also reported that there were a number of other small initiatives in Islamic banking and finance in Malaysia and Pakistan; however, they were not successful (Dusuki & Abdullah, 2014). The earliest attempts at establishing Islamic financial institutions can be traced back to the 1960s, with the set-up of Lembaga Tabung Haji in Malaysia (to assist people to save on a regular basis to pay for their pilgrimage to Mecca) and Mit Ghamr (1963–1967) in Egypt, devised based on German saving banks catering to rural farmers. Mit Ghamr was short-lived and later revived as Nasser Social Bank in 1972 (a public bank owned and governed by the government).

After these small initiatives in Egypt and Malaysia, a major growth in the development of Islamic banking and finance came with the support of the governments of a number of Muslim countries. In December

1975, the Islamic Development Bank (IDB) was established in Jeddah, after the proposal of constructing an international Islamic bank for trade and investment was presented. IDB serves the financial and investment needs of Muslim-majority countries, particularly those that are short of capital and are reliant on credit for development projects on the basis equity participation (ISRA, 2012). Dubai Islamic Bank (DIB) was established as the first Islamic commercial bank in 1975, followed by Faisal Islamic Bank, Sudan, and Kuwait Finance House in 1977. The first takaful (Islamic insurance) was founded in Sudan in 1979. An overview of the major developments is listed in Table 2.2.

Overview of the Global Developments in Islamic Banking and Finance

The development in Islamic banking and finance occurred globally and different jurisdictions adopted different models of developing and promoting Islamic banking and finance. In some countries, the government implemented active steps in advocating Islamic banking and finance. The role of a government, among others, is to provide enabling environments and provide the necessary infrastructure through the formulation of a comprehensive set of legal and regulatory framework for Islamic banking and finance. In other countries, it is the private sector that pushes the growth of the Islamic banking industry in the country. There are different models being practised in different countries in terms of the implementation of Islamic banking (ISRA, 2012):

1. Islamic banking system only—Iran and Sudan
2. Dual system (Islamic banking system operating in parallel with the conventional system)—Malaysia, Bahrain, Pakistan
3. Conventional plus system (conventional system with a few Islamic banking institutions operating on the fringe of the banking system)—UK, Thailand and Bangladesh.

Further Islamic banking has three governance structures:

1. Full-fledged Islamic banks
2. Islamic banking windows of conventional banks
3. Islamic banking subsidiaries of conventional banks either newly established or converted from existing Islamic windows.

Table 2.2 Overview of the global developments in IBF

1900–1930	• A majority of scholars subscribed to the position that interest in all forms constitutes prohibited *riba*
1930–1950	• Attempts were undertaken to outline *Shari'a-compliant* alternatives in the form of partnership
1950s	• Islamic scholars and theorists started to offer alternatives to Islamic banking and finance as a substitute of interest-based banking • By 1953, Islamic economists offered the first description of an interest-free bank, based on two-tier *Mudaraba* (banks to collect funds and extend financing on *Mudaraba* basis) • Later they should that financial intermediation can also be based on *wakala basis*
1960s	• Applications and practices in finance based on Islamic principles began in Egypt and Malaysia • The landmark events include the rise and fall of Mit Ghamr (Egypt) Savings Association during 1963 and 1967 and establishment of Tabung Haji, Malaysia, in 1963. Tabung Haji has since flourished and has become the oldest Islamic financial institution in modern times • Operational mechanisms for institutions offering Islamic financial services (IIFS) began to be proposed and a number of books on Islamic banking based on profit and loss sharing and leasing were published
1970s	• Islamic banks emerged with the establishment in 1975 of the Dubai Islamic Bank and the Islamic Development Bank • In 1975 fiqhi objection to conventional insurance become pronounced, laying the ground for an alternative structure • Financial *murabaha* was developed as the core mechanism for the placement of Islamic banks funds • Academic activities were launched with the first international conference on Islamic economics held in Makkah in 1976 • Faisal Islamic Bank, Sudan, and Kuwait Finance House, Kuwait, were set up in 1977 • The first research institution, namely the Centre for Research in Islamic Economics, was established by the King Abdul Aziz University in Jeddah in 1978 • Jordan Islamic Bank, Jordan, was set up in 1978 and Bahrain Islamic Bank, Bahrain, in 1979 • The first takaful company was established in 1979 in Sudan

(continued)

Table 2.2 (continued)

1980s	• More Islamic Banks and academic institutions emerged in several countries like Al Baraka was set up in 1982, Bank Islam Malaysia, Islamic Bank Bangladesh and Qatar Islamic Bank in 1983, Dar al Mal Islamic Trust, Geneva, in 1984 and ANZ Global Islamic Finance, UK, in 1989 • Pakistan, Iran and Sudan announced their intention to transform their financial system in compliance with *Shari'a* • The governors of central banks and monetary authorities of the Organisation of International Conference (OIC) member countries, in their fourth meeting held in Khartoum in 1981 called to strengthening of the regulation and supervision of IIFS • The Islamic Research and Training Institute (IRTI) was established by the IDB in 1981 • In 1980, Pakistan passed the legislation to establish *Mudaraba* companies • Malaysia and Bahrain initiated Islamic banking within the framework of the existing system • Islamic mutual funds and other non-banking financial institutions emerged towards the middle of 1980s
1990s	• The first corporate sukuk was issued by Shell MDS in Malaysia in 1990 • Accounting and Auditing Organisation for Islamic Financial Institutions (AAOIFI) was established and its first standards were issued in 1991 • The Harvard Islamic Finance Forum was set up • Large international conventional banks started operating Islamic windows • Islamic Bank of Brunei was set up in 1993 • The Dow Jones and Financial Times Islamic indexes were launched in 1999 • Bank Muamalat Malaysia Berhad was set up • Several countries introduced legislations to facilitate Islamic banking and its regulation and supervision • Systemic concerns and regulations, supervision and risk management issues gathered momentum

(continued)

Table 2.2 (continued)

2000–2006	• Sovereign and corporate sukuk as alternatives to conventional bonds emerged and are increasing rapidly in volume • Bahrain issued Financial Trust Laws. First sovereign sukuk issued in 2001 • Meezan Bank, the largest Islamic bank in Pakistan was set up • International infrastructure institutions such as the Islamic Financial Services Board (IFSB), International Islamic Financial market (IIFM), (General Council for Islamic Banks and Financial Institutions (CIBAFI) and the Arbitration and Reconciliation Centre for Islamic Financial Institutions (ARCIFI) as well as other commercial support institutions such as the International Islamic Rating Agency (IIRA) and the Liquidity Management Centre (LMC) were established • The systemic importance of Islamic banks and financial institutions has been recognised in several jurisdictions • The government of United Kingdom and Singapore extended tax neutrality to Islamic financial services • Islamic Bank of Britain (now named as Al Rayan Bank) was set in the UK in 2004 • World's first university dedicated to Islamic finance was established in Malaysia in 2006 International Centre for Islamic Finance Education (INCEIF)
2007–2014	• First institution dedicated to undertake research in Islamic finance was set up in 2008 by Bank Negara Malaysia known as International *Shari'a*h Research Academy (ISRA) • Islamic finance started to spread widely to other Arab countries including Jordan, Egypt and African continent • Many non-Muslim countries started to amend their laws to enable institutions to issue sukuk such as France, Germany, Malta, Turkey, South Korea, Japan and Hong Kong • International Islamic Liquidity Management Corporation (IILM) was established to facilitate cross-border liquidity management by Islamic financial institutions in 2010 • Islamic Inter Bank Offer Rate (IIBR) was launched by Thomson Reuters • Qatar banned windows to be operated as part of a bank in 2011 • Royal Decree to allow Islamic banking and finance in Oman was announced in 2011 • Sovereign sukuk were issues by UK, South Africa, Luxembourg and Hong Kong in 2014

Adapted from Dusuki and Abdullah (2014) and edited

2.5 Size and Growth of Islamic Banking and Finance

Islamic banking is the most developed element of the Islamic finance, and it is the fastest growing segment of the credit market in Muslim countries with Islamic banks (Zaher & Hassan, 2001). Islamic banks have been well positioned to attract investments; however, these institutions have not been able to invest efficiently in the past. This trend is now changing and Islamic banks are becoming more efficient and resourceful due to their increased involvement in the international market (Iqbal, 1997). Similarly, Islamic financial markets in the past have lacked liquidity enhancing instruments and have thereby not been of interest to a large segment of potential investors. However, this trend is changing and more liquid financial instruments are now emerging.

According to the Global Islamic Finance Report 2023, the size of the global Islamic financial services industry reached USD $3.805 trillion by the end of 2022. Saudi Arabia and Malaysia are the two countries that remain the leaders in the growth of Islamic banking and finance globally.

Figure 2.4 summarises Islamic banking and finance growth between 2008 and 2022. Notably, the global Islamic financial services industry has slowed down in the last 14 years—from the high annual growth rate of 28.6% in 2008 to 12.87% in 2022.

Banks continue to dominate in terms of assets under management (AUM) of Islamic banking and finance institutions, with 75% of the global Islamic financial assets held by Islamic banks and conventional banks in their Islamic window. The second largest sector in terms of AUM is sukuk, which comprises 15% of the global Islamic financial services industry. At 4%, Islamic investment funds have yet to see any significant growth and this is the case too for takaful and the emerging business of Islamic microfinance. The Islamic funds are divided into different types: equity funds, commodity, sukuk and leasing funds and the total AUM of them collectively has reached USD 120 billion (Islamic Financial Services Board Stability Report, 2023). More details on the recent developments in IBF industry are discussed in Research Analysis 2 in Chapter 6.

Islamic equity funds have the largest share within Islamic funds and are similar to the conventional funds. However, Islamic equity funds are required to go through a screening process known as *Shari'a* screening (ISRA, 2012), which ensures that the investments made correspond with *Shari'a*. The screening process ensures that the business, mode and capital

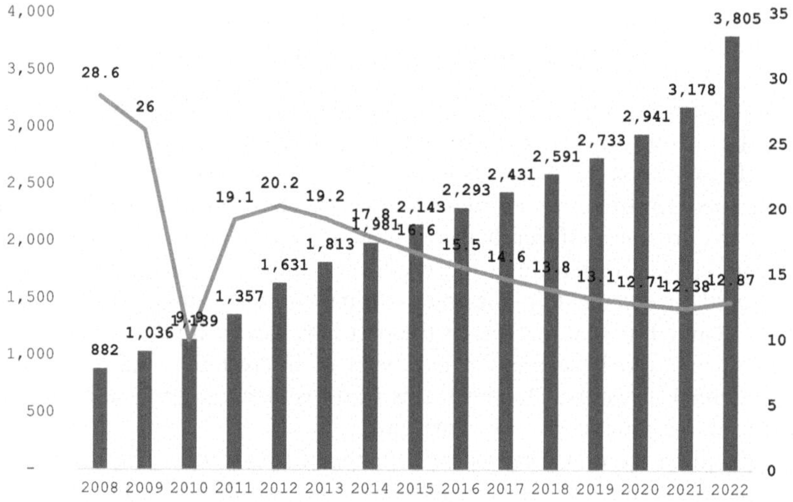

Fig. 2.4 Size and growth of Islamic banking and finance between 2008 and 2012 (US$ billion) (Adapted from GIFR [2023])

structure of the businesses the funds invest in are in compliant with *Shari'a*.

In order to determine whether a stock is *Shari'a* compliant, there are two key questions that need to be asked creating two screens:

1. Is the company involved in activities deemed by the *Shari'a* to be impermissible? This is known as the "business screen".
2. Is the financial management of the company involved in undertaking financial obligations that are not entirely in conformity with *Shari'a*? This is known as the "financial screen".

They are usually conducted consecutively with the business screens undertaken first. The guidelines underpinning the *Shari'a* assessment of stocks are provided by the *Shari'a* bodies (e.g. *Shari'a* advisory councils of AAOIFI Bahrain and SC Malaysia) and other *Shari'a* boards of financial institutions, which have delved into Islamic legal principles and precedents to determine the boundaries of investment. These guidelines regarding the activities of the company are present to prevent an investor being involved in something deemed impermissible. As this is the main topic of the research, it is discussed in detail in the next chapter, together with the literature review.

References

Ainley, M., Mashayekhi, A., Hicks, R., Rahman, A., & Ravalia, A. (2007). *Islamic Finance in the UK: Regulation and Challenges*. Financial Services Authority.

Akram, M., Rafique, M., & Alam, H. M. (2011). Prospects of Islamic Banking: Reflection from Pakistan. *Australian Journal of Business and Management Research, 1*(2), 125–134.

Dudley, N. (1998). Islamic Banks Aim for the Mainstream. *Euromoney, 349*, 113–116.

Dusuki, A., & Abdullah, I. (2014). *Fundamentals of Islamic Banking*. IBFIM

ECB. (2013). *Islamic Finance in Europe* (Occasional Paper Series No.146).

Forte, G., & Miglietta, F. (2007). *Islamic Mutual Funds as Faith-Based Funds in a Socially Responsible Context.* Bocconi University.

Global Islamic Finance Report (GIFR). (2023). Published by Cambridge Insitute of Islamic Finance. United Kingdom

Hayat, U., & Malik, A. (2014). *Islamic Finance: Ethics, Concepts and Practice.* CFA Institute Research Foundation.

Iqbal, M., & Moyneu, P. (2005). *Thirty Years of Islamic Banking: History, Performance and Prospects.* Palgrave Macmillan.

Iqbal, Z. (1997). Islamic Financial Systems. *Finance & Development.*

Islamic Financial Services Board Stability Report. (2023). Published by Islamic Finacial Services Board. Malaysia.

ISRA. (2012). *Islamic Financial System: Principles and Operations*. International *Shari'a*h Research Academy for Islamic Finance.

IFSB. (2011). *Financial Policy and Stability.* Constraints on Growth in Islamic Finance.

Kamali, M. H. (2005). *Principles of Islamic Jurisprudence.* Pelanduk Publications.

Siddiqui, R. (2007). Shari'ah Compliance, Performance, and Conversion: The Case of the Dow Jones Islamic Market Index^{SM}. *Chicago Journal of International Law, 7*(2), 495–519.

Usmani, T. (2002). *An Introduction to Islamic Finance.* Arab and Islamic Law Series, Brill.

Zaheer, K. *What Is Islamic and What Is Not?* http://www.khalidzaheer.com/essays/kzaheer/islamic%20shariah/what_is_islamic_and_what_is_not.html

Zaher, T. S., & Hassan, K. M. (2001). A Comparative Literature Survey of Islamic Finance and Banking. *Financial Markets, Institutions and Instruments, 10*(4), 155–199.

CHAPTER 3

Islamic Equity Investments

3.1 Introduction

The focus of this research is on equity-based modes of investments. Equity finance, or rather sharing in the profit and loss of a company, is considered ideal when partaking in Islamic finance transactions (Khan, 2010). While debt finance structures have predominated in the industry, there is a strong advocacy towards equity finance. There are usually two ways to finance any business venture, when one's own resources are not available or are insufficient: borrow money (debt based) or invite a partner (equity based). The unique feature of the Islamic equity industry compared to conventional equity investments is that investors can only invest in assets deemed *Shari'a* compliant. *Shari'a* compliancy is achieved through a decision by *Shari'a* boards of financial institutions. These *Shari'a* boards are highly respected and understand that the underlying transaction is *Shari'a compliant* (Grais & Pellegrini, 2006).

The chapter starts with consideration of the historical developments of Islamic equity investments industry in Sect. 3.2 before discussing the *Shari'a* legitimacy of shares and joint-stock companies. The chapter then develops to provide a detailed discussion on the introduction of *Shari'a-compliant* screening methodologies and the process involved. The chapter concludes by presenting a detailed consideration of the issues facing the *Shari'a-compliant* screening methodologies in 3.6 and the research focus for this book in Sect. 3.7.

R. Malik, *Shari'a Compliant Equity Investments*,
https://doi.org/10.1007/978-3-031-70822-0_3

3.2 Historical Development

Islamic equity investments began with the pronouncement of Fatwa by Justice Mufti Muhammad Taqi Usmani (Pakistan), Professor Saleh Tug (Turkey) and Sheikh Mohammad Al Tayyeb Al Najar (Egypt) in July 1987. It is also suggested that it started with the 1986 launch of the Amana fund in the United States; however, it is believed that the 1987 Fatwa was more transparent with detailed stated preconditions for investing in public listed equity securities (Securities Commission Malaysia, 2009). Siddiqi (2007) also stated that the Islamic equity investments are only 20 years old. The number of Islamic equity funds and the assets under management (AUM) in these funds remained small between 1986 and 1994. However, the number of Islamic equity funds reached 130 between 1994 and 2006, and the AUM grew to $6 billion in 2003 from $800 million in 1996. Furthermore, the International Fiqh Academy also issued a ruling in 1992 that approved investment in the stock of companies that do not engage in activities which would violate *Shari'a* principles (Wilson, 2004). This could be the reason behind the sudden increase in the AUM of the Islamic funds. Before this ruling, the *Shari'a* ruling on equity investments was unclear and hence the slow growth in AUM.

Islamic funds are still in their infancy, compared to conventional and socially responsible investment (SRI) funds, in terms of both its AUM and its growth in the market. As reported by the Islamic Finance Services Board (IFSB) Stability Report, the AUM of Islamic funds reached US$ 182.24 billion by the end of 2023, with a steady growth evident since the 2008 financial crisis. In terms of assets allocations, majority of funds are equity funds 40.70%, followed by commodity funds—33.60%, money market funds—21.22%, fixed income—11.70%. However, before the financial crisis, the Islamic funds industry had grown rapidly over the last 10 years to become an important segment of the global Islamic banking and finance industry. The growth in the Islamic asset management industry is mainly attributed to the increased awareness of the Islamic funds industry and wealth management solutions, increase in the investible asset classes and the increase in global wealth (Fig. 3.1).

According to the IFSB Stability Report 2023, the Islamic fund management industry represents almost 4% of the total Islamic banking and finance industry and it is expected to grow between 10 and 15% per annum. Furthermore, this industry is expected to reach US$ 150bn by the year 2027.

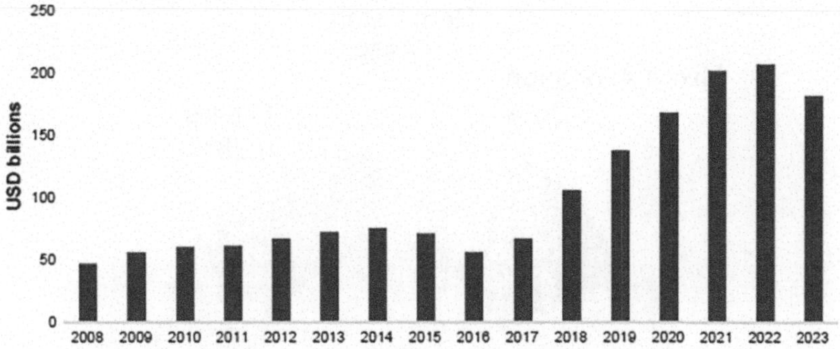

Fig. 3.1 Growth in Assets Under Management of Islamic Funds (2008–2023) (*Source* IFSB estimates based on data from Refinitiv for 2019–2023, including Iran. Data for the years 2008–18 from bloomberg database as per previous reports (excluding Iran due to data limitations))

Figure 3.2 also represents the growth in the different types of Islamic funds in the last nine years and clearly shows that the overall growth of equity type of funds is significantly more than the other types of funds. It is this equity investment that is the topic of this research and a review of the literature on the process of equity investments is conducted in the remainder of this chapter, together with a discussion on *Shari'a* investments, issues and gaps in the literature. Before exploring these issues, it is necessary to start with an insight into the nature of a modern-day company. This sub-section then examines the legitimacy of shares from the *Shari'a* perspective.

3.3 *Shari'a* Legitimacy of Shares and Joint Stock Companies

Companies can be formed in a number of different ways. There are three key considerations that the founder of a company has to determine: (1) the amount of funding needed to set up the company; (2) the amount of control the founder wishes to divest in the company; and (3) whether profits should be spread among a few or many. For instance, if a company requires funding from a third party, this may result in less control for the founder over company decisions. Conversely, the founder may want total ownership of the business but may have to sacrifice access to funds.

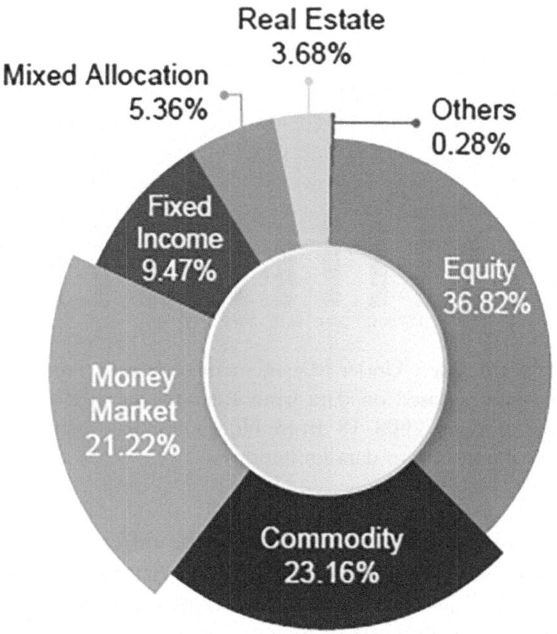

Fig. 3.2 Islamic Fund Assets by Asset Class (2023) (*Source* IFSB estimates based on data from Refinitiv; Islamic Finance Services Board Stability Report 2024)

A business entity can either be unincorporated[1] or incorporated.[2] The latter also includes public limited companies known as joint-stock companies, where individuals or entities own only a portion of the company.

Additionally, there are two ways that a company can raise capital funds: by borrowing (debt finance) and selling ownership (equity finance). Debt finance involves borrowing from a third party. The third party, as creditor, has only rights of repayment of capital in addition to earning interest. Equity finance grants the third party full or partial ownership of the

[1] An unincorporated business entity will be considered to have no separate legal personality of its own. The owners will bear the full risks and liabilities. Examples of unincorporated businesses include sole traders and informal partnerships.

[2] Incorporated businesses include companies that offer limited liability to shareholders such as limited liability partnerships and private and public limited companies.

company. The company divides its assets into indivisible units (shares) that investors can buy. The company often issues share certificates as an evidence of ownership of investors in the assets of the company. Equity investors receive a share of the profits generated by the company (dividends) and may additionally benefit from the sale of their shares. They can also contribute to the overall decisions the company makes in terms of strategy. The outcome of holding a share in the company is that investors can either benefit through the positive performance of the company, or suffer loss if the company experiences financial losses. In this manner, the investor is sharing in the profit and loss of the company. The shareholder has the option of disposing of their ownership by selling their shares. If the company is a public limited company, they will buy and sell their shares on the stock market. The first time when the company lists itself on the stock exchange will be through an initial public offering (IPO).[3] The buyer of the share can then sell the share on the secondary market. This creates a dynamic and ongoing trade activity that is evident in stock exchanges around the world. This activity may also act as an indicator of the performance of the economy.

Joint-Stock Company and Shari'a

The existence of joint-stock companies—and being a legal personality—is a relatively recent phenomenon and a European development. Roman law had some concept of the joint-stock company with a legal personality, but it was from the thirteenth century onwards that the concept was developed and refined. Still, it was not until the nineteenth century that the world witnessed a proliferation of joint-stock companies (Hickson et al. 2011). In classical Islamic law, there was no concept of a joint-stock company and only implicit recognition of limited liability. The idea that an intangible entity has rights is a modern idea (Hansmann et al., 2005). According to Elgari (1993), the "limited liability" characteristics of a joint-stock company may be the most significant yet most problematic according to *Shari'a*. Large corporations with indefinite life and multiple shareholders were not known, and therefore, no specific Islamic legal ideas were formed around the concept. In a limited liability company, a shareholder's loss is limited to the amount invested. Losses suffered

[3] An initial public offering (IPO) is a way of raising equity capital, where shares of stocks in a company are issued for the first time when the company is going public.

by a company, including creditor claims, cannot be borne by the shareholder. This feature allows shares to be traded in the market without being hindered by potential claims on a shareholder's own income.

In classical Islamic law, business entities were typically structured as partnerships (*sharikah*) of different variations. Partners would unite and invest either their capital or labour to a particular endeavour. Individuals could invest equal shares (*mufāwaḍah*) or unequal shares (*ʿinān*). A second type of business entity, besides the *sharikah* model, was the *muḍārabah*. The investor (*rabb al-māl* or capital provider) would provide the capital to a manager (*muḍārib*) of venture, who would undertake to invest the capital in a business transaction. Any liability would be limited to the capital invested. Here, we have an example of limited liability of the capital provider, unless there has been negligence on the part of the manager.

There is no standing of "limited liability" in the standard contracts of *Shari'a*; however, most of the *Shari'a* scholars who dealt with this issue concluded that the issue of joint-stock company is acceptable in *Shari'a* and hence "shares" as units of ownership are acceptable. The joint-stock concept is similar to a principle in the *Shafi'i* school of Islamic law where, in a business partnership with many different owners, zakat is levied on the whole of the assets and not on each individual. This means that the obligation of zakat is on the entity, making it similar to a legal personality as Elgari (1993)[4] said that a joint-stock company has an independent existence and identity from its owners.

Therefore, it was difficult to define the concept of joint stock from an Islamic perspective. For this reason, the concept of joint stock being a separate legal entity could not acquire approval from the scholars. Hence, they initially deemed this arrangement *Shari'a* non-compliant, until the OIC Fiqh Academy subsequently approved the concept of joint-stock company in 1992 (as discussed in Exhibit 3.1 below) and the concept was also approved by Sheikh Taqi Usmani in his discussions.

There are a number of differences between the Western concept of business partnership and traditional Islamic concepts. Business entities in classical Islamic law were usually short term and for specific transactions, whereas companies today transact on a number of deals usually without knowledge of the shareholders, although in an unrestricted *muḍārabah*,

[4] Elgari, M. (1993). Towards an Islamic Stock Market. *Islamic Economic Studies,* Vol. 1 No. 1 Dec.

agents can transact in any deal they see fit. Nevertheless, there were usually only a few parties to any given transaction who knew each other. In today's joint-stock company, there are many shareholders distributed worldwide. Decisions are usually made by the majority or those with preferential status. In classical Islamic entities, partners would make decisions in unison. However, in a *mufāwaḍah*, participants could act on behalf of the other as both agent and guarantor, but this was only accepted in the Ḥanafī school of thought, and, to some extent, the Mālikī school of thought (Borhan & Mohamad, 2009).

Thus, it can be said that under the classical concept of businesses, there were examples of limited liability and shareholders making decisions on behalf of others. However, there were three key differences to modern-day circumstances. First, most business transactions were small; second, any similarities were incidental rather than explicit; third, leading on from the second point, there was no explicit mention of a non-human entity having a legal personality. While there are still lingering doubts about the acceptability of limited liability and legal personality in Islam in academic debates, for practical purposes the debate was largely put to rest in 1992 when the OIC Islamic Fiqh Academy resolved that "*there is no objection in Sharīʿah to setting up a company whose liability is limited to its capital for that is known to the company clientele and such awareness on their part precludes deception*".

Currently, the capital markets have developed to such an extent that the joint-stock company is an established part of any country's economy along with the stock exchange in which shares of companies are regularly sold (through IPO) and traded. For an Islamic equity market to develop, it was necessary to address the legal gap on limited liability joint-stock companies with legal personality by finding precedents in classical Islamic law. Furthermore, the next steps would be to discuss the *Shari'a* permissibility of trading in these companies listed on the stock market.

Exhibit 3.1 *Shari'a* Legitimacy of Investment in Shares

The *Shari'a* ruling that approved equity investments was remarkable and vital for the expansion of the Islamic finance industry. The *Shari'a* ruling not only defined what company shares are but also specified the precise category of shares that could be purchased and sold by Muslim investors.

Initially, the concept of joint stock having a status of separate legal entity was new from the juristic point of view. In Islam, there has always been the idea of *mushārakah* (partnership). Therefore, it was difficult to define the concept of joint stock from an Islamic perspective.

The condition remained as such until the Organisation of the Islamic Conference (OIC) Fiqh Academy in May 1992 had approved the concept of joint stock stating that *"there is no objection in Shari'a for setting up a company whose liability is limited to its capital for that is known to the company clientele and such awareness on their part precludes deception"* (Resolutions and Recommendations of the Council of the Islamic Fiqh Academy 1985–2000, 2000: 130).

Besides the OIC Islamic Fiqh Academy approving the concept of joint-stock companies, in 1998 Sheikh Taqi Usmani also approved the concept, considering that a joint-stock company or a (joint) corporation is similar to partnership corporations and acknowledged the concept of separate legal entity by legalising it from a *Shari'a* perspective. This ruling was based on the practice of Islamic institutions like *waqf*, mosque and *bayt al-māl*. Because it is such an important ruling and single handedly legalised investment in stocks, below are details of Sheikh Usmani's arguments (2002) pertaining to joint-stock companies:

i. Once the property is declared as *waqf*, the donor cannot claim any sort of ownership on the *waqf* property. *"The beneficiaries of a waqf can be benefited from the corpus or the proceeds of the dedicated property, but they are not its owners"* (Usmani, 2002). Therefore, *waqf* institutions have a separate legal entity status. In addition, if any property is bought using the money of a *waqf* institution, the purchased property becomes the property of the *waqf* institution. This means that the ownership of the property will lie with the *waqf* as an institution. Regarding the donations given to those mosques that are managed by *waqf* institutions, such donations belong to the mosque only and cannot be a part of the *waqf*.

ii. The second argument was about *bayt al-māl*. Imām al-Sarakhsī (Al-Sarakhsi, al-Mabsut, 14:33) stated "*that bayt al-māl has some rights and obligations which may possibly be undermined*". Al-Sarakhsī stated that in the case of necessity, the head of an Islamic state can use *zakāh* funds for paying salaries to the army men when the funds available in *bayt al-māl* are not sufficient to meet such expenditures. However, the usage of *zakāh* funds is considered borrowing or loan taken by *bayt al-māl* (also called as *kharāj* department) and shall be repaid to the *zakāh* department.

iii. Thirdly, according to the Shāfiʿī school of thought, *zakāh* shall be calculated on the total stock of the partnership business wherein the assets of each partner are mixed with those of others. Hence, *zakāh* cannot be levied at the individual level. If any of the partners does not acquire enough assets (mostly shares) equivalent to the amount of *niṣāb* but the amount of total assets exceeds the *niṣāb* limit, *zakāh* is applicable on the total assets. This is based on the principle of *khulṭah-al-shuyūʿ* (it means mixing of assets by two or more partners in such a way that their ownership cannot be distinguishable except by way of apportionment) according to which in some cases a person has to pay more *zakāh* on the livestock, while in some cases less. Other classical jurists like Mālikī and Ḥanbalī had also accepted this principle. Therefore, as per the principle of *khulṭah-al-shuyūʿ "it is not the individual who is liable to pay zakāh. Again, it is the joint stock which has been made subject to the levy"*, indicating that joint stock has separate legal entity status.

iv. When a person dies without settling his debts and the ratio of debt is more than his property, his heirs do not get the ownership of his property as *"the debt on the deceased have a preferential right over the property as compared to the rights of the heirs"*, and so do the creditors. *"Being the property of nobody, it has its own existence and it can be termed as a legal entity. The heirs of the deceased or his nominated executor look after the property as managers"* (Usmani, 2002).

With regard to corporate shares, they are considered as partners' share in the company and testify the ownership of the partners in the paid up capital (in terms of assets and retained profits). Jurists have permitted the buying and selling of common shares; however, they have imposed a restriction on buying and selling of interest-bearing bonds, debentures and preference shares. It has been found that not all common shares are 100% *Shari'a* compliant. The question there is: is it permissible to trade the shares of such nature? In other words, what criteria should be used to determine whether it is permissible or not to trade stock in the case when the companies run a mix of permissible and prohibited activities?

A mixed company in this context means a company where its core or primary activities are permitted by *Shari'a*; however, there are some other activities in that company which may contain some small extent of prohibited activities/elements. According to Ḥanafi jurists, if the majority of something is permissible, then it becomes permissible in and of itself.

Based on this principle, the scholars have approved the concept of the stock market as well as trading of shares that are not 100% permissible.

In addition, the concept of *ṭahārah* (means purification) was also considered. Discussions on *ṭahārah* are commonly found in books of *fiqh* which cover the laws of cleanliness and purification in relation to many aspects of life. One of the topics examined pertains to purification of water. According to the laws of purification of water in *fiqh*, water is considered pure even if it contains some impure substances, provided the quantity of water reaches to "*qullatayn*" (refers to two large containers of water which is approximately 190 litres). For example, if the water in the lake contains impure substances like animals urine and others, people can still perform ablution (*wuḍūʾ*) using that water as the quantity of water is more than "*qullatayn*". However, if the impurity in the water changes the nature of water in terms of colour, smell or taste, then the water is deemed to be impure to perform ablution (*wuḍūʾ*).

The same analogy (*qiyās*) was used for companies' stocks. In order to buy company shares that are not 100% permissible, the nature of the company must remain pure, meaning it cannot have debt beyond the benchmark and the portion of non-permissible income should also be within the benchmark prescribed by *Shari'a* scholars. In order to identify non-permissible income, *Shari'a* scholars have developed *Shari'a* screening methodology for equity stocks (see detailed discussion on *Shari'a* screening in later sections).

Concept of Share

The Islamic Fiqh Academy of Organisation of the Islamic Conference (OIC)[5] thoroughly discussed the concept of share at a number of their meetings and agreed on the following definition: "a share is an undivided share in the assets of the company and the certificate is the instrument of the right to this share" (Amine, 2002).

AAOIFI also issued a *Shari'a* Standard that reiterates the position of Islamic Fiqh Academy with regard to the concept of share. Similarly, Elgari (1993) stated that shares are units into which a company's equity is divided and hence it represents an indivisible portion of the company's

[5] OIC—whose rulings are most respected with regard to Islamic finance and are largely followed by Islamic financial institutions.

total assets, real and monetary. Share-holders are the “owners” and yet the company has an independent existence from its “owners”. These shares can be transferred to others anytime. A joint-stock corporation is a type of business entity involving two or more legal persons (ISRA, 2012). Certificates of ownership are issued by the company, which represents undivided ownership in the company called shares. These joint-stock companies have become very important in the global economic and investment space. They have implemented several important tasks including construction, development and manufacturing projects (Yaquby, 2000). Elgari (1993), while stressing the importance of such joint-stock companies in the Muslim-majority countries, stated that “joint stock companies have become one of the most important financial innovations of modern times. Through this innovative form, it has been possible to raise enormous capital, which otherwise would not have been raised through other financial products. It has also made it viable to channel funds to viable investments and useful utilisation in the fields of industry, agriculture, real estate development projects”.

3.4 Trading in Equity Shares

As briefly discussed in Exhibit 3.1, tradability of shares in the secondary market is vital for the growth of equity market as otherwise liquidity concern will limit its growth. After establishing the permissibility of purchasing shares, the next question is whether the trading of shares is permissible or not.

McMillen (2013) stated that tests should be conducted to determine if the security itself is permissible. *Shari'a* scholars have allowed secondary market trading of shares by advocating shares as reflecting partnership interest where investment in shares can be interpreted as *Musharaka*. However, there are clear differences between a *Musharaka* and a modern-day share (as discussed in Sects. 3.3.1 and 3.3.2). These include share is assumed to have an infinite life, while *Musharaka* has a fixed time period, *Musharaka* partners share in profit while equity holders receive capital gain in addition to dividend (profit) and in *Musharaka* the agreement of all partners is needed while in an equity to stock market investments such decisions can be dealt with simple majority. The second is shares can be interpreted as ownership of enterprise, which subsequently means co-ownership of a company's net assets and owners are free to sell their ownership interest to third parties without permission of other co-owners (ISRA, 2012). The contemporary jurists are of the view that these requirements must be relaxed in the context of public limited companies. The stock markets allow shareholders to sell their shares in case they want to exit and hence there is no need for the liquidation of the company. Additionally, the modern-day equity valuation techniques help the partners receive the fair price of their shares in case they want to exit. Thus, the buying and selling of shares of the companies (whether private or public) is permissible, either on face value or at a price mutually agreed between the transacting parties. However, within the Islamic finance framework, some restrictions regarding the trading of shares would apply. For instance, *Gharar* and *maysir* are not allowed in *Shari'a*, but there is a strong tendency for these to occur in stock markets, which are causes for volatility in the markets. Therefore, investors and equity funds are recommended to avoid frequent purchases and sales on the market (ISRA, 2015). Moreover, it is not permitted to use future contracts,[6] options and swaps[7] while trading in shares[8] as all these contracts encourage speculation. It is also not permitted to be involved in the buying and selling of shares of a company whose assets are exclusively or predominantly cash as these are not tangible assets. It is furthermore not allowed to trade shares of a company whose assets are entirely or predominantly composed of debt or receivables. Lastly, another important restriction concerns selling shares that one does not own. This means that traditional short-selling is problematic in an Islamic financial framework.[9]

[6] Future contracts imply a delay in the delivery of an ascertained sold share—a matter which is prohibited under *Shari'a*. In addition, the seller usually does not own the asset at the time of entering into the contract and hence selling something that he does not own.

[7] The basis of impermissibility of swap contracts is because these include *riba* and in addition they include *gharar* because of the uncertainty about the amount of cash at the time of the contract.

[8] In the recent past, a number of *Shari'a-compliant* techniques have emerged to execute trading in shares in such a way that they generate economic effects of options and swaps but the use of such techniques is restricted to risk management and hedging and not for pure speculative trades.

[9] In the contemporary practice of Islamic finance, a limited number of techniques have emerged to replicate economic effects of short-selling in a *Shari'a-compliant* way. Their use remains limited, as they must be used for genuine hedging and risk management and not for speculative purposes.

Khatkhatay and Nisar (2007) stated that in the case of investing, the structure of equity share is acceptable according to *Shari'a* as they do not offer any fixed returns or benefits. The shareholders of equities are at risk of losing all their investments. Additionally, the equity investments do not necessarily involve the element of randomness that otherwise is found in gambling and games of chance. However, there can be possible problem or constraint, as in the nature of the counter-party or type of company you invest in. As you become a part-owner of the company and as an owner, the investor is responsible for anything that a company does against the *Shari'a*. Concurrently, as a minority shareholder, the investor is not expected to influence the decision of the company with regard to how they conduct their business.

Mufti Taqi Usmani commented "the contemporary *Shari'a* experts are almost unanimous that if all the transactions of a company are in full conformity with *Shari'a*, which includes neither borrowing on interest nor keeping surplus in an interest-bearing account, its shares can be purchased, held and sold without hindrance from *Shari'a* side". The *Shari'a* scholars are also in agreement that it is prohibited to invest in a company who's main line of business is based on prohibited elements—that is, involvement in *riba*-based transactions or involvement, facilitating, buying and selling of prohibited products and services (Al Amine, 2002).

Further, the OIC Fiqh Academy stated that "as a principle it is impossible to participate in companies that occasionally deal with prohibited transactions, such as usury, and the like, although their main business activities are primarily lawful".[10] Similarly, Elgari (1993) noted that a joint-stock company is permissible so long as the following conditions are evident:

"If a company avoids all prohibited activities, which include selling, distribution or production of alcohol, or activities giving rise to interest or gambling". After the debates with contemporary scholars, it was agreed that companies should be *Shari'a compliant* in their capital structure. Consequently, they should not borrow on interest or deposit their funds in interest-bearing accounts. However, some scholars exempted this as the minority shareholders are not able to influence the company's decision, such that the company avoid such activities. This issue is discussed in detail in the next sections.

[10] OIC Resolution No.64/1/7, subsection (1) (c).

Treatment of Companies Involved in Mixed Businesses

Section 3.3 above highlighted the limited Islamic financing availability for joint-stock companies in Western countries as well as Muslim-majority countries. Resultantly, these companies eventually have to deposit with and borrow funds from a conventional bank. Furthermore, the treatment of companies whose main business lines correspond with *Shari'a* but occasionally generate income from *Shari'a* non-compliant activities (mixed businesses) was unclear. Hence, the important question was whether *Shari'a* allows participating or trading in the shares of such companies (Yaquby, 2000). A lot of deliberations occurred and a number of research papers were presented at different events and workshops. Al Amine (2002) stated that scholars differ in the implementation and details of the treatment of companies in mixed businesses; some state that investment in such businesses is only allowed if the intention is to transform the *Shari'a* non-compliant business into *Shari'a compliant* in the first general meeting, while some prefer that the process continues until the third meeting.

On the other hand, some scholars have agreed a fixed percentage of non-permissible income and shareholders should do their best to calculate the haram element and give it away to the charity that is not to generate any benefit from the *Shari'a* non-compliant revenue. The process of purging unlawful gain is known as "purification" and is a very important element in *Shari'a-compliant* equity trading. Purification means deducting that part of the revenue which is generated from *Shari'a* non-compliant activities. In the case of equity investments, it refers to interest earnings and incidental income from other non-permissible sources of income including the sale of alcohol and pork; yet there remain scholars who strictly do not allow investment in companies with mixed businesses (Elgari, 2000). The advocates of permissibility base their arguments on the following legal maxims as stated by Yaquby (2000).

i. **That which is independently impermissible becomes permissible when done in conjunction with the permissible**

An analogy can be made for investing in a questionable company with the sale of an unborn offspring of an animal. This is impermissible unless the animal and its offspring are sold together. Similarly, it should be permissible to purchase ownership of a company which generates revenue through both permissible and impermissible means.

ii. **General need takes the ruling of specific necessity**

If Muslims are not allowed to purchase shares, then they would be obstructed from improving their livelihoods, which could cause hardship. Today, the stock markets generate millions for not only individual investors but also for funds, governments, among others. For instance, pension funds are the repository of saved income to be used once an individual retires. Pension funds invest actively on the stock market generating further income for eventual pensioners.

iii. **Majority has the ruling over the whole**

If the marginal activities constitute a negligible part of a company's revenue, then it is permissible to invest in the company.

iv. **What is inescapable is tolerable**

This is linked to necessity but acknowledges that in today's commercial markets, most companies will have some trace of impermissible income. It follows from the Prophetic hadith: *"There will come a time when you will not be able to find a single person in the world who will not be consuming ribā. And if anyone claims that he is not consuming ribā then surely the dust of ribā will reach him"* (Mishkāt al-Masābīh, 2818). By investing in companies, one cannot avoid the fact that there will be certain parts of the company's transactions which will be considered impermissible.

Needless to say, other jurists rebut the interpretation of these maxims that accord with the permissibility of investing in shares. Moreover, what can be garnered from the scholarly debates, and from the maxims mentioned above, is that it is not optimal to purchase shares even in companies whose peripheral activities are considered impermissible. According to the Jeddah-based Islamic Fiqh Academy, during its 7th session, resolution No. 64/1/7 sub-section (1)(c) was passed that states the following:

> As a principle, it is impermissible to participate in companies which occasionally deal with prohibited transactions, such as usury, and the like, although their main business activities are primarily lawful.

Additionally, the advocates and scholars who argued against the permissibility based their arguments on Quranic verses prohibiting usury "O you who believe! Fear Allah, and give up what remains of your demand for usury, if you are indeed believers" (2:278) and the hadith of Prophet (P.B.U.H) like "one usury-based dirham income that is knowingly earned by a person is more unlawful and worse in degree than thirty six adulteries" narrated by Ahmad and al-Tabarani. These are two clear authentic sources.

Having analysed the perspectives of scholars on both sides, Yaquby (2000) concluded that the arguments of those suggesting that investing in companies with mixed businesses is permissible is stronger than the scholars who prohibit it. Hence, allowances can be made as it is felt that Muslims, Islamic countries and Islamic financial organisations will suffer if they are not involved in the equity markets. Therefore, there is a resentful consensus about the permissibility of purchasing shares in companies whose marginal activities are impermissible. He further stated that an indication of this conclusion is that some of the scholars who initially opposed the idea have since changed their views and joined those who permit such transactions (investment is allowed as long as impermissible revenue is minor). Furthermore, the view of permissibility of investing is more beneficial to the growth of Islamic finance.

Jurists have also imposed restrictions on investments in these companies. This will be explored in the *Shari'a* screening section below.

3.5 *Shari'a* Screening for Equity Investments

Ahmed (2009) stated that a multi-stage screening process is involved in order to create a *Shari'a-compliant* portfolio. This portfolio is constructed by investing in companies that pass certain screening criteria. Htay et al. (2013) stated that since not all the assets or businesses a company is involved in are *Shari'a* compliant, regulators, *Shari'a* boards of banks and index providers have laid rules and tenets to ensure *Shari'a* compliance. These screening criteria need to adhere to *Shari'a*, which stems from three sources: Quran, Hadith and Ijtihad (Derigs & Marzban, 2008). To derive rules from the sources, the Islamic legislative model places the responsibility on trained jurists. Jurists typically undergo years of training developing the reasoning tools required to interpret the sources and apply to practical questions. Consequently, Islamic financial institutions have to hire trained *Shari'a* scholars (DeLorenzo, 2000) to interpret the sources and specify a set of checkable *Shari'a* guidelines to be used to differentiate halal[11] assets from haram.[12] Ahmed (2009) stated that these scholars have created various guidelines for the screening processes. These different screening strategies are due to varying interpretations of different *Shari'a* scholars following different schools of thought,[13] which can also be influenced by the cultural norms. Grais and Pellegrini (2006) noted that *Shari'a* compliance is recognised through a decision by a *Shari'a* authority that is highly respected and confirms that a given transaction adheres to *Shari'a*. The industry recognises the pitfalls of relying on the opinions of a single scholar. In order to ensure objectivity, Islamic financial institutions typically have three or more scholars to adjudicate on a financial practice. Together, they form the *Shari'a* supervisory board (SSB).[14]

Shari'a screening has been divided into business screening (qualitative screening) and financial screening (quantitative screening), also known as business of the enterprise and structure of the enterprise (Khatkhatay & Nisar, 2007). The business screening process looks to avoid companies which are deemed non-*Shari'a compliant* in terms of business activity. Financial screening is focused on reducing exposure to companies with high interest-bearing debt and a high proportion of intangible assets.

Business Screening

Business screens are sector screens reducing exposure to those businesses that undertake activities deemed non-permissible under *Shari'a* are excluded (Derigs & Marzban, 2008). Norman, T. (2006) listed these prohibited activities as:

[11] *Shari'a* compliant.

[12] *Shari'a* repugnant or *Shari'a* non-compliant.

[13] There are five school of thoughts, Shafi, Hanafi, Hambli, Maliki and Jaffari.

[14] Usually consist of three or more *Shari'a* scholars.

- Companies that produce, sell, distil or supply alcoholic beverages and products.
- Companies that produce, sell, distribute or slaughter pork and pork-related products.
- Companies involved in gambling, casinos, lotteries and related games.
- Companies whose basic activity is in the entertainment production like movies and cinemas.
- Companies engaged in producing adult entertainment such as pornography and obscenities in any type.
- Companies producing weapons.
- Companies that produce tobacco and tobacco-related products.
- Companies engaged in products related to aborted human foetuses.
- Companies engaged in human cloning.
- Companies with bad and harmful environmental record.
- Conventional banks, financial institutions and insurance companies.
- Companies with any impure activity exceeding 5% of revenues (Norman, 2006).

The above prohibited activities listed are uniform across all *Shari'a* screening methodologies. Naughton and Naughton (2000) reviewed the permissibility of stocks, bonds, futures and options and concluded that short selling, speculation and margin trading are prohibited under *Shari'a*. Additionally, there are some businesses that may be regarded *Shari'a* non-compliant, such as entertainment, defence and weapons (ISRA, 2012). Hence, investment in shares of such companies whose main line of business is in such activities is not allowed under *Shari'a*. Furthermore, there will be instances where the company's main line of business is *Shari'a* permissible but over time indulges in activities that are *Shari'a* repugnant.[15] Furthermore, there may be a company involved in *Shari'a* permissible activities but has acquired a subsidiary involved in *Shari'a* repugnant business (Siddiqui, 2007).

Khatkhatay and Nisar (2007) stated that the most conservative of the scholars do not allow even a small amount of revenue generated from haram activities, while others allow investments as long as the main line

[15] An example of such businesses includes a supermarket selling grocery items as well as alcoholic beverages and pork-related products. Other examples include hotel selling alcohol.

of business of the company is not *Shari'a* repugnant and the revenue from *Shari'a* repugnant business is only a minor part of the overall business. Such companies are also known as mixed companies (ISRA, 2012). An interesting suggestion by the authors was that in terms of business level screening, any business with even a small proportion of non-*Shari'a compliant* should not be allowed in the portfolio, thus moving towards a more conservative opinion. Typically, Islamic investment methodologies such as AAOIFI accept up to 5% threshold for companies to generate revenue from *Shari'a* repugnant businesses (AAOIFI, 2010) and are regarded incidental. Derigs and Marzban (2008) stated that the investable universe reduces after applying qualitative screens to the portfolio as the *Shari'a* repugnant businesses are excluded, therefore resulting in reduction of the overall investment universe.

Most of the screening methodologies accept the businesses generating revenue from prohibited elements up to 5%; however, Derigs and Marzban (2008) stated that DJIMI, S&P and Azzad follow most conservative opinion and consider a company *Shari'a* non-compliant if there is even small revenue generated from *Shari'a* non-compliant activities.

These are categorical prohibitions, but there are uncertainties regarding certain sectors. For instance, entertainment is a broad sector encompassing movies, animation, sports, computer games and others. Investing in production companies may be considered impermissible, whereas football clubs may be considered permissible. Therefore, different organisations and *Shari'a* boards will have different opinions.

Difficulties also arise where a company has mixed activities. The primary activity may be *Shari'a* compliant but one or a few of the subsidiary activities may be considered *Shari'a* non-compliant. An in-depth analysis of the company's activities is required in order to accurately decide whether the stock should be considered compliant or non-compliant. A number of scenarios can occur, which obscures whether a stock can be deemed *Shari'a* compliant.

In the contemporary world of Islamic finance and investing, detailed *Shari'a* guidelines have been developed to address the issues highlighted above. Such guidelines permit investments in companies where only a small percentage of the revenue is generated from non-compliant activities. The level of tolerance is determined by a benchmark. Most institutions and standard setting bodies, such as the AAOIFI, state that if the revenue generated by an organisation from *Shari'a* non-compliant activities is more than 5% of the firm's revenue, it is prohibited to invest in these companies. SEC Malaysia has imposed more progressive benchmarks that account for the type of good offered, and could rise to 20%. The percentage thresholds have no textual basis and are dependent on the institution.

Even with these benchmarks, problems arise despite the imposition of this limitation. The following are some of the commonly observed problems:

Availability of Information

> In some cases, information might not be available. The breakdown of revenue from which to determine the acceptable percentage may not be publicly available, making it difficult for the auditor to assess the *Shari'a* compliance of the company. For instance, it may be difficult to determine how much revenue of a supermarket is generated from alcoholic beverages. In which case, the *Shari'a* auditor would have to directly contact the company in order to request the revenue breakdown. In certain jurisdictions like Malaysia, the regulatory body (SC Malaysia) has the authority to request details from listed companies which then resolves the issue of non-availability of information.

Change of Business Focus

> Over time, business focus can change. It may be that the initial analysis of the company showed that the company had less than 5% of revenue in *Shari'a* non-compliant activities. However, over time, this percentage may exceed the threshold. Consequently, *Shari'a* auditors have to be constantly vigilant regarding the activities of the company. In the case of Malaysia, for instance, SC Malaysia recommends for the business screening assessment to be undertaken every year.

Customer Exclusivity

> A *Shari'a*-compliant company may be predominately producing goods for a *Shari'a* non-compliant company or goods that are facilitating *Shari'a* non-compliant activities. However, unless or until it is found that there is this exclusivity, then the company is deemed *Shari'a* compliant.

A *Shari'a* auditor is thus required to analyse company information from a number of sources, including company accounts. Occasionally, they may need to go beyond this information and contact the company directly. Vigilance is also required as a company's strategy and conditions can change quickly. The *Shari'a* auditor would be keen to ensure that the investor divests quickly of the stock once it becomes clear that the stock is *Shari'a* non-compliant.

Financial Screening

To fund an expansion or to maintain enough liquidity for working capital purposes, most companies borrow from conventional financial companies meaning they are indebted and have to pay interest. Entities also deal with intangible assets. If the company is procuring too many financial products as part of its financial management, this can generate *Shari'a* concerns.

The second stage of screening is the financial screening (Ahmed, 2009). The reason for employing financial screening is due to the fact that *Shari'a* forbids involvement in *riba*, trading of money and hence it is necessary to analyse how deeply companies are involved in such practices (Derigs & Marzban, 2008). The aim is to capture how much interest-based income the company receives and how much interest it pays on its debt. Many successful listed companies based in both Muslim- and non-Muslim-majority countries[16] may place excess funds in interest-bearing accounts, own certificates of deposits (CDs), bonds and other interest-bearing securities and hence cause incurrence of impermissible income (interest), which will also become part of total earnings of the company. This impermissible income makes the company *Shari'a* non-compliant that otherwise was a *Shari'a-compliant* company. Similarly, many companies on occasions may borrow on interest such as by issuing bonds, and hence pay interest. Khatkhatay and Nisar (2007) stated that from a *Shari'a* perspective three aspects are to be considered: debt owed by the company, interest and other non-permissible income, and cash and receivables of the company. Furthermore, the money cannot be traded in *Shari'a* as it does not have any value,[17] the level of cash and cash equivalent has to be measured and compared to the maximum allowable threshold (Derigs & Marzban, 2008). Companies are expected to

[16] Apart from Iran and Sudan whose financial economy is based on *Shari'a* as they declare.

[17] Money is not an asset and does not have a value on its own and cannot be traded. It has to meet a tangible product to be called an asset.

have tight debt controls and limits to the amount of financial assets on their balance sheets. In this way, investors will have the comfort that the companies they invest in are not highly leveraged, nor are they exposed to unbridled corporate speculation. These problems caused the eventual collapse of Enron and Worldcom, two companies that would have been considered *Shari'a* compliant from a business point of view. However, both stocks were removed from the Dow Jones Islamic Market Index months before their crash due to their financial situations. It succeeded in protecting *Shari'a* sensitive investors from the precipitous fall of their share prices (Chorafas, 2005).

Siddiqui (2007) states that this is a relaxed form of the strictest application of *riba* ban in the complex financial world. *Shari'a* scholars implicitly acknowledge the fact that a pure Islamic economy or pure Islamic capital market does not exist and it is difficult to find a company that is not involved in interest-bearing transactions, involving cash deposits, loans or credits (ISRA, 2012). Very few companies operating in the global markets are *Shari'a compliant* in their debt profile and cash management; that is, all listed companies directly or indirectly get involved with the conventional banking and financial institutions. Furthermore, Wilson (2004) stated that the Muslim investors will not be able to participate in the capital markets if the strictest form is followed. *Shari'a* scholars use different sources of *Shari'a* to further interpret such situations, resulting in the creation of different thresholds, which limit the amount of *riba*-based revenue acceptable to *Shari'a* scholars (Derigs & Marzban, 2008, Khatkhatay & Nisar, 2007). *Shari'a* opinion in this regard is that while the current financial structure of a company is not optimal, investment should still be permitted. The rationale for using such thresholds and allowing minor impermissible activities has been stated above.[18] Some *Shari'a* scholars are of the view that if the main line of business of a company is *Shari'a* permissible and exposure to *riba* and other prohibited business is limited, they argue that judgement should be based on majority, as majority deserves to be treated as a whole (AAOIFI, 2004). Further, the aim of the tolerance or relaxation of the rules is based on the aim of removing hardship, acknowledging the general need for interest-based activities, and does not necessarily mean acceptance of *riba* or other *Shari'a* impermissible activities (AAOIFI, 2004). Yaquby (2000) states

[18] *Shari'a* investors are only minority shareholders and hence they do not have the power to force the company to operate completely in *Shari'a-compliant* manner.

that, given the lack of Islamic banks in many Muslim and non-Muslim-majority countries, these companies use conventional banks to finance their ventures. Hence, such companies are left with limited choice but to use conventional banks to borrow funds or deposit cash.

In order to safeguard investors from high leverage, poor financial management and payment of interest, a number of financial ratios have been formulated. Each financial ratio must meet a certain threshold. According to AAOIFI standard No.21, in order for a company to be permissible to invest in there are certain financial screening ratios which must be met, if the nature of the business is *Shari'a* permissible (AAOIFI, 2004). In order to assess as to what extent a company is involved in *Shari'a* non-compliant activities, a thorough financial analysis has to be carried out using financial statements published by the companies on a regular basis (Derigs & Marzban, 2008).

There is no real consensus on the right financial ratio. Islamic banks and financial institutions, including regulators, agree on certain criteria in assessing the *Shari'a* compliancy of the companies and to assess which companies to invest in. Regulatory bodies, index providers, funds and Islamic banks can have different criteria for the same ratio, or different ratios altogether; however, the aim remains to capture interest income and interest expense. Generally, there are three ratios used: measuring debt, liquid assets and interest income and forth being the non-permissible income (Derigs & Marzban, 2008).

Hence, in a state of interim tolerance, a little impermissibility is acceptable to majority shareholders as long as the community continues to achieve *Shari'a* purity. Siddiqui (2007) defines the current state of *Shari'a* compliancy as tolerating little impermissibility, but going forward it should reach a new paradigm (*Shari'a* enabling).

The following financial ratios or screens are commonly used: liquidity screen, debt screen, interest-bearing investments screen and impermissible business revenue screen.

Liquidity Screen

Liquid assets include current assets, cash and cash equivalents, short-term investments, and account receivables. Not all companies are generally in a position to make full cash payments; hence companies agree to pay on an instalment basis which gives rise to receivables for seller company (Siddiqui, 2007). Siddiqi (2004) stated that liquid assets should be traded at par, hence a company that has a majority assets comprised of cash or debt assets (receivables) cannot be traded either above or below the book value (Khatkhatay & Nisar, 2007). This is the case as *Shari'a* scholars have considered a company as the bundle of assets and liabilities, including fixed assets, investments, cash, receivables and payables. The share price paid is hence considered as a price paid for the assets and liabilities of the company. If the fixed assets (tangible assets) of the company are negligible and majority assets include debt and receivables (intangible assets), the company may have value of the company above the par value. This is due to the fact that the company is driven by future expectations of prices and not by book value. To overcome this issue, *Shari'a* scholars have put in place a limit on the amount of tangible assets and intangible assets (Khatkhatay & Nisar, 2007). AAOIFI has also introduced a liquidity screen; it employs the condition that the market value of tangible assets and benefits should not be less than 30% of the total assets or else the rules of sarf[19] will be observed (AAOIFI, 2010); intangible assets can be up to 70% of total assets. This ratio is 33%, according to DJIMI. According to Siddiqui (2007), *Shari'a* allows investing in a company if the main line of business is *Shari'a compliant* and cash, and receivables do not represent a majority of the total assets. He further stated that if the receivables of the company are more than 50%, this means that the company is in fact trading in money and not in assets, which is not permitted. It is known that a company with high receivables may face high credit risk, which may ultimately affect the stock prices negatively.

Level of Debt

Corporations depend on borrowing from banks on a short- to long-term basis to fund its growth and developments. On a short-term basis, it may take the form of loans that may arise due to working capital needs, and on a long-term basis, it may arise in the form of issuing a bond for infrastructure development or expansion. Hence, for these reasons, it may become inevitable for companies to avoid having debt on their balance sheet. Siddiqui (2007) stated that, although companies do not benefit by making interest payment as result of this debt, such activities are not permissible according to *Shari'a* as both interest income and expense are not allowed. Derigs and Marzban (2008) stated that not only

[19] Gold is to be paid for by gold, silver by silver, wheat by wheat, barley by barley, dates by dates and salt by salt—like for like, equal for equal, payment being made on the spot. If the species differ, sell as you wish provided that payment is made on the spot.

the receiving of interest is banned but also interest payments are generally not permissible. The level of interest payment for debt is also measured and limited by a threshold level, since a larger number of companies have exposure to interest-based finance (Wilson, 2004).

Furthermore, as the *Shari'a-compliant* alternatives at the time of *Shari'a* screening methodologies were limited, *Shari'a* scholars have allowed the interest-bearing debt to market cap to be 33%. Ahmed (2009) also confirmed that usually the acceptable leverage ratio is 33% of total assets or market capitalisation.

Interest-bearing Securities

The general practices at most companies are that excess cash is deposited in the bank accounts, which may generate a nominal interest. Additionally, at times companies may purchase fixed income securities or CDs as part of treasury management activity. Such investments in interest-based deposits, interest-based securities including treasury bills, government and corporate bonds, and preferred stocks are not *Shari'a compliant* (Elfakhani et al., 2005). However, in the current circumstances, it might be very difficult to avoid them as almost all firms have a relationship with the bank which might generate some form of interest.

The aim of this threshold is to assume that investment in interest-bearing securities is at an acceptable level. *Shari'a* scholars have allowed investing in such interest-bearing securities as long as it makes up a small portion of total income. The threshold acceptable for such variable is also 33%. Furthermore, from an investor's perspective, interest-bearing securities to market capitalisation or total assets may provide an interesting insight into the management's use of cash for the growth of the company[20] (Siddiqui, 2007).

Non-Permissible Income Screen

This screen is usually used for companies with mixed businesses where the primary line of business of the company is permissible; however, they indulge in *Shari'a* non-compliant businesses as well. However, most *Shari'a* boards tolerate a small amount of impermissible income as long as the main line of business is *Shari'a* compliant. Additionally,

[20] A high interest-bearing securities to market cap ratio may indicate the company does not have sufficient investment opportunities which in turns signal lower growth and hence negative affect on the stock price.

finding companies that are fully *Shari'a compliant* are scarce. According to AAOIFI (2010), such a screen requires that non-*Shari'a-compliant* activity should be less than 5% of the total income of the company.

Khatkhatay and Nisar (2007) conducted a critical analysis of three screens: Dow Jones, Meezan Bank and Securities Commission of Malaysia. Their conclusion was that all three screening methodologies need further modification. They opined that the much-used screen (cash and receivables to market capitalisation) is not required. The book also concluded that the use of market capitalisation as a denominator in screening methodologies is not appropriate and it should be replaced by a more stable variable that is total assets. Furthermore, the first screening methodology introduced was DJIMI which is based on balance sheet information. The interest income and interest expense are assessed by using balance sheet items like total receivables to market capitalisation and total debt to market capitalisation. McMillen (2013) states that these are at best rough measures and do not take into account the actual interest income and expense. He further suggests that at the time of DJIMI the information available was rather limited; however, with developments in accounting standards and requirements of disclosure, more information has been made available. Hence, going forward the ratios should be based on actual interest income and expense rather than using debt and total receivables figure. This will assist with issues facing the market capitalisation figure which in the financial crisis has been volatile. However, there has not been any consensus on using the actual interest income and expense figures. Similarly, there is a difference of opinion among the *Shari'a* scholars on the use of the 5% threshold as to the type of impermissible income that should be captured. Attention has been given to the type of impermissible income; however, it all depends on the available information. The important question remains what needs to be done if information is not available.

Table 3.1 highlights different screens used; there are different thresholds used for different screening methodologies. There is no collective consensus on the use of level of tolerance thresholds as it varies from one methodology and *Shari'a* board to the other. However, the commonly used thresholds for interest-bearing debt and cash and interest-bearing debt is 30%–33%, while for cash and receivables it is 33%–50% (BinMahfouz & Ahmed, 2014).

Derigs and Marzban (2008) stated that as these ratios define the *Shari'a-compliant* universe, it is important for *Shari'a* sensitive investors

Table 3.1 *Shari'a-compliant* screening methodologies

	AAOIFI[21]	*SEC Malaysia*[22]	*DJIM*[23]	*MSCI Islamic*[24]	*FTSE Islamic*[25]	*Russell Jadwa*
Year of Launch	**2010**	**2013**	**1999**	**2007**	**1999**	**2009**
Business screening	5%	5%–20%		5%	5%	5%
Financial screening ratios						
– Interest-bearing debt/Market Capitalisation	30%					
– Interest-bearing securities/Market Capitalisation	30%					
– Cash & receivables/total assets	70%					
– Total debt/total asset		33%		33.33%	33%	
–Cash and interest-bearing/total asset				33.33%	33.33%	
– Account receivable and cash/total asset				33.33%	50%	
– Total Cash/Total assets		33%				
– Debt/24 months average Market Capitalisation			33%			
– Cash and interest-bearing/ 24 month average Market Capitalisation			33%			

(continued)

21 Accounting and Auditing Organisations for Islamic Financial Institutions.

22 Securities and Exchange Commission Malaysia.

23 Dow Jones Islamic Markets.

24 Morgan Stanley Capital International.

25 Financial Times Stock Exchange Islamic Index Series.

Table 3.1 (continued)

	AAOIFI	*SEC Malaysia*	*DJIM*	*MSCI Islamic*	*FTSE Islamic*	*Russell Jadwa*
– Account receivable and Cash/24 month average Market Capitalisation			33%			
– Interest-bearing debt/12 month average Market Capitalisation						33%
– Total cash, deposits and receivables/12 month average Market Capitalisation						70%
– Total cash, deposits and interest-bearing securities/12 month average Market Capitalisation						33%

to find out where these ratios are derived from. The screening process is not explicitly mentioned in the Quran or Hadith. The most frequent screen used for debt and interest is at a level of 33%. Obaidullah (2005) stated that this is based on a hadith where Prophet (P.B.U.H) advised a companion not to donate more than one-third of his wealth and stated that "One Third is too much" (*Al Thuluth Katheer*). Furthermore, he stated that the use of the above Hadith is debatable as it was used in a very different context, since the situations differ widely from the screening processes in which they are used. Additionally, from fiqhi rule of a commodity that is part gold and part silver, it is considered gold and rules of *riba* apply if the part gold is more than 33% (Derigs & Marzban, 2008). Additionally, the range 33% and 50% is agreed from the *Shari'a* maxim associated with the rule of majority; the majority can be classified as a "simple majority" in the case of 50% and a super majority in the case of more than 67%. The *Shari'a* boards of FTSE, S&P, HSBC and Azzad Islamic funds used these thresholds, and view that the illiquid portion of assets should be higher than liquid portion. The ratio of 70% for liquid assets AAOIFI and 33% for MSCI is used for the liquid assets of the company. A ratio of 80% is also used for liquidity screen and followed by Meezan Islamic funds and is based on Hanafi school of thought. Here, the argument is that portion of liquid and illiquid assets is not critical until the total illiquid assets are of insignificant quantity and the liquid assets per share are higher than the market price of the company. This ensures that the price difference is due to the illiquid assets. In case, the value of liquid assets per share is higher than market price, and the stock is considered *Shari'a* non-compliant as money can only be traded at par. In case of Meezan, net liquid assets are used, which are obtained by subtracting current liabilities from current assets. On the other hand, the 5% threshold used for impermissible income is based on the Ijtihad of scholars and is not based on any Quranic reference or Hadith (Derigs & Marzban, 2008).[26]

Furthermore, there are two types of denominators used in the financial screening: (i) market capitalisation and (ii) total assets. There are discussions in the literature on the use of both. Proponents of total assets state that market capitalisation which is dependent on the stock price is very volatile, while total assets represent true value of the company. However,

[26] However, the non-*Shari'a-compliant* income needs to be purified for it to be considered halal.

the proponents of market capitalisation argue that total assets do not capture the value of intangible assets like goodwill.

Some of the existing Islamic screening methodologies are as below:

Purification Requirements

Shari'a opinion remains uncomfortable with even a small percentage of impure income. Consequently, it is a strict requirement that this impure income should be divested in order to purify the company's revenue.

The idea of purification of revenue has strong foundations in Islamic law. The obligatory payment of *zakāh* (alms-giving) under the *Shari'a* is considered a purification of a person's income. Purification of the revenue is in addition to the *Shari'a* screenings imposed on *Shari'a*-compliant stocks. This amount is typically distributed to charities or other philanthropic endeavours. It is strictly prohibited to use the purification funds for the benefit of the investor, either using the funds for any tax benefit or as part of *zakāh* obligation.

To calculate the amount that should be paid for purification is wrought with difficulties. A central problem is calculating the percentage of the income generated from non-*Shari'a* activities. It may be obscured and aggregated into other categorisations of revenue. For instance, in the accounts of a supermarket, porcine products would be aggregated under revenue generated from food and beverages. This creates challenges in calculating the exact amount of revenue that should be purified.

Even if the total revenue generated from the non-*Shari'a-compliant* activities can be determined, the return that accrues to the investor can come from dividends or capital gains. Scholars have preferred dividend purification where a portion of the dividend to an investor is divested. In this case, AAOIFI advocates the following method for purification:

1. Identify the total number of common shares of the company.
2. Divide the total prohibited income by the total number of shares issued to get non-compliant dividend per share.
3. Multiply these by the total number of shares owned by the investor.
4. This final amount should be reduced from the dividends.

The "dividend purification" technique is only suitable for companies that pay out all of their income as dividends. This is not a common practice particularly with growth companies that prefer to reinvest a large proportion of the dividends as investments which overtime might increase the value of the company. This means the revenue for purification will be reduced. If the non-compliant income is 4%, of which 2% is reinvested into the company, it will be on the remaining 2% that purification will occur.

Another problem is that stocks may have exchanged hands a number of times before the time of purification. It would mean that the last holder of the stock before purification would bear the burden. Such treatment may encourage selling of stocks just before the last day of the financial year creating unwanted price volatility. Hence, this approach has been argued as an incomplete form of purification. Investment income would need to be cleansed to complete the purification. The second approach is called the "investment purification", where the non-compliant income is purified irrespective of whether it makes any profit or not. This approach is a more conservative approach and is used by a number of financial institutions in the GCC.

3.6 Issues Within Existing *Shari'a* Screening Methodologies

Shari'a screening methodologies are used by different institutions for various purposes. These include fund managers, index providers, investors and market intelligence providers. These users have different objectives, which are reflected from the choice of methodology they select. The aim of any portfolio manager is to select a stock that provides high return or the objective in line with the investment philosophy. However, for an Islamic fund manager, there will be an extra layer of compliance and ensuring that the underlying stocks not only provide high return but are also in compliance with the *Shari'a*. Similarly, Khatkhatay and Nisar (2007) believe that index providers may have their own objective of providing a picture that reflects the overall state of the market. Hence, their selection criteria will be in favour of highly traded and large cap stocks. They provide a measure of the market compared to earlier days. Indices can also assess how a stock is performing compared to the market or index; hence for them, what is important is the price and market capitalisation of the stock; the higher the market capitalisation stock, the more important for index provider.

The regulators will have an objective of ensuring the smooth and healthy development of the market without sudden shocks and volatility. At times, national policy about a particular industry, such as alcohol industry in a particular Muslim country, can change. The regulators will have to monitor these stocks and provide regulatory concessions to promote regulators policy.

Concurrently, when conservative *Shari'a* scholars would like to define screening methodologies to identify *Shari'a-compliant* stocks, the concern will be to select those stocks which have minimum *Shari'a* non-compliant element.

This section critically reviews the *Shari'a* screening criteria and issues associated with implementing the screening processes. The issues will include discussions from the existing literature on business screening, credibility, inconsistency, financial ratios screening tolerance thresholds and social responsibility.

Imprecision

Shari'a screening methodologies were introduced as a need of time, to establish a control factor on how much a *Shari'a* sensitive investor can be involved in impure businesses. The first *Shari'a* screening methodology DJIMI institutionalised the principle that some degree of impermissibility is tolerated.

The ratios that became part of DJIMI screening methodology were based on the information available at the time. The aim of the financial ratios was to capture interest income and interest expense of a company. This is captured using balance sheet items, like the ratio of debt and receivables to market capitalisation. After DJIMI, other *Shari'a* screening methodologies (including the most recent ones like AAOIFI, Russel Jadwa) have adopted similar balance sheet items to capture the prohibited income and expense. However, McMillen (2013) stated that these measures at best are approximate and do not take into account the actual interest income and expense rates and amounts. Furthermore, he stated that the *Shari'a* board of DJIMI stressed the importance of adopting more precise financial tests should they become available, in order to ensure that *Shari'a* compliance is measured using the most accurate information available.

DJIMI was introduced in 1999 and since then there has been a lot of developments in the financial industry, regulatory requirements and disclosure on annual statements. Screening methodologies have remained stagnant and failed to evolve with a view to improve the ratios.

There is a need to review the existing screening methodologies to ensure that the precise prohibited element, the interest income and interest expense can be captured in an efficient manner. The alternative screening methodology should depend on the actual prohibited element and not on imprecise figures.

Further, there are issues with regard to the implementation of business screens for companies involved in mixed businesses and hence generate impermissible income in addition to interest income. For example, a company involved in producing beverages (both alcoholic and non-alcoholic) is regarded *Shari'a compliant* as long as the revenue generated from alcoholic beverages is less than 5%. However, what happens if the information is not available on the revenue of alcoholic beverages. Furthermore, the treatment of a company that produces furniture to be used by conventional financial institutions has a difference of opinion among *Shari'a* scholars.

There is also a difference of opinion among various screening methodologies on the exemption of different businesses, as some of these screens were introduced by borrowing concepts from the SRI industry. There is a lack of authentic Islamic source prohibiting investing in defence and tobacco. She further avers that not only is there a lack of direct *Shari'a* source of prohibition, but also there are various verses in the Quran that allow Muslims to protect themselves in the state of war. Similarly, there is a lack of a clear *Shari'a* source that prohibits investing in companies producing tobacco-related products.[27]

Standardisation

Since the introduction of the DJIMI methodology, all other methodologies are derivatives of DJIMI and are equally *Shari'a compliant* as they have been approved by *Shari'a* board or scholars. However, they differ

[27] AbdRahim stated that there is a difference of opinion among the scholars on smoking cigarettes while there is a Fatwa issued by Permanent Committee of Academic, Research and Fatwa Saudi Arabia, classifying tobacco as haram, the Body of Muslim scholars in Indonesia has issued an opinion classifying cigarettes smoking merely an act to be avoided and not haram.

from each other slightly on the use of financial thresholds. A key difference is the use of market capitalisation or total assets as the denominator. This has resulted in no uniformity among the screens used and there is no universal code of investment agreed upon by the scholars. Derigs and Marzban (2008) undertook a research on the current screening methodologies used by different institutions, including fund managers, banks and indices. The points raised in the book are very crucial for a sustainable development of Islamic fund management industry. They concluded that *Shari'a* scholars are allowing certain stocks to be *Shari'a compliant* under one methodology and non-compliant under the other methodology. They argue that such inconsistencies can contribute towards the insecurity of the investors in Islamic fund management industry. They opined that "the development of a unified and standardised screening framework that takes into account the different existing *Shari'a* guidelines and allows a controlled and understandable classification will certainly enrich the credibility and consistency of Islamic equity products" (Derigs & Marzban, 2008). Cognisant (2012) studied the complexities the fund manager has to handle when assessing the compliancy of a stock. Different results transpire from different methodologies, which leads to the conclusion that there needs to be consistency in the way financial ratios are interpreted otherwise it might lead to further confusion for the fund manager. The fund managers also benefit from the type of *Shari'a* screening methodology that is being followed as certain methodologies may render more stock *Shari'a compliant*, compared to methodologies that shrink the *Shari'a* universe the most.

Derigs and Marzban (2008) opine that there are two possible reasons for the difference of opinions among the *Shari'a* scholars in terms of screening methodologies. First, *Shari'a* screening and equity investment is a new phenomenon and hence the practices are based on *ijtehad* of *Shari'a* scholars who have a difference of opinions arising from personal reasoning or the school of thought they follow. In particular, the financial screening criteria are not mentioned in the *Quran* or *Sunnah*. Second, there is no higher authority among Muslims that is responsible for *Shari'a* rulings that can be followed by all Muslims. There is no final arbiter on a decision. This said, BinMahfouzooz and Ahmed (2014) stated that although there are no higher authorities for Muslims, Islamic Fiqh Academy, as a credible universal *Shari'a* authority can set up a global *Shari'a* screening methodology—which should be followed by all stakeholders of *Shari'a* sensitive investments. They further suggested setting up national level *Shari'a* boards that ensure *Shari'a* consistency and ensure acceptability of the criteria.

Additionally, when various screening methodologies used by different fund managers are analysed, the portfolio of stocks constructed after screening will differ from each other. This means that although all these Islamic screening methodologies are considered to align with the dictates of the *Shari'a*, the results will differ based on the constituents of the methodology (Ahmed, 2009). For example, to constitute the Dow Jones Islamic Market Index, the denominator for the ratios used is market capitalisation. Based on this, a particular stock may be *Shari'a* compliant. On the other hand, if the FTSE methodology (which uses total assets as a divisor) is used for the same stock, it might not be *Shari'a* compliant. With the ongoing maturation of the Islamic banking and finance industry, such inconsistencies need to be phased out. Ho et al. (2014) conducted a quantitative book of 21 *Shari'a-compliant* screening methodologies used throughout the world by a number of Islamic finance users and concluded that different users have different objectives and based on that they choose a different screening methodology. The authors assert that a great mean can be achieved if these screening methodologies are harmonised.

Credibility

Although the *Shari'a* authenticity of screening methodologies is intact, there is criticism in the literature that it has not received the approval of a credible, independent and universal *Shari'a* authority like Islamic Fiqh Academy. The Islamic Fiqh Academy has only approved investment in stocks whose business is fully incompliance with *Shari'a*—that is, the most conservative view (BinMahfouz & Ahmed, 2014). On the other hand, AAOIFI—a *Shari'a* standard body—has issued the *Shari'a* screening methodology which has been approved by its *Shari'a* board who are independent of the industry. To complicate matters further, the *Shari'a* board members sit on a number of *Shari'a* boards in Islamic financial institutions or are part of *Shari'a* board of a screening methodology. BinMahfouz and Ahmed (2014) further stated that Islamic Fiqh Academy is a higher authority, responsible for all general religious rulings and represent all Muslim countries, and AAOIFI on the other hand is only specialised to issue *Shari'a* principles to standardise Islamic finance industry. Hence, discussions need to be undertaken between AAOIFI and Islamic Fiqh Academy to reach a solution to this.

Financial Screening and Tolerance Thresholds

Yaquby (2000) analysed the view of scholars who argued that it is not permissible to participate in business of company that generate even a small percentage of their revenue from *Shari'a* non-compliant activities. Dissidents argue that the issue of *riba* cannot be tolerated in Islam as evident by Quranic verse (2:279) where Allah has declared war on the people who deal with it (BinMahfouz & Ahmed, 2014). They further cited this as one of the reason why it has not been approved by Islamic Fiqh Academy.

However, the screening practices approved under *Maslahah*[28] allow investment in companies whose revenue from *Shari'a* impermissible activities is incidental and negligible. Furthermore, the screens allow investment in companies that deal with interest-bearing debt or securities and their exposure is up to 33%. Threshold of 33% is debatable as Dusuki (2009) questions the *Shari'a* authenticity of these screening methodologies, and mentions that if, under *Shari'a,* even a small amount of interest is prohibited then what are the justifications to allow the threshold to be 33% and up to interest income to be 5%.

The threshold of 33%, or one-third, is taken from a hadith of Prophet (P.B.U.H); however, Obaidullah (2005) stated the hadith above was used in the context of inheritance and hence it is being used out of context in the screening process. Second, the 5% threshold is based on the *ijtehad* of *Shari'a* scholars in order to define minimum acceptable share (or classify something as minority) and is centred on the fact that individual shareholder does not have control over the whole business.

Islamic banking and finance has developed immensely since the screening methodologies were first introduced in 1999 and hence Islamic financing availability has enhanced. BinMahfouz and Ahmed (2014) argue that tolerating interest-bearing debt and securities based on the law of necessity is not valid anymore (particularly in Muslim-majority countries) or countries where Islamic finance has developed. They also argued that conventional debt and instruments should gradually be replaced with

[28] For the state of general need and public interest, rule of exception for removing hardship for an interim period, until the Islamic banking and finance industry is developed.

Shari'a-compliant alternatives. Wilson (2004) stated that lower thresholds should be used for such countries, as this will motivate companies to use Islamic financing instead of conventional debt or securities. However, in countries where Islamic financing availability is limited, higher thresholds can be used. Khatkhatay and Nisar (2007) stated that the tolerated level of debt should be based on unavoidable level of debt such as working capital. They further stated that the existing levels of tolerance are too liberal as in an ideal world it should be zero.

Securities Commission Malaysia did not include any financial screening thresholds until 2013 and were regarded as the most liberal organisation. Since then, this has changed to include financial screens based on interest-bearing debt and interest-bearing cash to market capitalisation. This inclusion of financial screens will motivate local companies to seek financing in a *Shari'a-compliant* manner and thus increasing the assets of Islamic banking and finance industry. BinMahfouz and Ahmed (2014) stated that DJIMI and S&P employ a liberal screening methodology, since they do not take a view on interest-based income. They concluded that such liberal views are not based on any strong *Shari'a* source; rather, the companies employ them to enhance their range of investible universe of stocks.

Regarding the use of liquidity filter, it is argued in the literature that such a filter is not required as companies whose share price is traded above their book value indicates a premium paid above the market price (Khatkhatay & Nisar, 2007). Investors usually pay a premium above the book value if the company can generate future abnormal returns that can compensate for the risk taken irrespective of the value of liquid assets. They further argued that it is not right to treat modern-day companies as a bunch of assets and liabilities as defined on its balance sheet. Some other assets like intangible assets including goodwill, brand, distributional networks and access to markets are not reflected on the balance sheet. Abnormal returns may be generated by the intangible assets.

BinMahfouz and Ahmed (2014) stated that most *Shari'a* boards avoid investing in companies whose liquid assets are traded above par; this is due to the fact that, according to *Shari'a,* cash and debt must be traded at par or face value. Further, it is worth noting that AAOIFI screening methodology does not include a liquidity screen; however, AAOIFI requires that the value of tangible assets of the company should be at least 30% of the total assets.

Another important point is that the level of liquidity holding is very much dependant on the overall market and the business cycle a business is in (Wilson, 2004). Hence, it is difficult to impose a fixed ceiling on cash and other liquidity holdings. In the time of market down turn, some businesses may like to hold on to the liquidity that they have to better strategise themselves. Similarly, in a bullish market, businesses may utilise the liquidity they have for expansion, research and development purposes. BinMahfouz and Ahmed (2014) agreed with Khatkhatay and Nisar (2007) in concluding that such a screen is not necessary to include such criteria in the screening methodologies.

Market Capitalisation vs Total Assets

Different screening methodologies either use market capitalisation or total assets as a denominator to calculate the true value of the company. Proponents of market capitalisation argue that total assets do not capture all the assets of the company like intangible assets or goodwill. Hence, the total assets tend to underestimate the true worth of the company (Derigs & Marzban, 2008). They further stated that another disadvantage of using total assets is that it may only be reported once a year compared as reported on their annual reports, while market capitalisation is available on a daily basis.

Khatkhatay and Nisar (2007) argue that total assets as a divisor to measure debt are more rational since the total assets of a company are financed by shareholder's equity and debt. This is due to the fact that due to the changes in the market perception, which resulted in change in the market capitalisation can make a *Shari'a* non-compliant stock; *Shari'a compliant* while the debt has remained the same (Dar Al Istithmar, 2009). Additionally, it is argued that market capitalisation as a divisor is a more volatile financial ratio compared to total assets as market capitalisation depends on general business cycles and may be high during a bull market and low during a bearish market (Wilson, 2004). Hence, without a change in the figure of numerator, the use of market capitalisation as a divisor is likely to increase the investment universe during bullish market and reduce it during bearish market. Resultantly, like DJIMI and others using market capitalisation have to smooth out the ratios by using average 24 months or 36 months average market cap. Derigs and Marzban (2008) further state that the use of total assets is more conservative as DJIMI and

S&P, which uses market capitalisation, have a larger number of *Shari'a-compliant* companies in their universe compared to those indexes and funds that use total assets.

Khatkhatay and Nisar (2007) suggested using a divisor based on the aim and purpose of the ratio; for example, when calculating the liquidity ratio market cap should be used since the aim is to ensure that liquid assets are not traded above par. Similarly, Al Rajhi Bank has applied a maximum of total assets or market capitalisation. Furthermore, Dar Al Istithmar (2009) proposes using shareholder equity as a divisor since it is a well-practised and used ratio and is known as leverage ratio.

Development in Islamic Banking and Finance
Islamic finance has developed immensely in the last 40 years particularly in Muslim-majority countries such as GCC countries and Malaysia. This has resulted in better availability of *Shari'a-compliant* financing in these countries than countries where Islamic finance is in developing stage (BinMahfouz & Ahmed, 2014). However, the screening methodologies have not taken into account this development and enhancement in Islamic financing availability. Hence, there is a need to revisit the *Shari'a* tolerance levels particularly in Muslim-majority countries. Lowering the thresholds for screening is ultimately suggested to be one of the ways of moving towards more conservative opinions from the scholars. This will assist in the growth of IBF industry, as companies will be pushed towards borrowing and investing in a *Shari'a-compliant* manner and thereby increasing the size of the overall IBF industry.

Socially Responsible Principles and Shari'a Screening Methodologies

Socially responsible investment (SRI) like Shari'a compliant investments has its roots in religion and started as faith-based investments.[29] The

[29] Ethical investing has its origins in Jewish, Christian and Islamic traditions. Judaism has teachings on how to use money (see, e.g., Maimonides Mishneh Torah, Laws of Gifts to the Poor 10:7). In medieval Christian times, there were ethical restrictions on loans and investments based on Old Testament (see Exodus 22:25). Further, the Catholic Church imposed a universal prohibition on interest in 1139, which was relaxed in nineteenth century. In England, the Act Against Usury which prohibited excessive interest on loans from 1571 to 1624. During reign of Henry VIII (1491–1547), usury was defined as a loan with interest rate higher than 10%.

earliest reference is found in the Quakers' movement and their avoidance of investing in companies involved in weapons and slavery business in the seventeenth century (Colle & York, 2008). Further, the initial investment policies were organised around avoiding companies involved in sinful acts like tobacco, alcohol and gambling. The first responsible investment fund in US "The Pioneer" fund was launched in 1928 and was driven by the motive of excluding investments in companies involved in alcohol and tobacco, i.e. avoiding sin stocks (Eurosif, 2012). The first SRI mutual fund was the Pax World Fund founded in 1971 by Luther Tyson and Jack Corbett for investors who opposed the Vietnam War, the fund avoided investing in weapon contractors. In the 1980s–90s, there was an increased focus on environmental issues including the establishment of United Nations World Commission on Environment and Development in 1983 and the Earth Summit in 1992 (Eurosif, 2012).

The Shari'a compliant investments are socially responsible (Elgari, 2002), as it forbids investments in unethical industries (alcohol, gambling and pornography;) however, there is no direct focus on social responsibility. That is, Shari'a compliant investments do not invest in companies committed to socially responsible businesses to support environment, human rights and employee rights (Forte & Miglietta, 2007). Both Shari'a compliant investments and SRI started as faith-based; however, the latter evolved to include more social and environmental issues (positive screening), away from core religious issues and the former apply exclusion criteria (negative screening) only and has thus remained just faith-based investments.

The growing concerns and awareness on social and environmental risks are compelling regulatory authorities and investors to integrate wider social issues into the investment decisions. These are vital for hedging risks and ensuring long-term sustainable growth (Clarke et al., 2015). Ahmed (2009) indicates that Vedanta Resources, a diversified metals and mining company from India listed on the London Stock Exchange and part of FTSE 100 index and the FTSE Shariah Index UK, was found to be seriously violating ethical practices, i.e. violations of human rights and environment. As a result, the Norway Government Pension Fund divested the stock from the fund, yet it remained part of FTSE Shariah Index

UK. The Church of England also disinvested from Vedanta Resources in the year 2010 after the practices of the company were found not at par with ethical standards. BinMahfouz and Ahmed (2014) applause Ahmed (2009) on raising a very vital question, i.e. how can a company that violates serious environmental and human rights be part of a Shari'a portfolio. Is it not against Shari'a to disrespect human rights and cause damage to the environment? Are the investors devoid of any further responsibilities if a company has an Islamic corporate structure and is not involved in any prohibited business activities according to Shari'a? Ahmed (2009) suggests that it is vital for Islamic finance to expand and include SRI principles in its investment guidelines. Like SRI investment which started with negative screening and moved to include wider ethical issues; positive screening, Islamic finance should follow similar steps and move Islamic investments from achieving Shari'a compliancy to achieving objectives of Shari'a. Clarke et al. (2015) state that environmental and social principles rooted in SRI funds are also in line with the tenets of Islam; however, they are not applied to Shari'a compliant funds. This contradicts Islamic finance's own ontological assessment of itself as being socially responsible, based on fairness, justice and equity. There is a need to develop the existing screening methodologies to account for more social issues than otherwise promoted by Shari'a and where institutions that are striving to give back to the society are supported, in addition to being Shari'a compliant.

Islamic Finance and Socially Responsible Investments: Synergies

To understand Shari'a one needs to understand its objectives that allow flexibility and dynamism. According to Imam Al Ghazali, "The objective of Shari'a is to promote wellbeing of all mankind, which lies in safeguarding their faith (din), their human self (nafs), their intellect (aql) their posterity (nasl) and their wealth (mal). He further states that whatever ensures safeguarding of these five serves the public interest (maslaha) and is desirable".

Dusuki (2009) states Al Shatibi's view who follows the taxonomy of Imam Ghazali and classifies maslahah in three categories: daruriyyat (essentials),[30] hajiyyat (complementary)[31] and tahsiniyat (embellishments).[32]

The Islamic economic and finance system is perceived as a socio-economic finance system that requires incorporating ethicality and morality in economic activities, with its ethical values such as fairness, justice and equity (Obaidullah, 2005). Islam's concept of SRI encompasses a broader meaning, being God-conscience by which corporations and individuals assume their role as a vicegerent on earth. Dusuki (2009) state that corporations should do "good" to the society irrespective of the financial outcome. They also state that when Al Satibi's three classifications of Maslaha are placed in a pyramid structure, the most important is the daruriyat by which essential needs are provided. These include safety of employees, welfare, life, environment, intellect and posterity. At the second level, hardships are removed and at the highest level corporations are expected to pay back to the society in terms of social good and that which may lead to perfection of public life. As a whole, the maslaha pyramid implies the need for organisations to engage in and manage their businesses and CSR activities according to priorities evolved from deep understanding of Shari'a.

To summarise, the concept of social responsibility is not new to Islam as it is deeply inscribed in the Shari'a (Kamali, 2005). Hence, any corporation that follows Shari'a principles should naturally incorporate SRI principles as well. Dusuki (2009) believe that Islamic corporations should endeavour to be at the forefront in the business world in promoting socially responsible practices.

Hasan (2008) analysed the current screening methodologies of SRI and Islamic funds; he concluded that "Islamic equity funds should arguably put stress on the positive criteria for selecting companies rather than simply listing prohibitions". Islamic banking and finance (IBF) involves wider ethical and moral issues than just interest-free transactions. This makes it more efficient than conventional banking and at the same

[30] These are self-interest upon which people depend on such as faith, life, intellect, posterity and wealth, i.e. elements that are absolutely necessary for the proper functioning of person's religious and other affairs.

[31] These are those interests which if avoided lead to hardships but not to total disruption.

[32] These are those interest which if realised will lead to refinement and perfection in the customs and conduct of people at all levels (better ethics within society).

time promote greater economic equity and justice (Khan, 2010). This will assist the Islamic fund management industry to move away from being just religious-based screening to more objective-based screening. Further, there is not much difference between SRI and Islamic investment as the end objective of both is similar, investing or financing activities that are beneficial to humanity and society (Central Bank, 2013). DeLorenzo (2000), a Shari'a scholar, states that Islamic investors can only invest in businesses that are "responsible" and "committed" to good causes, principles that both Islamic investing and SRI share.

Ahmed (2009) stated that in terms of excluding investments both SRI and Islamic screening have some overlap. Some of the common businesses excluded under Islamic and SRI screens are alcohol, tobacco, gambling, weapons and adult entertainment. He further states the need to build on the existing Shari'a investments principles by integrating social, environmental and responsible businesses. Miglietta and Forte (2011) conducted a book on the similarities and differences between Islamic and SRI screening methodologies. They are of the view that the most important goal for the Islamic investors is the compliance of eligible assets to Shari'a, followed by performance whereas for the SRI funds, importance is on sustainability and the environment before financial performance.

It is believed that for the Islamic finance industry to succeed there has to be more collaboration between the Islamic finance and SRI industry. The Holy Quran instructs "*Eat and drink from the provision of Allah, and do not commit abuse on the earth, spreading corruption*" *(Quran 2:60)*. It is important for the Islamic fund management industry to include factors related to environment, labour and human rights and other SRI issues in their decision-making process for Islamic investments. Abdullah et al. (2007) stated that incorporating SRI principles can have two significant benefits for the Islamic funds industry. First, it will increase the portfolio of Shari'a compliant investments by attracting investments from ethical sources. Second, it will allow SRI investors to diversify their portfolio into Islamic investments which tend to be less risky than their conventional counterparts.

3.7 Research Focus

This research focuses on the gap in the literature on historical reasoning for the introduction of *Shari'a* screening methodologies by Dow Jones in 1999 (McMillen, 2013) and how the existing practices can be enhanced.

In a changing world, both in terms of available information and with people becoming increasingly more informed of the social and other norms, it is only helpful that an assessment of current practices is undertaken. In doing so, opinions of *Shari'a* scholars who approved the DJIMI and other experts are sought; how they see the current practices and how they can be enhanced to ensure that we move towards progression as the IBF industry grows, which ultimately was the aim of introducing the *Shari'a* screening methodologies (more discussed in Methodology and Data Chapter 4).

First, the existing literature on *Shari'a-compliant* screening methodologies is scarce. There are opinion pieces written from industry practitioners and some academic papers on the methodologies itself. Greater focus has been given to the investment results by using different statistical tools. To the best of the author's knowledge, there is no single academic paper that has received opinions from the *Shari'a* scholars who approved the first screening methodology that is DJIMI and how they would like this equity investments industry to be developed. Neither are there discussion papers with other *Shari'a* scholars on how the current practices can be enhanced to take into account the IBF industry growth in the last 18 years.

Through this research, the author aims to enhance the understanding of the rationale behind the *Shari'a* screening methodologies and analyse how they can be enhanced. Based on the interviews with *Shari'a* scholars, the research intends to develop on the analysis to ensure that some of the issues facing the *Shari'a* screening methodologies are resolved. The research particularly aims to undertake an exploratory book on some equity portfolios and screen them based on the actual interest income and interest expense and compare them with current practices of screening based on source of funds. Furthermore, the research aims to create an IBF Index, which quantifies the development and growth in the IBF industry globally. As discussed above, the *Shari'a* screening methodologies were only introduced for a temporary basis, until an alternative to conventional finance is developed. As such, the IBF industry has developed immensely in a number of countries and hence these screening thresholds should account for these developments and move towards their aim of ultimately not allowing even a small percentage of *Shari'a* non-compliant revenue—zero tolerance. Hence, in line with IBF developments in different countries, the research aims to propose financial screening thresholds that account for the IBF development in that particular country. More details on the research questions, research methodology, design and data are provided in the next chapter.

References

AAOIFI. (2004). Shariah Standard 21. *Financial Papers*. AAOIFI.

Abdullah, F., Hassan, T., & Mohamad, S. (2007). Investigation of Performance of Malaysian Islamic Unit Trust Funds: Comparison with Conventional Unit Trust Funds. *Managerial Finance*, *33*(2), 142–153.

Accounting and Auditing Organisation for Islamic Financial Institutions. (2010). *Shari'a Standards for Islamic Financial Institutions*. AAOIFI.

Ahmad, Abū Dāwūd, an-Nasā'ī, Ibn Mājah; Mishkāt al-Masābīh, 2818.

Ahmed, I. (2009). *Incorporating Socially Responsible Investing in Islamic Equity Investments*. Cass Business School, UK.

Al Amine, M. B. M. (2002). *Comments of Muhammad Al Bashir Muhammad Al Amine on Reviewing the Concept of Shares: Towards a Dynamic Legal*. Perspective by Faisal Ahmed Manjoo [online]. http://www.kantakji.com/media/163527/file521.pdf. Accessed on 14 December 2013.

BinMahfouz, S., & Ahmed, H. (2014). Shariah Investment Screening Criteria: A Critical Review. *Journal of King Abdulaziz University: Islamic Economics*, *27*(1), 3–38.

Borhan, J. T., & Mohamad, M. T. (2009). Conducts of Partners in al- Sharikah al Mufawadah: An Analysis from Hanafi's Classical Sources presented at *District Level Economy Seminar* [Unpublished].

Central Bank. (2013). *Islamic Finance in Europe*. Occassional Paper Series.

Chorafas, D. N. (2005). Wealth Management. *Elsevier Monographs* (1st ed.). Elsevier.

Clarke, G., et al. (2015). *From the Stockholder to the Stakeholder*. [Online] https://arabesque.com/research/From_the_stockholder_to_the_stakeholder_web.pdf. Accessed on 02 September 2015.

Cognisant. (2012). *Sharia Stock Screening: A Fund Manager's Conundrum*.

Dar Al Istithmar. (2009). *A Universal Platform for Shari'a-Compliant Equity Screening*. Oxford Islamic Finance.

Delorenzo, Y. (2000). Shariah Supervision of Islamic Mutual Funds. In *Proceedings of the Fourth Harvard University Forum on Islamic Finance*. Harvard University.

Dergis, U., & Marzban, S. (2008). Review and Analysis of Current Shariah-Compliant Equity Screening Practices. *International Journal of Islamic and Middle Eastern Finance and Management*, *1*(4), 285–303.

Dusuki, A. W. (2009). *Challenges of Realizing Maqasid al Syariah (Objective Shariah) in Islamic Capital Market: Special Focus on Equity Based Sukuk*.

Elfakhai, S., & Hassan, M. K. (2005). Performance of Islamic Mutual Funds. *Economic Research Forum, 12th Annual Conference*, 1–33.

Elgari, M. (1993). Towards an Islamic Stock Market. *Islamic Economic Studies, 1*(1).

Elgari, M. A. (2000). Purification of Islamic Equity Funds: Methodology and *Shari'a* Foundation. In *Proceedings of the Fourth Harvard University Forum on Islamic Finance*. Harvard University.

Elgari, M. A. (2002). Towards an Islamic Stock Market. *Islamic Economic Studies, 1*(1).

Eurosif. (2012). *European SRI Book 2012*. [Online] www.eurosif.org. Accessed on 17 August 2013.

Forte, G., & Miglietta, F. (2007). *Islamic Mutual Funds as Faith-Based Funds in a Socially Responsible Context*. Bocconi University.

Grais, W., & Pellegrini, M. (2006, November 1). *Corporate Governance and Shari'a Compliance in Institutions Offering Islamic Financial Services*. World Bank Policy Research Working Paper No. 4054.

Hansmann, H., Kraakman, R., & Squire, R. (2005). *The New Business Entities in Evolutionary Perspective, Rev. 5*.

Hasan, M. S. (2008). Stock Returns, Inflation and Interest Rates in the United Kingdom. *European Journal of Finance*.

Hickson, C. R., Turner, J. D., & Ye, Q. (2011). The Rate of Return on Equity Across Industrial Sectors on the British Stock Market, 1825–70. *The Economic History Review*, *64*(4), 1218–1241. http://www.jstor.org/stable/41262528

Ho, C., Abd Rahman, N., Yusuf, N., & Zamzamin, Z. (2014). Performance of Global Islamic Versus Conventional Share Indices: International Evidence. *Pacific-Basin Finance Journal*, *28*, 110–121.

Htay, S. N. N., et al. (2013). Towards Standardisation of Shariah Screening Norms and Practices. *International Journal of Humanities and Social Sciences Invention, 2*(11), 23–30.

ISRA. (2012). *Islamic Financial System: Principles and Operations*. International *Shari'a*h Research Academy for Islamic Finance.

ISRA. (2015). *Shari'a Stocks, Islamic Capital Markets: Principles and Practices*. Chapter 13, Kuala Lumpur. International *Shari'a*h Research Academy for Islamic Finance.

Kamali, M. H. (2005). *Principles of Islamic Jurisprudence*. Pelanduk Publications.

Khan, F. (2010). How 'Islamic' Is Islamic Banking? *Journal of Economic Behavior and Organisation, 76*(2010), 805–820.

Khatkhatay, M. H., & Nisar, S. (2007). *Shari'a*h Compliant Equity Investments: An Assessment of Current Screening Norms. *Islamic Economic Studies, 15*(1).

McMillen, M. (2013). *Islamic Finance and the Shari'ah*. Riverstone Publishing Group.

Miglietta, F., & Forte, G. (2011, April 22). A Comparison of Socially Responsible and Islamic Equity Investments. *Journal of Money, Investment and Banking ISSN, (21). ISSN 1450-288X.*

Naughton, S., & Naughton, T. (2000). Religion, Ethics and Stock Trading: The Case of an Islamic Equities Market. *Journal of Business Ethics, 23*, 145–159.

Norman, T. (2006). *Islamic Investment Funds*. Euromoney Books.

Obaidullah, M. (2005). *Islamic Financial Services*. King Abdulaziz University.

Securities Commission Malaysia. (2009). *Resolutions of the Securities Commission Malaysia Shariah Advisory Council*. Securities Commission.

Siddiqi, M. N. (2004). *Riba, Bank Interest and the Rationale of Its Prohibition*. Visiting Scholars Research Series No. 2, Islamic Research Training Institute, Islamic Development Bank.

Siddiqui, R. (2007). Shari'ah Compliance, Performance, and Conversion: The Case of the Dow Jones Islamic Market Index^{SM}. *Chicago Journal of International Law, 7*(2), 495–519.

Usmani, T. (2002). *An Introduction to Islamic Finance*. Arab and Islamic Law Series, Brill.

Wilson, R. (2004). Screening Criteria for Islamic Equity Funds, Islamic Asset Management: Forming the Future for *Shari'a*-Compliant Investment Strategies. In S. Jaffer (Ed.), *Euromoney Institutional Investor*. PLC.

Yaquby, N. (2000). Trading in Equities: A *Shari'a* Perspective. In *Proceedings of the Fourth Harvard University Forum on Islamic Finance: Islamic Finance: The Task Ahead Cambridge, Massachusetts* (pp. 119–128). Center for Middle Eastern Studies, Harvard University.

York, J. G., & De Colle, S. (2008). Why Wine Is Not Glue? The Unresolved Problem of Negative Screening in Socially Responsible Investing. *Journal of Business Ethics, 85*(1), 83–95.

CHAPTER 4

Methodology and Data

4.1 Introduction

An effective research outcome is based on how detailed a research problem is investigated and how comprehensive the research analysis has been conducted. In this regard, it is vital that the research is planned so as to generate results that produce meaningful, reliable findings and conclusions. Accordingly, this research examines the existing *Shari'a* screening methodologies, from a historical, present and futuristic perspective with a view to enhance them in line with the development of the IBF industry.

This chapter elaborates on the research methodology employed in this book. The chapter begins with a brief overview and outline of the intended scope; subsequently, the general plan of the book is explained in the research design and the analysis framework then discussed in the research strategy section. The chapter continues with a focus on the research methods used in the book, including the purpose of the methods, the research tools used and the data analysis approach taken. The chapter then ends with a conclusion.

4.2 Research Design

A research design provides a general structure for the collection and analysis of the data, clarifying how the research questions will be answered. The choice of research design reflects a decision about the priority

R. Malik, *Shari'a Compliant Equity Investments*,
https://doi.org/10.1007/978-3-031-70822-0_4

provided to a range of dimensions of the research process (Bryman & Bell, 2007). These include an expression of causal connections between variables, generalising to large groups of individuals in addition to those forming part of research, understanding behaviour and having overtime appreciation of social phenomena and their interconnections. According to Saunders et al. (2007), research design assists in making an informed decision about the research methodology, which helps in the collection, analysis and process involved to ensure the research is conducted in an effective manner. It also assists in catering the constraints that may arise and the selection of the research methods appropriate for the book. The primary aim of the research should be to increase knowledge of a particular area that may consequently assist in resolving relevant problems. According to Bryman and Bell (2007), the terms research design and research methods are usually confused. A research method is a technique of collecting data with the help of instruments such as interviews or questionnaires, while research design is the framework that guides the process of data collection followed by analysis of the data. According to Saunders et al. (2007), the purpose of the research can be exploratory, descriptive and explanatory or any combination of the three, while a research piece can also have multiple objectives—depending on the way the research question is designed. Additionally, the purpose of the research may change over time (Saunders et al., 2007, cited Robson, 2002).

Descriptive studies are suitable if the purpose is to provide precise profile of persons, events or situations. The aim is to examine a phenomenon that occurs at a specific place and time (Robson, 2002 cited in Saunders et al., 2007, p. 134). These studies are usually recommended and efficient methods for collecting information that will explain the relationships and the world as it exists. Correlational research, causal comparative research, case book, ethnography and document analysis are examples of descriptive research methods.

Interpretive studies provide descriptive accounts targeted at understanding a phenomenon using data that might be collected in different ways such as interviews, observations and document review. Interpretive approaches give the research greater scope to address issues of influence and impact and to ask questions such as "why" and "how" particular technological trajectories are created (Deetz, 1996). Walsham (1993) asserts that the purpose of the interpretive approach in information science is to produce an understanding of the context and the process whereby information science influences and is influenced by the context. Interpretivism often addresses essential features of shared meaning and understanding whereas constructivism extends this concern with knowledge as produced and interpreted.

Explanatory studies, on the other hand, aim to explain the interaction or relationship that exists between the variables (Saunders et al., 2007). The focus here is on a situation or a problem. Statistical methods are used to analyse the relationships between variables. Additionally, qualitative data collection tools can also be implemented to scrutinise the relationships. This strategy is particularly useful if the research objective is to receive greater insight and understanding of a particular situation.

Contrastingly, exploratory research is an important means of acquiring new information and insight, asking questions and clarifying problems, particularly if the information and knowledge of a particular subject is limited. Advantages of this book are its flexibility and adaptability to change when new data appear; the research starts with a broader scope and narrows as progress is made (Saunders et al., 2007). An exploratory research book can be conducted in three ways: a search of the literature, interviewing experts of the subject area and conducting focus group interview (Saunders et al., 2007, cited Adams & Schvaneveldt, 1991). They further related the exploratory research to the activities of an explorer and that the researcher must be willing to change direction as the way forward develops due to new information and insights that are accrued. Adams and Schvaneveldt (1991) also argue that the flexibility inherent in exploratory research does not imply absence of direction; however, it means that to start with the focus is broad and then it becomes narrower as the research progresses.

Based on the nature of subject area being investigated and the research process involved, the overall research design is evaluative and the book can be categorised as an exploratory book with a descriptive and analytical research purpose. The first part of the research book attempts to assess the current *Shari'a* equity screening methodologies from a historical perspective to understand why they were introduced originally and how they can be enhanced to better align with *Shari'a* going forward. In this regard, semi-structured interviews are conducted with DJIMI *Shari'a* board—this was the first *Shari'a* board to introduce the screening methodologies in 1999, in addition to interviewing a number of other scholars from different jurisdictions.

In line with the feedback from the *Shari'a* scholars in the first stage, the second section conducted an analytical analysis of different portfolios based on an interest-based methodology. The research then develops on the possibility of basing the screening thresholds in line with the developments in the Islamic banking and finance industry in different countries. In doing so, the research uses the exploratory factor analysis technique to design an IBF index, which quantifies the development in different Islamic banking and finance industries in different countries. Based on this, the research proposes revised screening thresholds. It is suggested that the *Shari'a* screening thresholds in a country should depend on the development in Islamic finance in that particular country. In this manner, the industry will progress towards achieving its goal: where these thresholds or tolerance is reduced to absolute zero. Hence, two types of data will be collected, namely primary data (semi-structured interviews) and secondary data (portfolios screening). Furthermore, two types of analyses will be undertaken to examine the data: qualitative analysis and quantitative analysis. This chapter continues with the research methods of this book in the following section. Figure 4.1 presents an overall conceptual framework of this research book.

Conceptual Framework

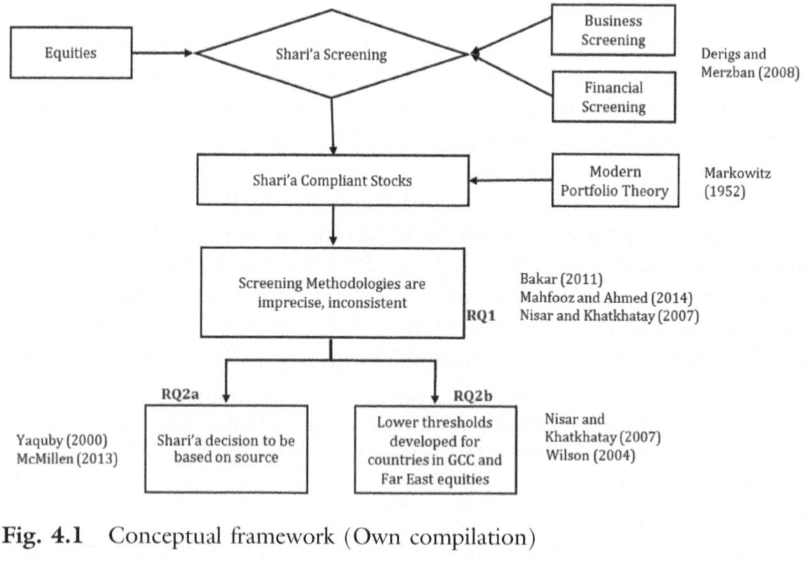

Fig. 4.1 Conceptual framework (Own compilation)

4.3 Research Methods

There are range of qualitative and quantitative methods in social sciences research. Both sets of methods have their advantages and disadvantages. Due to the nature of this research, it will employ both the qualitative and quantitative research methods. More specifically, semi-structured interviews will be used as part of qualitative method, while an exploratory factor analysis will be used as research tools for the quantitative method. Both methods are discussed below in detail.

The Qualitative Research Method

Qualitative is naturalistic; it aims to explore and discover issues at hand as very little is known about the subject (Domegan & Fleming, 2007). It is a systematic inquiry into the nature of complex social groups by using interpretive and naturalistic approaches. It aims to be unbiased and takes into account collected views of the participants as the purpose is to have an objective outcome. Qualitative research is appropriate when the researcher wants to have a deep understanding of how people think of a topic and to explain in detail the perspectives of the research participants. The research design is descriptive and interpretive that is analysed using qualitative research methods as explained in Sect. 4.2.

The qualitative method employed in this research attempts to explore the *Shari'a-compliant* equity investments industry with a focus on *Shari'a-compliant* screening methodologies. The aim is to enhance the existing *Shari'a-compliant* screening methodologies used by investment managers and *Shari'a* sensitive investors accessing the stock market. This is achieved by receiving opinions and other relevant inputs from the *Shari'a* scholars who approved the first formal *Shari'a* screening methodology introduced by Dow Jones Islamic Market Index (DJIMI) in the year 1999. In doing so, the objective is to understand the history of *Shari'a-compliant* screening methodologies; that is, from the *Shari'a* scholar's perspective why was there the need to introduce such screens and what discussions were held when formulating the first methodology and confirmation on thresholds used? This particular section of the book aims to fill the important gap in the academic literature by documenting the discussions and opinions of *Shari'a* scholars on the use of the existing screening methodologies. Furthermore, the book further receives opinions from *Shari'a* scholars on the existing practices and how they can be developed going forward to account for the developments in the Islamic banking and finance industry since the launch of DJIMI. Presently, there are numerous *Shari'a* screening methodologies; while all of them are equally *Shari'a* compliant, it has led to different portfolio combinations which in essence increase the cost of fund managers. This book aims to seek opinions on how the existing practices can be standardised. Some of the criticisms regarding the use of screening thresholds and ratios which have led to different screening methodologies are also discussed. These *Shari'a* screening methodologies were introduced as a contemporary need as *Shari'a-compliant* financing availability in the industry was limited. However, the Islamic financing availability has subsequently enhanced but the *Shari'a* screening methodologies are yet to take this into account. Detailed opinions from the *Shari'a* scholars who actually formulated these screening methodologies are very valuable to this book as the inputs can be used to enhance the existing practices to take into account the developments in the industry and move towards progression, something envisaged when these methodologies were first introduced.

Based on the opinions of the *Shari'a* scholars on some of the criticisms of the existing practices in *Shari'a* screening methodologies, this research aims to propose an alternative screening methodology that is based on the prohibited income itself and not the source of funds as is practiced at present. Furthermore, in the second part of the research, an IBF index will be created to quantify the developments in IBF in various countries with the aim of reducing the screening thresholds for the countries where IBF has developed.

Semi-structured Interview Method

The research book uses face-to-face semi-structured interviews as a research tool conducted with *Shari'a* scholars in different parts of the world, namely Bahrain, UAE, London and Malaysia. The exception is a few interviews where the interviewers were sent questions and wrote their replies in response. According to Bryman and Bell (2011), research interviews are a prominent data collection tool in both quantitative and qualitative research studies. Interviews are defined as purposeful discussions between two or more people (Kahn & Cannell, 1957) where the aim is for the interviewer to generate information regarding the interviewee's own behaviour, attitudes, norms, beliefs and values or those of others (Bryman & Bell, 2011). There are different types of interviews, namely:

(a) Structured interview: also known as standardised interview (Bryman & Bell, 2011). In this interview method, all the interviewees are given exactly the same context of questions. Here the questions are usually very specific and offer the interviewees a range of answers. These are usually used in social survey research.
(b) Semi-structured interview: this generally refers to a context where the interviewer has a series of questions but is able to change the sequence of them. The questions are generally less structured than a structured interview and the interviewer generally has the freedom to ask more questions in response to the replies of the interviewees.
(c) Unstructured interview: In this type of interview, the style of questioning is usually informal and the interviewer will only have a list of topics or issues to be covered.
(d) Oral history interview: generally, an unstructured or semi-structured interview where the interviewee is asked to recall events from his or her past and reflect. The research book usually has a specific research interest so there is a focus on particular incidents.
(e) Life history interview: this is like oral the history interview but the aim of this unstructured interview is to receive information on the entire history of each interviewee.

For the purpose of this research semi-structured interview, face-to-face interviews are selected. However, for a few interviewees, a list of questions was distributed to enable them to reply in their own time. Face-to-face interview method is preferred over telephone interviews, survey questionnaires and internet surveys due to the following reasons:

(a) Face-to-face interviews allow the flexibility of asking more questions than otherwise planned so that issues can be discussed in detail and the sequence of questions can be altered accordingly, so as to account for the replies of the interviewees. This is not possible with other forms of interviews, like survey questionnaires.
(b) As receiving responses from *Shari'a* scholars is vital for this book, face-to-face procedure eases the process.
(c) Face-to-face interviews further allow the interviewee to understand the body language in the replies received. Hence, an equal focus should be allotted to the respondent's body language and any signs

of unease. This also ensures that respondents are replying to the questions clearly and honestly and thus minimising error. Other types of interview methods may not be able to achieve this.

(d) Since the focus of the book is on detailed analysis, other type of interview method like telephone interviews may not permit this (Bryman & Bell, 2011).

(e) Face-to-face interviews permit the chance to seek any clarifications necessary or rephrase any ambiguous questions, reducing errors in the data obtained. This gives a significant advantage of interviews over other modes of data gathering methods, such as questionnaires or electronic surveys.

The main focus of the research book is on the *Shari'a* screening methodology of Dow Jones Islamic Market Index (DJIMI) as it was the first formal screening methodology introduced for *Shari'a* sensitive investors. Other screening methodologies widely used in the Islamic banking and finance industry are designed based on DJIMI. Hence, the interview process begins with the selection of the *Shari'a* scholars who approved the DJIMI, which consisted of five founding *Shari'a* board members while one *Shari'a* scholar joined later. These are:

(a) Justice Mufti Dr Taqi Usmani
(b) Sheikh Nedham Yaquby
(c) Dr Mohamed Ali Elgary
(d) Sheikh Abdus Sattar Abu Gudah
(e) Dr Yousuf Talal DeLorenzo
(f) Dr Daud Bakar (Joined later)

All the above *Shari'a* scholars are based in different parts of the world, so it was challenging to visit them in their respective countries to conduct these face-to-face interviews. However, it was discussed and agreed that the interviews will be conducted either in London when they visit or at a mutually agreed location. Initially, all of the above scholars were sent a letter, inviting them to take part in the interview, out of which four agreed. This constitutes a success rate of 66.67%, which is deemed acceptable. Additionally, to enhance the book, some of the above *Shari'a* Scholars also asked to conduct an interview with Mr Rushdie Siddiqui, the lead person at DJIMI in 1999 who worked on introducing a *Shari'a-compliant* benchmark for *Shari'a* sensitive investors. Further interviews with Sheikh Essam Ishaq and Dr Akram Laldin, renowned *Shari'a* scholars, Dr AbdulAzeem Abozaid, an academic at Qatar Foundation, the management of Saturna Capital (who launched the first Islamic mutual fund in 1986) and one more scholar were also recommended. After their acceptance, interviews were organised depending on their availabilities in different parts of the world.

Before conducting the interview, the interviewees were informed and reminded of the focus of the research book, and further assurance was provided on the confidentiality of the information i.e. any information provided would solely be used for the purpose of this research book. Each interview lasted between 45 and 90 minutes, and the interviews were recorded using the researcher's audio recorder. The recorded interviews reduce the chance of missing information during the data transcription process. Since the interviews were fully recorded, any significant non-verbal cues from the respondents were also recorded. The recorded interviews were then transcribed before the coding process; data analysis and report writing.

In order to safeguard the respondent's interest, the full transcripts of interviews were kept safe and coded accordingly. Once the research is complete, all the recorded data will be safely destroyed at an appropriate time.

Template Analysis: An Analytical Tool for Semi-structured Interviews

As the first part of the book uses semi-structured interviews, a set of questions was prepared to stimulate the interview and to ensure that all relevant data were collected without losing the focus.

Each interview lasted between 45 to 90 minutes and was recorded using an audio device. After conducting the interviews, all the interviews were transcribed. The qualitative data in the form of transcription and notes were obtained to undertake the analysis using the coding analysis based on the template analysis method.

Template analysis is a technique of thematically organising and analysing qualitative data. The data used are generally interview transcripts, textual data, including focus groups, diary entries, electronic interviews or open ended question responses to a written questionnaire (Brooks & King, 2012). Saunders et al. (2007) defines template analysis as an analysis of qualitative data that involves creating a hierarchical template of data codes representing themes revealed in the data collected and the relationships between these. The process of template analysis starts with developing codes after the initial review of the data and refines and modifies them during the analysis process (Crabtree & Miller, 1999). According to King (2004), the template analysis approach involves creating a code manual, coding the text by hand or computer, organising and sorting the text in one place and reading the segments making links between the themes. Brooks and King (2012) state that the templates analysis can be used in the real world for a number of epistemological positions; a key debate in qualitative research is the extent to which the method provides access to the personal world of research participants. Further template analysis can also be used within a "contextual constructivist" term (Madil et al., 2000; cited by Brooks & King, 2012), which assumes that there is always more than one interpretation from any phenomenon and it depends on the researcher and specific social context.

Template analysis allows the researchers to define some of the initial themes prior to the research process known as "a priori" code; however, these codes should only be regarded tentative and are subject to removal and redefinition. These initial codes can be helpful to relate to important concepts and perspectives (Brooks & King, 2012). It further emphasises the use of hierarchical codes but balances a high degree of structure in the process of analysing the textual data with the flexibility to adapt it to the needs of a book. It is a very flexible approach with regard to the style and format of the template and encourages the researcher to adopt and develop themes more extensively where the richest data are found. Saunders et al. (2007) define the steps involved in template analysis. After the priori themes, the next step is read through the text and highlighting the parts that in some way relates to the research question. If the text is found relevant to priori themes, the codes are applied, or else new themes are defined to include relevant material and organised into an initial template, something undertaken after the initial coding of the subset of a data. This initial template is applied to the whole data set, and the template is used as a basis for the researcher's interpretation of the data set. Template analysis further allows the categories and codes to be arranged hierarchically in order of their importance to assist in the analytical process. The main topics that formed the Interview Questions are given the higher order codes (Capitals-upper case) while the subset questions indicate the depth of the analysis and are given lower-order codes (lower case). The codes are subjected to further revision if needed until all data have been coded and analysed. Furthermore, the process involves unitising the data according to the list of codes currently being used which is a verification process to justify any modification and to examine how it had an implication on previous coding activity. The method uses both deductive and inductive approaches to qualitative analysis since it requires the codes to be determined before the analysis and which are subject to revision.

Template analysis differs from grounded theory in a sense that the latter does not allow the priori codes and is more structured (Stauss & Corbin, 2008; citied by Saunders et al., 2007).

Other advantages include:

i. Flexibility of template is among the reason of employing this method compared to other methods like grounded theory approach; as such, the codes will be revised as and when necessary ensuring that there will be no loss of data and new information will be analysed.
ii. It is a convenient method and may not necessarily need computer-aided data analysis software (CAQDAS) or Nvivo. However, for the purpose of this research we have used Nvivo to assist in the process of coding.
iii. Lastly, since semi-structured interviews are expected to generate a lot of qualitative unstructured data, the analysis method chosen should be able to deal with complex, non-standardised transcripts. A reason why template analysis is preferred over content analysis is that it is more suitable for analysis involving documents, meeting minute's reports and other forms of data (Bryman & Bell, 2011).

The following section elaborates the chronology of events in the fieldwork activities.

Semi-structured Interviews Process

The fieldwork involved three main stages, namely planning, execution and post-execution. Each of the stages is explained below:

i. Designing the Semi-structured Interviews Questionnaire

The idea of conducting interview analysis with *Shari'a* scholars emerged after considering the vital role they play in determining a product being *Shari'a-compliant* or otherwise. *Shari'a* scholars or advisers are defined by AAOIFI as specialised experts in Fiqh-al-Muamalat and entrusted with the duty of directing, reviewing and supervising the activities related to Islamic finance in order to ensure that they are in compliance with *Shari'a* rules and principles. Their views are considered binding in the specific area of supervision. In this respect, the *Shari'a* scholars play a crucial role on behalf of the investors in determining a transaction *Shari'a* compliant. The role of the *Shari'a* scholars is becoming more important as the Islamic banking and finance industry is developing, and it is crucial for the scholars to have a good understanding of financial literacy in addition to their *Shari'a* knowledge. Hence, their participation would contribute significantly to this book, particularly in providing a valuable input regarding the enhancements with the screening methodologies, which secondary data or any other professionals will not able to facilitate.

The interview process began in September 2013 with the drafting of interview questions (completed in October 2013 after numerous discussions and amendments). The set contains 16 questions on what this analysis seeks to investigate. Due to the availability of the *Shari'a* scholars, it was planned that the fieldwork would be undertaken between March 2014 and April 2015 on the sides of international Islamic finance conferences in London, Bahrain, Malaysia and Qatar, whichever they attended.

The next step in the planning stage was to collate the contact details of all the *Shari'a* scholars, after which they were sent an invitation letter outlining the purpose of the book and stating the intention to invite the *Shari'a* scholar to take part in the analysis. The letters were sent using both the general post as well as email in December 2013, specifying the proposed date and location for the interview. The fieldwork began in March 2014 as planned. The following section highlights the activities involved in the execution stage. To start with a pilot test was conducted, which assisted in improving the interview questions.

ii. **Administering the Semi-structured Interviews Questionnaire**

The interview process involved 9 respondents, comprising of *Shari'a* scholars, academics and a technical expert. Prior to the interview sessions, all respondents were reassured of the confidentiality of the conversation and information revealed during the interview. Additionally, they were also reminded that they could exercise their discretion when answering any of the interview questions. The interviews were conducted at different places in four countries, including mosques, conferences and homes; each lasted between 45 and 90 minutes.

The interviews were recorded using a digital audio recorder and stored in a laptop for easy retrieval. The use of digital audio recorder reduces distraction caused by the need to take interview notes and allows a full focus on the interviewing process itself. Furthermore, the digital recorder also minimised the data loss as it recorded the interview conversation in its entirety. Since the interviews were fully recorded, the remaining task for interviewer during the interview session was to observe any significant non-verbal cues from interviewees; these were duly entered into interview notes. The process was then continued in the post-execution stage as below.

iii. **Post-execution of the Semi-structured Interviews Questionnaire**

The post-execution stage involved the process of data transcription, coding, data analysis and report writing, as shown in Fig. 4.2. Indeed, this was the most crucial stage of the fieldwork process as it involved actual analysis from the very time-consuming data transcription process to the coding analysis and data display processes and eventually the writing of the analysis itself. Despite these difficulties, the entire process had to be undertaken carefully to ensure the accuracy of the analysis. The interview recordings were initially transcribed from audio form into written form without any alteration. This was to preserve the authenticity of the data before an analysis using template analysis method involving coding and decoding processes. The transcription was indeed a lengthy and time-consuming process since most recorded words had to be repeated several times for clarity. The outcome from the data transcription process was a written document containing the entire conversation for each of the

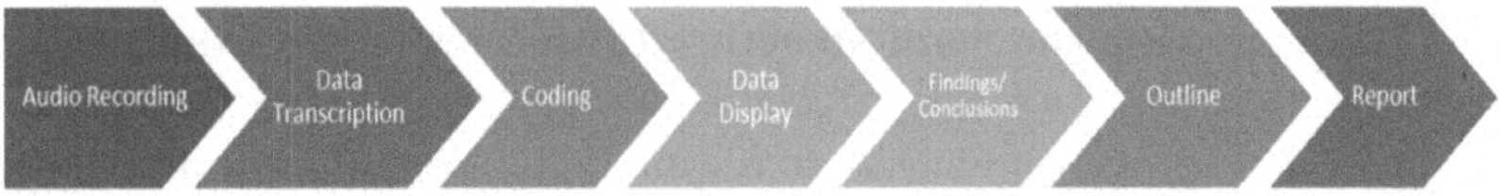

Fig. 4.2 Post-execution activities in the interviews process

interview sessions. To obtain a general view of the interview results, a reply summary sheet was created which clearly indicated the respondent replies to all of the interview questions. In order to develop a comprehensive list of *first-level* codes, each interview document was examined and scrutinised several times, and reflective, as well as marginal, remarks were introduced into the documents to better explain the meaning of words or phrases from the respondents. The initial codes were then grouped into specific sets of themes or constructs to produce pattern codes, which revealed the relationship among the codes, thus allowing for a richer interpretation of the data. Hence, both the reflective and marginal remarks allow for a more accurate interpretation, beyond the simple meaning of the original words or phrases used by the respondents.

The next step in the post-execution stage was to display the data through a mapping technique. The mapping is simply a graphic approach in data presentation that clearly highlights the interaction of different themes or constructs identities in the coding process. This significantly enhances the understanding of a particular subject and research question being investigated since it provides a better overview of the analysis and broadens the researcher's perspective. Mapping further assists in establishing the nature of the relationship between codes, themes and constructs would greatly improve the reliability of the research findings and conclusions. The final step in the post-execution stage is the report writing. The report preparation begins with the outline of the report based in the coding analysis and data mapping. The report outline consists of title headings and a summary of its contents that later form the basis of the writing. Indeed, the writing implies that the entire process of this qualitative analysis has been completed.

iv. **Ethical Consideration**

This research project was conducted with full compliance of research ethics norms during different phases of data collection, recording and analysis. During the research the interviewees provided their informed and voluntary consent for participation in the research. Throughout the research where there was a contact with the human the questions did not entail any personal information. The questions were not sensitive in nature and all interviewees were comfortable to be included in the analysis. In all cases the confidentiality of information and anonymity of respondents was respected. No one other than the researcher has access to the data.

Designing of Semi-structured Interviews Questionnaire

A total of 16 semi-structured interview questions are used. These 16 questions were grouped into five broad questions based on the five important topics. The five topics are history of Shari'a screening methodologies their weaknesses and issues highlighted in the literature, possible integration with SRI investments, purification of impure income and how they can be modified and enhanced. These five questions are explained in the following:

i. **What is the history of *Shari'a-compliant* screening methodologies, how and why they were introduced and what is rationale behind the use of the screening thresholds?**

This interview question attempts to understand the history of *Shari'a* screening methodologies since they were formally introduced for the first time in 1999 with the launch of Dow Jones Islamic Market Index (DJIMI). Before DJIMI, there were no official screening methodologies and *Shari'a-compliant* investments lacked an Islamic benchmark. However, it is believed that at an individual level, some efforts were conducted to align investments with *Shari'a* principles with the help of *Shari'a* advisors and boards. This is evident with the launch of the first Islamic fund—Amana Growth Fund in 1986 approved by renowned *Shari'a* scholars in the USA. Similar practices were undertaken in other parts of the world, including Malaysia. This interview question also aims to understand some of the discussions that were conducted at the time of DJIMI where the consultation started in 1993 and the index was launched after 5 years, when debating the criteria of the screening methodologies, what were some of the discussions at the time. Furthermore, the aim is to understand the rationale and reasoning behind the usage of the thresholds, namely 5% for *Shari'a* non-compliant business and 30–33% for the financial ratios as there is a very limited academic literature on the subject.

ii. **How is *Shari'a* screening process undertaken and what are the issues facing the screening methodologies?**

This interview question focuses on the issues that the *Shari'a* screening methodologies are facing and aims to understand the thoughts of the interviewees and how they can be minimised. The *Shari'a* screening process is conducted in two steps; business screening and financial screening. Business screening avoids businesses that are not in compliance with *Shari'a* while the financial screening ensures that those stocks remain *Shari'a-compliant* in their capital structure. Furthermore, this interview question aims to understand how the existing issues, criticisms and weaknesses can be eradicated and what needs to be done to improve them?

Some of the issues and criticisms in business and financial screening include:

(a) **Business Screening:**

a. Presently, the screening methodologies do not screen for elements such as derivatives; do you think the existing screening methodologies should also look at this?
b. What is your view on the companies that generate their revenue from arms and defence and tobacco industry (like the body of Muslim scholars in Indonesia to avoid cigarettes and it is not haram)?
c. 5% rule for *Shari'a* non-compliant businesses.

(b) **Financial Screening:**

a. One of the criticisms of current screening methodologies is the lack of standardisation. Resultantly, one stock may be *Shari'a-compliant* under one methodology while it may be *Shari'a* non-compliant under another methodology. Resultantly, an investor may benefit or bear loss just because of the methodology they are following; should there be standardisation? (i.e. use of market cap and total assets) and if there should be just one methodology?

b. The existing screening methodologies and ratios have been criticised in the literature, particularly on the use of **liquidity screen** (cash and receivables to market cap). There is discussion that there is no need for such a screen, as the main line of business is not indulging or making money from the change in the value of debt or receivables. Hence, this screen should not be part of it. Similarly, how does one assess that the debt has not been traded at par? Is it relevant for non-financial companies?

c. Can the financial rations be increased or lowered? (i.e. 33%)

The existing screening methodologies do take a view on the source of funds and not the prohibited income itself. For instance, the view is taken on the interest-based debt to market capitalisation or interest-based receivables to market capitalisation while in *Shari'a*. It is the interest that is *Shari'a* non-compliant, and debt that is to be repaid. According to *Shari'a* scholars, how these screening methodologies can be developed to take this into account. Further if it is even feasible.

iii. **Is there a need to incorporate socially responsible principles promoted by *Shari'a* within existing screening methodologies? This will also assist in tapping into the SRI industry—US$33 trillion industry.**

This interview question attempts to understand the views of the interviewees on the incorporation of socially responsible principles in the *Shari'a* screening methodologies. Islamic funds are regarded as ethical yet the socially responsible principles—also promoted by *Shari'a*—are not included in the *Shari'a* screening methodologies. The research will further look at the commonalities and differences between the *Shari'a* principles and the ethical principles and draw a plan on how they can be included in the screening methodologies. Furthermore, if *Shari'a-compliant* investments take into account the socially responsible principles then the conventional socially responsible industry will be keen to invest in the *Shari'a-compliant* investments (i.e. increasing the AUM of the *Shari'a-compliant* investments).

iv. **How can the existing *Shari'a* screening methodologies be enhanced?**

The *Shari'a* screening methodologies fulfilled the contemporary need; due to the lack of *Shari'a* financing availability, a compromised solution was agreed. This was allowing companies with up to 5% *Shari'a* non-compliant business revenue and up to 33% of *Shari'a* non-compliant debt or receivables to allow them to be part of *Shari'a-compliant* portfolio. However, since 1999 the *Shari'a* financing availability has enhanced as the Islamic banking and finance has developed in different parts of the world, mainly the GCC and Malaysia. The Islamic banking and finance industry represent a major chunk of the industry for a number of countries in the OIC bloc. Hence, how can the existing *Shari'a* screening methodologies be developed to take this industry development into account—so that going forward we achieve the perfect model of *Shari'a* screening that is otherwise desired?

v. **What is the preferred way of purification?**

Purification is an important concept in Islam and is considered one of its five pillars, Zakat—which also means "purification" (i.e. purification of wealth). When the existing *Shari'a* screening methodologies were approved, the *Shari'a* scholars placed an enormous effort on the purification. This is to remove the *Shari'a* non-compliant income, otherwise derived from up to 5% *Shari'a* non-compliant businesses and from allowing up to 33% of interest-based debt. Fund managers and investors calculate the impure income received throughout the year from their investments and remove it from their earned income. The purified income is donated to charity and hence the investors should not benefit from it. This question aims to understand the purification method that is preferred by the interviewees and if there is a way to improve it.

The five interview questions were carefully designed based on five important topics to explore the issues facing the *Shari'a* screening methodologies, particularly with regard to the history of these screening methodologies, standardisation, weaknesses and existing criticisms highlighted in the literature. Furthermore, how these *Shari'a* screening methodologies can be developed to take into account the development in Islamic banking and finance and the integration of socially responsible principles in the *Shari'a* screening methodologies. The interview transcripts are next examined in the data analysis stage as explained in Chapter 5.

The Quantitative Research Method

Based on the qualitative analysis conducted, it has been proposed by the *Shari'a* scholars to conduct an exploratory research based on the actual interest income and interest expense ratios. Furthermore, to analyse the development in Islamic banking and finance in different countries and propose screening thresholds in line with these developments. Hence, the main part of the quantitative analysis method is to determine how the newly proposed screening methodology affects the existing *Shari'a-compliant* portfolios. Additionally, explore the possibility of lowering the existing thresholds, which has not been attempted in any research. Hence, if the portfolio combination based on the development in Islamic banking and finance results in an investible universe, it will be a monumental achievement in Islamic equity markets. The main research and analytical tools are discussed below:

There are two parts to this book; hence, two different research tools are implemented. First, the analysis based on the interest income and interest expense and secondly the analysis based on the development in different Islamic banking and finance industries.

Analysis Based on Interest Income and Interest Expense as Screening Thresholds

Based on the criticism in the literature on the imprecise use of the screening thresholds (McMillen, 2013), the research analysis in the qualitative part discussed this with the *Shari'a* scholars being interviewed. Among the scholars, the majority of them supported the idea of screening the stocks based on more precise criteria, should there be one. During the interviews, the below proposed ratios were very much supported and it was suggested to conduct a research book on a different portfolio and analyse the difference it makes to the portfolio combination. *Shari'a* scholars further stated that if this proposed methodology achieves the objective and is practical enough (i.e. has enough *Shari'a-compliant* universe) then they will endorse it extensively. The two ratios are:

1. Interest Income Ratio $= \frac{\text{Interest Income}}{\text{Total Revenue}} \ngtr 5\%$
2. Interest Expense Ratio $= \frac{\text{Interest Expense}}{\text{Total Expenses}} \ngtr 5\%$

The two ratios are selected as it is the interest income and interest expense that is prohibited under *Shari'a* and hence captured through the financial screening using the ratios such as debt to market capitalisation. However, according to McMillen (2013), the existing screens are imprecise as they are based on source of funds and not the prohibited element itself.

In this regard, three different indices, namely Nasdaq 100, FTSE 100 and S&P 500, are screened based on the newly proposed thresholds above. The above-selected indices were then screened against the *Shari'a* screening methodologies followed by these indices. For example, S&P 500 was screened based on the S&P *Shari'a* screening methodology, while the FTSE 100 was screened based on FTSE *Shari'a* screening methodology. Nasdaq 100 does not have its own methodology; however, for their Nasdaq 100 *Shari'a* index they use AAOIFI *Shari'a* screening methodology, which has been employed in this analysis.

The Nasdaq 100 and S&P 500 are US-based indices, where Nasdaq 100 index includes 100 of the largest domestic and international non-financial securities listed on the Nasdaq stock market based on market capitalisation. The index reflects companies across major industry groups including computer hardware and software, telecommunications, retail or wholesale trade and biotechnology. It excludes banks and non-bank financial organisations, including investment companies. The AAOIFI methodology used is as follows:

- Interest-based debt to market capitalisation <30%
- Interest-based securities to market capitalisation <30%
- Cash and receivables and other liquid assets <70%

The Standard & Poor's 500 or S&P 500 is a US stock market index based on the market capitalisation of 500 large companies having stocks listed on the New York Stock Exchange (NYSE) or Nasdaq. It is different from other US stock market indices, such as Down Jones Industrial or the Nasdaq Composite, in terms of its diverse constituency and weighting methodology. It is one of the most common followed equity indices and is also considered one of the best representations of the US stock markets and the economy as a whole. The market capitalisation of the index is US$18.5 trillion. The screening methodology used is as follows:

- Interest-based debt to market capitalisation (36 months avg) <33%
- Interest-based receivables to market capitalisation (36 months avg) <49%
- Interest-based cash and securities to market capitalisation (36 months avg) <33%

The FTSE 100 (UK based) is the third and last index selected for this part of the analysis. It is composed of the 100 companies listed on the London Stock Exchange with highest market capitalisation. It was developed in 1983 and has a total market capitalisation of US$1.7 trillion. The screening filters used are as follows:

- Interest-based debt to total assets <33%
- Interest-based cash and securities to total assets <33%
- Interest-based receivables and cash to total assets <50%
- Interest income and impermissible income to revenue <5%

The results are then compared to analyse the differences in the portfolio combinations. The portfolios and financial results for all the three indices were obtained from Bloomberg on 10th of June 2016. The newly proposed screening filters are:

- Interest Income to total Revenue <5%
- Interest Expense to total Expenses <5%

The rationale for selecting these indices is based on the potential outcome envisaged. It is well understood that developed countries such as the UK and USA have well-developed regulatory, governance and accounting standards. As such, all the underlying companies listed on the stock exchanges will be following the rules and standards of reporting and disclosure. Hence, from the literature and interviews, we know that information on interest income and interest expense is something that does not require disclosure and as such companies would generally publish the net interest income or expense figures or would show total income or total expenses without disclosing the details. Hence, through the analysis of these portfolios, we would be able to relate it to other countries and as such if there is sufficient information available to form the conclusion upon. For all our data in the Research Analysis 1, the information is extracted from secondary source Bloomberg.

Screening Analysis Based on development in Islamic Banking and Finance Industry

The Islamic banking and finance has developed significantly compared to its humble beginning 5 decades ago. As far as the academic literature is concerned, there is not a single book that has quantified the development in Islamic banking and finance in different countries in an objective and systematic manner. However, there are two attempts conducted by Global Islamic Finance Report published by Edbiz Consulting (IFCI) and Global Islamic Finance Development Indicators (IFDI) published by Thomson Reuter; however, their methods have limitations (discussed in the last paragraph).

Concurrently, there are various studies in the conventional financial industry that quantifies the development in the financial sector. Through these research studies, it is established that the financial sector development is positively related to levels of income and growth. Furthermore, Creane et al. (2004) stated that financial sector development is a good leading indicator of growth, physical capital accumulation and productivity growth, after accounting for a number of factors. Even when relying on quantitative information, it is important that conclusions are not based on univariate analysis. Among the masses, a common perception is based on univariate analysis. Univariate analysis is the usual way of assessing countries against another based on one or more variables. However, in doing so, each variable is studied and analysed in isolation from others and hence it is not possible to assess from the definitive collective view. Mere dependence on individual observation to a particular question of interest could be misleading if due weight is not attached to each observation in an objective manner. Furthermore, there are some studies that have used a multi-variable approach; however, their methods of weights assigning has been very subjective.

Creane et al. (2004) stated that assessing the development in the financial sector requires good measures. Empirical works are usually based on standard quantitative indicators, including ratios as liquid liabilities to GDP, deposit money bank assets to banking sector assets and credit to private sector GDP. Zhuang et al. (2009) quoted the book conducted by King and Levine where they constructed four indicators of financial development using (i) ratio of liquid liabilities to GDP, (ii) ratio of commercial bank domestic credit to the sum of commercial bank domestic credit and the central bank domestic credit, (iii) the ratio of credit issued to non-financial private firms to total credit; and (iv) the ratio of credit issued to non-financial private firms to GDP.

Gelbard and Leite (1999) progressed beyond the standard quantitative indicators, using measures of market structure, financial products, financial liberalisation, institutional environment, financial openness and monetary policy instruments to construct a comprehensive index for 38 countries from the sub-Saharan countries. Similarly, Abiad and Mody (2003) created an index for 35 countries. There indicators included measures of policy liberalisation in the areas of credit controls, interest rate controls, entry barriers, regulations and securities markets, financial sector privatisation and restrictions on international financial transactions.

Creane et al. (2004) conducted a book on financial development in MENA region using two different methods of multivariate analysis. In one method, the authors used subjective weights based on their qualitative judgement to identify and assign relative weights to different components of financial development. In the second method, the authors used principal component analysis, which examines the statistical correlations across different variables and assigns largest weights to those indicators of financial development most correlated with the other indicators in the dataset. The six themes, each of which reflects a different aspect of financial development, included (i) development of monetary sector and monetary policy; (ii) banking sector development; (iii) development of the non-financial sector; (iv) regulation and supervision; (v) financial openness; and institutional quality. These detailed measures and methods provide more detailed description of financial development and motivate our measures of Islamic financial development based on the availability of data and similar statistical methodology of exploratory factor analysis using principal components analysis (PCA).

The Islamic banking and finance industry is a small part of the overall financial industry and, as such, the data on most of the above components is not easily accessible. Hence, this research uses a number of different variables to collect as much information as possible to gauge the depth and incidence of Islamic finance across the globe. As such, it uses a similar methodology of data collection employed by the IFCI and IFDI. By doing so, the research attempts to measure the overall size of the Islamic finance industry and highlight the role individual components play in developing the industry going forward. More precisely, the research uses a similar methodology to IFCI, namely factor analysis to create the index; however, IFCI was based on only eight variables and the weights used have remained the same since first introduced in 2011. On the other hand, IFDI—created by Thomson Reuters—uses different variables to create a weighted composite index, a method, which has been criticised in the literature for its subjectivity.

This book, therefore, aims at developing a unique and completely objective Islamic Banking and Finance Index (IBFI) for various countries, based on all the available information and form a collective view, using a methodology that has little subjectivity. In the academic literature of Islamic banking and finance, this is the first attempt using these many variables for different countries whereby each category of information is assigned weights based on an analytical system in a purely statistical manner.

Quantitative Data Analysis Method

The current book aims to enhance the screening methodologies based on the development and growth in Islamic banking and finance in different countries using a multivariate analysis in a purely objective manner to avoid any personal bias or a priori judgement affecting the outcome. In order to quantify the development, an IBFI index using statistical technique of factor analysis using PCA is developed, which is a single measure that captures the holistic assessment of the Islamic finance industry across all sectors.

It is vital that the data health is ensured before any statistical technique is applied to analyse the data for the purpose of quantification of demand. The book ensures that the collected data are accurate and in the right format, by employing all the standard practices and procedures in terms of observing the data in the form of simple data description and cross tabulation. This ensures that any inaccuracy in data inputting is detected (and remedied) and that any inconsistency is removed from the data set, without compromising its integrity.

Against this background, as explained in Chapter 2, the construction of the IBFI started with the collection of data on 25 variables across 95 countries in the world having some operations in Islamic banking and finance. These included all the OIC countries, as well as non-OIC countries with a presence of Islamic financial assets or institutions. However, the heterogeneous nature of each of these countries and limitation in the availability of data, limited the IBFI to only 41 countries. Additionally, the variables were reduced from 25 to 18 as there was a lot of missing information on some variables while other variables had anti-image correlation value lower than the bare minimum of 0.5 (Field, 2011). The data have been collected from various secondary sources that are publicly disclosed only, including central regulatory bodies, global agencies (World Bank, IMF, IFSB), published accounts of IFIs and technological data providers such as Bloomberg and Thomson Reuters. The employment of disclosed information ensures the reliability of data and consistency of results. The data were gathered on all 18 variables (Table 4.1) for all the 41 countries included in the IBF index. The data was then coded and organised to enable multivariate analysis and construction of the IBF index using SPSS.

In terms of selection criteria for the variables, it was important to keep in mind the ultimate objectives of creating an index; (1) developing an objective indicator based various variables that quantifies the development in Islamic banking and finance in a particular country. (2) Ensuring that the relevant information is captured that allows the index to be gauged to base the equity screening thresholds upon. In line with these two objectives, it was important that information was collected not only on the Islamic financial health (generally an assumed indicator of the well-being of an industry) but also on other variables that are equally important for the development of the Islamic banking and finance industry and thereby create an index based on holistic concept. Some of these recommendations have been provided in a document "Islamic Financial Services Industry Development": Ten Year Framework and Strategies' prepared by Islamic Research and Training Institute and the Islamic Financial Services Board in 2008. Hence, the key variables are listed in Table 4.1.

Among the different variables, the quantitative variables are an essential measure of the industry; they provide the size, depth and long-term sustainability of the sector overall. Financial institutions are regarded as the backbone of the industry given their size and track record. To assess the quantitative development of the industry, it is vital to examine the development from different angles; this includes both the number of IFIs as well as the size of the assets across both banks and non-banking

Table 4.1 IBF index variables and description

Variables	*Description*
Number of Institutions involved in Islamic Finance Industry	Represents both banking and non-banking institutions involved in Islamic finance in a country
Size of Islamic Financial Assets	Represents all assets relating to the industry in a country
Number of Islamic Banks	Represents all the banks involved in Islamic finance; both fully fledged Islamic banks as well as windows in a country
Size of Sukuk	Represents total outstanding sukuk amount in the country
Islamic Banking Assets	Represents all the Islamic banking assets in the country
Takaful and Re-takaful	Represents the Takaful and Re-takaful assets both from fully *Shari'a-compliant* insurance company as well as conventional insurance offering *Shari'a-compliant* products in a country
Number of Takaful and Re-takaful institutions	Represents the number of Takaful and Re-takaful institutions both from fully *Shari'a-compliant* insurance company as well as conventional insurance offering *Shari'a-compliant* products in a country
Other Financial Institutions Assets	Represents the *Shari'a-compliant* assets from pension funds, advisory companies and other financing institutions in a country
Number of Other Financial Institutions Assets	Represents the number of *Shari'a-compliant* assets from pension funds, advisory companies and other financing institutions in a country
Value of Islamic Funds	Total value of Islamic Funds (active) in a country
Number of Islamic Funds	Total number of funds (active) in a country
Value of Islamic Financial Transactions	The value of Islamic financial transactions in a country in a country
Number of Islamic Financial Transactions	Number of Islamic financial transactions in a country
Liquid Assets	Value of liquid assets both banked and non-banked institutions

(continued)

Table 4.1 (continued)

Variables	*Description*
Regulatory Environment	Represents the presence and support of regulatory and legal environment enabling IFI to operate in the country on a level playing
Central *Shari'a* Supervisory Regime	Represents the presence of a state-representative body to look after the *Shari'a*-compliancy process across the IFI in a country
Education and culture	Represents the presence of an educational institution and cultural environment conducive to operations of IFIs
Regulatory and Legal Infrastructure Framework	Represents the presence of regulations and legal systems that facilitate the operations of Islamic banking and finance

institutions. The underlying variables include the "Size Islamic Financial Assets"—this represents a sum of all the *Shari'a-compliant* assets. This, together with "Number of Institutions involved Islamic Finance Industry", provides a holistic picture of the overall industry. However, what it lacks is the role each underlying sub-sector plays in the development of IBF. Hence, to understand the relationship underlying sub-sector play, data were collected on "Islamic Banking", which consisted of all institutions licensed as banks operating in a *Shari'a*—compliant manner including investment, retail and wholesale specialised banks (including Islamic windows), both in terms of their assets and numbers. Islamic bond or sukuk is an important component of the industry, particularly due to its recent growth where a number of Muslim minority countries—including UK, South Africa, Hong Kong and Luxembourg—have issued them. The research captures the value of outstanding sukuk. Other quantitative indicators included "Takaful and Re-takaful", "Islamic funds" and "Islamic financial transactions". Information on these variables was collected, both in terms of the size and number of institutions.

"Other financial institutions" are the support institutions licensed to provide financial services other than banking activities; they include the investment, leasing, asset management and advisory companies. Furthermore, in line with the purpose of the basing screening thresholds on the development in IBF, information on "liquid assets" was also captured. This is based on the premise that the more liquid assets the IBF industry has, the more it can provide financial support to other institutions. Thus, institutions wishing to raise financing can do so through these *Shari'a-compliant* alternatives.

The non-quantitative variables include "regulatory environment" and "regulatory and legal infrastructure" which represents a score countries have received based on the presence and support of regulatory and legal environment, which enables IFIs to operate at equal level *vis-à-vis* conventional finance. This includes the Islamic banking act, Islamic capital markets' act, takaful act and double stamp duty act. Hence, it is not merely measuring the industry's development that matters but also the regulatory support that the *Shari'a* governance system receives. Furthermore, "Central *Shari'a* Supervisory Board" capture if a particular country has a centralised *Shari'a* supervisory board that overlooks the development in *Shari'a* governance on a national level and ensures that a similar set of practices are followed across various institutions. Moreover, it becomes easier to develop rules and procedures to review the conduct of IFIs with only one body responsible for the interpretation. Lastly, the IBF development in any country is a function of how knowledgeable and skilful the human resources is to develop and advance the industry in a particular country. Under "Education" variable, we assess the knowledge development of the IBF industry by reviewing if a particular country runs undergraduate, postgraduate or professional courses in IBF. Once the above variables complete the factor analysis process, they will be reduced to a lower number of themes. The underlying themes will have these 18 variables distributed among them based on the statistical properties of each.

After developing the index, different portfolios have been selected to screen the stocks based on the newly proposed thresholds. To ensure that we assess the equity investments industry in various countries, we selected Dow Jones Islamic Market Index (DJIMI), which has more than 2400 stocks from more than 60 countries. However, some of the stocks are from the countries that were not part of our IBF index. Concurrently, we know from the literature that most developed countries in terms of IBF are the countries in GCC,[1] Malaysia and Indonesia; consequently, a

[1] GCC includes Bahrain, Saudi Arabia, UAE, Kuwait, Qatar and Oman.

special focus has been placed on these countries. In line with this, when we analysed the stocks from these IBF-developed countries, it was ascertained that stocks from Bahrain, Saudi Arabia and UAE (both Dubai and Abu Dhabi) are not well represented in DJIMI. As such, it will not provide us with a meaningful research outcome; hence, we included all the stocks listed on the exchanges of these three countries in our research analysis to ensure that all countries are represented adequately. Furthermore, the stocks listed on these three stock exchanges needed to encounter a *Shari'a* screening process, which was not the case for DJIMI as it is a *Shari'a-compliant* index. As such, we screened these stocks based on the AAOIFI methodology before using them in our research analysis.

Further, the research proposed to use different thresholds for different countries based on the development in IBF. The analysis then compares the changes newly proposed thresholds make to the existing portfolio combination. The intelligence behind this proposal is that as the IBF industry grows, the thresholds used for *Shari'a* sensitive investments should become increasingly more conservative; this will allow the existing practices to correspond with the best practices of *Shari'a* and also assist the IBF industry in its growth. This is due to the fact that the companies that are part of a *Shari'a-compliant* portfolio were able to have up to 30% or 33% *Shari'a* non-compliant financing. Thus, in case the proposed methodology move the existing thresholds from 33 to 25% then companies in the particular countries will be pushed to borrow in a *Shari'a-compliant* manner if they are to remain in the *Shari'a-compliant* portfolio.

This next section explains the statistical techniques used to quantify the progress of IBF and develop a methodology that screens the stocks based on the development and growth in various countries.

A brief explanation of the factor analysis using PCA is described below.

Exploratory Factor Analysis

Factor analysis is a method for investigating whether a number of variables of interest—such as V_1, V_2, V_3—are linearly related to a small number of unobservable factors—such as F_1, F_2, F_3 (Tryfos, 1997). It is primarily used to reduce variables and understand the relationship between these different variables. It does this by seeking underlying unobservable (latent) variables that are reflected in the observed variables. There are three main uses of this technique: (a) to understand the composition of the variables, (b) to design a questionnaire to measure the underlying variable and (c) to reduce the set of variables to a more manageable size while retaining the maximum original information (Field, 2011).

There are two main approaches to factor analysis; exploratory and confirmatory. Exploratory factor analysis (EFA) is usually used in the early stages of research where the aim is to gather information or explore the relationships among different variables. Confirmatory factory analysis (CFA), on the other hand, is used in the later stages of the research and is designed to confirm a hypobook or theories that relate to the underlying variables.

The aim of this research is to explore the development and growth of IBF in different countries and hence exploratory factor analysis is used.[2]

There are three main steps in carrying out a factor analysis.

i. **Assessment of the Suitability of the Data for Factor Analysis**

There are two main issues to consider in determining whether particular data are suitable for factor analysis: (a) sample size and (b) strength of the shared variance between the variables. It is a technique that requires a large sample size as it is based on the correlation matrix of the variables involved and correlation usually requires a large sample size. Comrey and Lee's (1992) advice regarding the sample size was: 1000 and more is excellent, 500 is very good, 300 is good, 200 is fair, 100 is poor and 50 is very poor. Generally, a minimum of 10 observations per variable is necessary to avoid computational difficulties. The second issue concerns the strength of intercorrelations among the items. Another important alternative is the Kaiser-Meyer-Olkin measure of sampling adequacy (KMO), which can be calculated for individual and multiple variables and represents the ratio of the squared correlation between variables to the squared partial correlation between variables. The KMO measures vary between 0 and 1. A value of 0 indicates that the sum of partial correlations is large relative to the sum of correlations, indicating diffusion in the pattern of

[2] There are two main approaches to factor analysis—exploratory and confirmatory. Exploratory factor analysis is often used in the early stages of research to gather information about (explore) the interrelationships among a set of variables. Confirmatory factor analysis, on the other hand, is a more complex and sophisticated set of techniques used later in the research process to test (confirm) specific hypotheses or theories concerning the structure underlying a set of variables.

correlation (hence factor analysis is likely to be inappropriate). A value close to 1 indicates that patterns of shared variance are relatively compact and, therefore, factor analysis should yield distinct and reliable factors. Kaiser (1974) recommends accepting a value greater than 0.5 as barely acceptable. Furthermore, values between 0.5 and 0.7 are mediocre, values between 0.7 and 0.8 are good, values between 0.8 and 0.9 are great and values above 0.9 are superb (Hutcheson & Sofronio, 1999).

In this research analysis, the KMO value was 0.732, which is regarded as good, and hence fulfils the requirements in terms of the sample size and the correlations (Kaiser, 1974).

Additionally, Bartlett's test is used to test homogeneity of variances, indicating whether the correlation matrix is suitable for factor analysis. It tests the null hypobook that the original correlation matrix is an identity matrix (all pair wise correlation is zero).

H_0 = all pair wise correlation is equal to zero.
H_A = not all pair wise correlation is equal to zero.

For factor analysis to work, there needs to be a relationship (correlation) between the variables implying that there is a need to reject the null hypobook and if the R-matrix[3] were an identity matrix then all correlation coefficients would be zero, which means that factor analysis will not work (as the grouping will be based on the correlation). Therefore, it is important to have this test to be significant (i.e., significance value less than 0.05), which means that correlation between the variables is not zero. Bartlett's test confirms that the R-matrix is not an identity matrix; that is, the variables are sufficiently correlated with each other. The data for the research are significant; namely it ($p < 0.001$) rejects the null hypobook and hence factor analysis can be used.

ii. **Factor Extraction**

Once the adequacy and sample of data are checked, the next step is to run the factor analysis to extract the factors. Factor extraction involves

[3] R-matrix is just a correlation matrix; it is table of correlation coefficients between pairs of variables. The diagonal elements of an R-matrix will be one because each variable correlates perfectly with itself.

determining the smallest number of factors that can be used to best represent the interrelations among the set of variables. There are a variety of approaches that can be used to extract the number of underlying factors or dimensions. However, for the purpose of this research, the principle component method is chosen.[4] It is subjective to determine the number of factors that best describe relationships among the variables. This requires balancing two conflicting needs: the need to find a simple solution with as few factors as possible and the need to explain as much of the variance in the original data as possible. For the purpose of this research, Kaiser (1960) has been used, which recommends retaining all factors with eigenvalues greater than 1.[5] Eigenvalues are a group of values related with a linear system of equations known as characteristic roots, characteristic values or latent roots. It shows the variance in all the variables, which is accounted for by that factor. The ratio of eigenvalues is the ratio of explanatory significance of the factors with respect to the variables.

The first part of factor extraction is to determine linear components within the data set by calculating eigenvalues of the R-matrix. When several variables are measured, the correlation between each pair of variables can be arranged in R-matrix. It is just a correlation matrix: a table of correlation coefficients between variables. The diagonal elements on R-matrix are always one because each variable will correlate perfectly with itself. The off diagonal elements are the correlation coefficients between pairs of variables or questions. The existence of groups of large correlation coefficients between subsets of variables suggests that those variables could be measuring aspects of the same underlying dimension. These underlying dimensions are known as factors. By reducing a data set from a group of interrelated variables to a smaller set of factors, factor analysis explains a maximum amount of common variance in a correlation matrix using the smallest number of explanatory constructs. In factor

[4] Other methods include, Principle Factor, Image Factoring, Maximum Likelihood Factoring, Alpha Factoring, Unweighted Least Squares, Generalised Least Squares and Principle Component Analysis.

[5] This criterion is based on the idea than eigenvalues represents a substantial amount of variation. There are a number of techniques that can be used to assist in the decision concerning the number of factors to retain. Most commonly used techniques are Kaiser criterion, screen test and parallel analysis.

analysis, the aim is to reduce this R-matrix down to its underlying dimensions by scrutinising which variables seem to cluster together in a more meaningful manner. This is achieved by looking at variables that correlate highly with a group of other variables, but do not correlate with variables outside of that group. In this research, a set of 18 variables has been reduced to 4 factors with the help of PCA. PCA is the most widely used method for determining the set of loadings that bring the estimate of the total communality[6] as close as possible to the total of the observed variances.

According to the eigenvalues, 4 factors were selected, which explain 83.4% of the variance. It is suggested that the factor analysis is usually considered effective if the total retained factors explain at least 70% of the overall variance of the variables. There are 4 linear components within the data set and the eigenvalues associated with each factor represent the variance explained by that particular linear component, and here it is presented as a percentage of variance explained.

Once the factors have been extracted, it is important to check how much of the variance of the variables is explained by these underlying factors; this is achieved through checking the communalities. Communality explains the amount of (common) variance in each variable that can be explained by the factors. A variable with a communality value 1 means that it does not have any unique variance, whereas a communality value of 0 means that there is no common variance in the variable and all the variance is unique (Field, 2011).[7] This is because before extraction there are as many factors as variables, but after extraction only 4 factors are retained and hence some of the information is lost. This means that the underlying factors will not be able to explain all the information but they

[6] The total variance for a particular variable will have two components: some of it will be shared with other variables or measures (common variance) and some of it will be specific to that measure (unique variance). Unique variance refers to variance that can be attributed to only one measure. However, there is also variance that is specific to one measure but not reliably so; this variance is called random variance. The proportion of common variance present in a variable is known as communality. A variable that has no specific variance (or random variance) would have a communality of 1; a variable that shares none of its variance with any other variable would have communality of 0 (Field, 2009).

[7] A main difference between the Principal component analysis (PCA) and factor analysis is that the former assumes that all the variance in the variable is common, whereas the later assumes that there are two types of variances in a variable, i.e. unique and common variance and it is the common variance that factor analysis is interested in.

will be able to explain some. It is also important to assess that reasonable common variance explained by the underlying factors.

iii. **Factor Rotation and Interpretations**

After factor extraction, it might be difficult to interpret and name the factors on the basis of their factor loadings.[8] This is due to the criterion of principal component analysis where the first factor accounts for the maximum part of the variance; this will often ensure that most variables have high loadings on the factors with high variance, and small loadings on all other factors (Field, 2000). This makes interpretation of the factors difficult. Factor rotation is one way of tackling this problem where this method alters the pattern of the factor loadings and improves interpretation. The factor rotation does not change the underlying solution; it is an attempt to improve the interpretability of the factors. It maximises the loading of each variable on one of the extracted factors while minimising the loading on all other factors. It presents the data in a manner easier to interpret. Factor analysis does not interpret each of the factors for the analyst; it just shows which variables clump together.

There are two main approaches to rotation: (1) orthogonal rotation and (2) oblique rotation.

a. **Orthogonal rotation**

It is a rotated component matrix that shows the factors loading for each variable onto each factor. This matrix contains the same information as the component matrix, except that it is calculated after rotation. According to Tabachnick and Fedell (2001), orthogonal rotation results in solutions that are easier to interpret; however, they do require the researcher to assume that underlying constructs are independent. Before rotation, all factors are independent and orthogonal rotation ensures that the factors remain independent. For the purpose of this research, orthogonal rotation (or varimax) has been preferred and used because all variables are independent of each other.

[8] This correlation between original variables and the factors is called factor loadings. Squared factor loadings indicate what percentage of the variance in an original variable is explained by a factor.

b. **Oblique rotation**

In an oblique rotation, the factor matrix is split into two matrices: the *pattern matrix* and the *structure matrix*. The pattern matrix contains the factor loadings and is similar to factor matrix interpreted for orthogonal rotation. The structure matrix, on the other hand, takes relationships between factors (in fact it is the product of pattern matrix and the matrix containing the correlation coefficients between factors). It is also understood that researchers prefer oblique rotation because it contains information about the unique contribution of a variable to a factor.

Once the above is completed, the next step involves identification of factors. As mentioned above, the factor analysis reduced the 18 variables used into 4 factors. The factors are normally named roughly, because constituting variables are not necessarily from the groups with similar economic interpretations. After factor identification, the next step involves quantification of demand for Islamic banking. This necessarily implies construction of an index that includes the individual factors determining development, weighted by the individual contributions of these factors. A generalised development index is given in the following:

$$\text{Development} = \sum_{i=1}^{4} \alpha_i X_i$$

where α_i are the weights given to different factors X_i.

The above measure of development is the most objective quantification of development, given the data set at hand. It includes the factors that determine development for Islamic banking through factor analysis by minimising the level of subjectivity.

Once the development index was created, portfolios from various countries (primarily GCC, Malaysia and Far East) are screened to enhance the screening thresholds that have been used.

iv. **Limitations of Factor Analysis**

The methodology employed in this research was EFA, as it was the most suitable for the purpose of the research; however, one should be aware of the limitations or constraints of using it.

Firstly, the primary goal of the EFA is to identify latent variables and reducing a large set of variables to a smaller set of factors, which would then help in the development of the theory. However, this is not always the case, Armstrong (1967) conducted a research book and subsequently argued that factor analysis has limited use in developing a theory, and, due to this, it could not be relied upon to provide meaningful information about the data.

Additionally, EFA requires the researcher to make a number of decisions as to how the analysis should be conducted. These include the variables to be incorporated and the sample size; it is understood that for factor analysis to work, the minimum sample size should be 100. This requirement has been fulfilled in this research; however, this means that EFA does not suit a smaller sample size. It is also important to ensure that the variables included in the research relate to the area of interest; otherwise, this will result in irrelevant information. Hence, it is important for researchers to carefully define the parameters of the research and choose variables accordingly (Fabrigar et al., 1999). This will help in overcoming specification error.

Second, the researcher must ensure that EFA is the best model for raison d'être of the research; as the nature of this research is exploratory, where the aim is to reduce the variables to smaller factors or groups this method was decided to be the most suitable.

Third, how many factors should be included in the model? In this research, the factors are selected with the help of eigenvalues above. However, this method of choosing factors has also been challenged as some researchers preferred other methods of choosing factors or some prefer using multiple methods in selecting factors. Additionally, there is a need to decide the method of rotation to make the interpretation easy: the main ones are orthogonal and oblique. It is suggested that to receive meaningful information from a factor, it should include a minimum of four variables in it.

Furthermore, the data used in the EFA require some multicollinearity between the variables; its absence will not permit undertaking factor analysis. Some of the eigenvalues are negative; these do not mean anything and hence need to be avoided. The variables used can also be sample specific as a unique quality possessed by a group of people and hence cannot be generalised.

4.4 Concluding Remarks

To summarise, this chapter explains the research methodology used in this book. Based on the nature of the subject of interest being investigated and the research processes involved, this book can be categorised as an exploratory research. The research strategy used in this combined both deductive and inductive approaches. This book involved two types of data collection at different times and from different sources, namely primary data (collected from semi-structured interviews) and secondary data (historical stock prices and other economic data). The primary data are analysed using qualitative analysis, while the secondary data are analysed using quantitative analysis.

The results obtained from both the quantitative and qualitative analyses are used for making inferences on the how the existing *Shari'a* screening methodologies were introduced and how they can be enhanced to account for the market developments and to achieve objectives of *Shari'a*. Furthermore, the book aims to test the value addition that the *Shari'a* portfolio brings to an SRI portfolio. Hence, it is expected that the book will contribute positively to the development of the Islamic fund management industry. Figure 4.3 presents the research outcome.

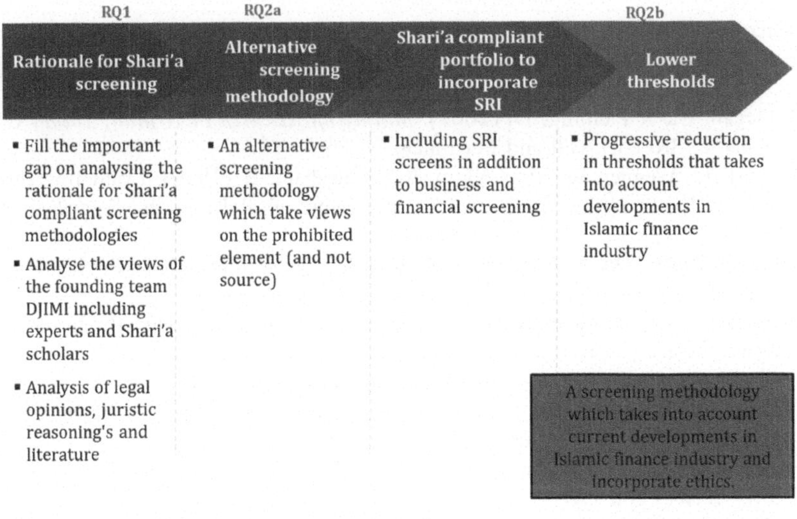

Fig. 4.3 Research book outcome

References

Abiad, A., & Mody, A. (2003). *Financial Reform: What Shakes It? What Shapes It* (IMF Working Paper, WP/03/70).

Adams, G., & Schvaneveldt, J. (1991). Obtaining Data: Documents of the Past. In G. Adams & J. Schvaneveldt (Eds.), *Understanding Research Methods* (2nd ed., pp. 291–314). Longman.

Armstrong, J. S. (1967). Derivation of Theory by Means of Factor Analysis or Tom Swift and His Electric Factor Analysis Machine. *The American Statistician, 21*, 17–21.

Brooks, J., & King, N. (2012, April 18–20). Qualitative Psychology in the Real World: The Utility of Template Analysis. *British Psychological Society Annual Conference*. London, UK (Unpublished). http://eprints.hud.ac.uk/13656/

Bryman, A., & Bell, E. (2007). *Business Research Methods* (Rev. ed.). Oxford University Press.

Bryman, A., & Bell, E. (2011). *Business Research Methods*. Oxford University Press.

Comrey, A. L., & Lee, H. B. (1992). *A First Course in Factor Analysis*. Erlbaum.

Crabtree, B. F., & Miller, W. L. (1999). Using Codes and Code Manuals: A Template Organizing Style of Interpretation. In B. F. Crabtree & W. L. Miller (Eds.), *Doing Qualitative Research* (2nd ed.). Sage.

Creane, G., Goyal, R., Mobarak, M., & Sab, R. (2004). *Financial Sector Development in the Middle East and North Africa* (IMF Working Paper WP/04/201).

Deetz, S. (1996). Describing Differences in Approaches to Organisation Science: Rethinking Burrell and Morgan and Their Legacy. *Organisation Science, 7*(2), 191–207.

Domegan, C., & Fleming, D. (2007). *Marketing Research in Ireland, Theory & Practise* (3rd ed.). Gill and Macmillan.

Fabrigar, L., Wegner, R., MacCallum, R., & Straham, E. (1999). Evaluating the Use of Exploratory Factor Analysis in Psychological Research. *Psychological Methods, 4*(3), 272–299.

Field, A. (2000). *Discovering Statistics Using SPSS for Windows*. Sage Publications Ltd.

Field, A. (2009). *Discovering Statistics Using SPSS* (3rd ed.). Sage Publications Ltd.

Field, A. (2011). *Discovering Statistics Using SPSS*. Sage Publications.

Gelbard, E., & Leite, P. (1999). *Measuring Financial Development in Sub-Saharan Africa* (IMF Working Paper 99/105).

Hutcheson, G., & Sofroniou, N. (1999). *The Multivariate Social Scientist: Introductory Statistics Using Generalized Linear Models*. Sage Publication.

Kahn, R. L., & Cannell, C. F. (1957). *The Dynamics of Interviewing; Theory, Technique, and Cases*. John Wiley & Sons.

Kaiser, H. F. (1960). The Application of Electronic Computers to Factor Analysis. *Educational and Psychological Measurement*, *20*, 141–151.

Kaiser, H. F. (1974). An Index of Factorial Simplicity. *Psychometrika, 39*, 31–36.

King, N. (2004). Using Templates in the Thematic Analysis of Text. In C. Cassels & G. Symon (Eds.), *Essential Guide to Qualitative Methods in Organizational Research* (pp. 256–270). Sage.

McMillen, M. (2013). *Islamic Finance and the Shari'ah*. Riverstone Publishing Group.

Saunders, M., Lewis, P., & Thornhill, A. (2007). *Research Methods for Business Students* (4th ed.). Pearson Education Limited.

Tabachnick, B. G., & Fidell, L. S. (2001). *Using Multivariate Statistics*. Allyn and Bacon.

Tryfos, P. (1997). *Methods of Business Analysis and Forecasting: Text and Cases*. John Wiley & Sons.

Walsham, G. (1993). *Interpreting Information Systems in Organisations*. Wiley.

Zhuang, S., Shao, H., Guo, F., Trimble, R., Pearce, E., & Abmayr, S. M. (2009). Sns and Kirre, the Drosophila Orthologs of Nephrin and Neph1, Direct Adhesion, Fusion and Formation of a Slit Diaphragm-Like Structure in Insect Nephrocytes. *Development, 136*(14), 2335–2344.

CHAPTER 5

A Review of the History and Existing Practices of the *Shari'a* Screening

5.1 Introduction

This chapter focuses on the analysis of face-to-face interviews conducted with the *Shari'a* scholars and other industry experts. The main objectives of the qualitative analysis are to understand the historical background of the *Shari'a* screening methodologies; discuss the issues highlighted in the literature regarding the current practices; and understand how the existing practices can be enhanced to ensure the screening methodologies are serving the purpose and lastly take into account the growth and developments in the IBF industry. The subject interest of this analysis includes history of *Shari'a* screening methodologies (including the relevance to *Shari'a* and fatwa allowing investment in stock market, practices before the launch of DJIMI, why the need existed, and the rationale behind the thresholds), *Shari'a* screening process issues (including issues facing business screening and financial screening), source of funds (i.e. why we are screening stocks based on source of funds and not the *Shari'a* non-compliant activity interest income or expense), socially responsible investments (how can we include the principles of socially responsible investments within *Shari'a* screening methodologies), purification, and finally the ways in which future screening methodologies can be enhanced to take into account IBF developments.

R. Malik, *Shari'a Compliant Equity Investments*,
https://doi.org/10.1007/978-3-031-70822-0_5

The outcome of the analysis will be used to further develop and enhance the research analysis in the second part; quantitative analysis. Hence, incorporating the input obtained directly from the *Shari'a* scholars and other experts will certainly add significant value to the depth and reliability of the overall book and further give direction as to how the existing screening methodologies can be developed. This chapter encompasses two parts, namely data analysis and results discussion.

5.2 Data Analysis

The data analysis attempts to extract valuable and meaningful information from the interview transcripts through the coding analysis technique by conducting a qualitative perception analysis. The coding analysis starts with the creation of descriptive codes to provide basic meaning and categories for words or phrases used by respondents in the interview transcripts. Subsequently, first-level codes were created to give interpretive meaning to the words or phrases. The final task in the coding stage is to assign pattern codes to enhance the inferential or explanatory power of words or phrases retrieved from the descriptive and first-level codes. A "List of Codes" is shown in Table 5.1.

History of Shari'a-Compliant *Screening Methodologies and How and Why They Were Introduced and Rationale Behind the Use of the Screening Thresholds*

This section analyses the responses given by the participating *Shari'a* scholars and other experts in Islamic finance on the history of *Shari'a* screening methodologies and how they were introduced. The coding analysis reveals that the responses can be categorised into six focused coding groups from which the general background of the *Shari'a* screening methodologies can be established. The six focused coding groups are: *Shari'a*, practice before DJIMI, stock market investments, investment in mixed businesses, use of thresholds and changes to screening methodologies. The coding analysis is summarised in Table 5.2a.

Table 5.2b describes the *Shari'a* ruling on the stock market investments and the companies that deal in interest or receive revenue from businesses that are not in compliance with *Shari'a*. In general, it is well-understood that *Shari'a* does not allow even a minimal amount

Table 5.1 List of codes

	Descriptive codes	*1st level codes*	*Pattern codes*
History of Shari'a *Screening Methodologies*		*HIST*	
HIST	*Shari'a*:	HIST-SHA	
	Quranic verdict on interest		HIST-SHA-QVI
	Fatwa by OIC		HIST-SHA-FOIC
	Solution to Fatwa		HIST-SHA-SOLF
	Shari'a as a facilitator		HIS-SHA-SHAFAC
HIST	Practice before DJIMI:	HIST-PRC	
	Private indexes		HIST-PRC-PRVIND
	Discussions		HIST-PRC-DISCS
	Not documented screening		HIST-PRC-NDSC
HIST	Stock Market Investments—the need of screening methodologies:	HIST-SMI	
	Benchmark		HIST-SMI-BENCH
	Internet growth		HIST-SMI-INTGR
	Business objective		HIST-SMI-BUSOBJ
	No market for 100% *Shari'a-compliant* companies		HIST-SMI-NMSHACC
HIST	Investment in mixed businesses:	HIST-MIX	
	Rulings of scholars		HIST-MIX-ROSCH
HIST	Use of thresholds	HIST-THRSH	
	33 percent		HIST-THRSH-33
	5 percent		HIST-THRSH-5
HIST	Changes to screening methodologies:	HIST-CHNG	
	Changes to DJIMI		HIST-CHNG-DJIMI
	Changes to SEC Malaysia		HIST-CHNG-SECM
Screening process issues		SPI	
SPI	Business Screening:	SPI-BS	
	5% rule		SPI-BS-5
	Tobacco and arms		SPI-BS-TOBARM
	Ghabn		SPI-BS-GHB
	Derivatives		SPI-BS-DER
SPI	Financial Screening:	SPI-FS	

(continued)

Table 5.1 (continued)

History of Shari'a *Screening Methodologies*	*Descriptive codes*	*1st level codes* *HIST*	*Pattern codes*
	33% rule		SPI-FS-33
	Ratios:		
	Debt-to-market cap		SPI-FS-DMC
	Liquidity Ratio		SPI-FS-LIQR
	Debt contract		SPI-FS-DEBC
	Interest income to total revenue		SPI-FS-ININCTR
	Trading in cash		SPI-FS-TRACSH
SPI	Other issues:	SPI-OISS	
	Standardisation		SPI-OISS-STAN
	Market cap vs total assets		SPI-OISS-MKTTA
	Enterprise value		SPI-OISS-ENTVAL
	Interest expense		SPI-OISS-INTEXP
	Weakness/ debt culture		SPI-OISS-DEBCUL
Source of Funds		SOF	
SOF	Screening on source of funds:	SOF-SOF	
	Possible on actual interest		SOF-SOF-PAINT
	Being considered already		SOF-SOF-BCONSA
SOF	Feasibility:	SOF-FEAS	
	Open to new ideas		SOF-FEAS-ONID
	Pilot test to see the difference		SOF-FEAS-PTSD
SOF	Issues:	SOF-ISS	
	Window dressing		SOF-ISS-WIND
	Netting effect		SOF-ISS-NETEFF
Socially responsible investments		SRI	
SRI	Maqasid *Shari'a*:	SRI-MAQS	
	Tayeb & Preferred		SRI-MAQS-TAYP
	Different levels of SRI		SRI-MAQS-DIFLSRI
	Not required by *Shari'a*		SRI-MAQS-NRSHA
	Whose responsibility		SRI-MAQS-WRES
SRI	Investors Preference:	SRI-INVPREF	

(continued)

Table 5.1 (continued)

History of Shari'a *Screening Methodologies*	*Descriptive codes*	*1st level codes* *HIST*	*Pattern codes*
	Market needs and Investors demand		SRI-INVPREF-MNID
	Different for different countries		SRI-INVPREF-DIFDIFC
	Muslims are concerned about SRI		SRI-INVPREF-MCSRI
	Not wise for all stocks		SRI-INVPREF-NWSTOC
SRI	Build bridges with SRI industry:	SRI-BBSRI	
	Investment opportunities		SRI-BBSRI-INVOPP
	Increase in AUM		SRI-BBSRI-INCAUM
Purification		PU	
PU	Purification:	PU-PU	
	Capital Gain		PU-PU-CAPG
	Dividend purification only		PU-PU-DIVPU
	Does not make sense		PU-PU-DNOTSECN
	Preferred model		PU-PU-PREFM
Future screening		FS	
FS	Business Screening Changes:	FS-BSC	
	Different criteria for tech and mining sector		FS-BSC-SIFCTMS
FS	Financial Screening Changes:	FS-FSC	
	Changes to 33%		FS-FSC-C33
	Interest expense		FS-FSC-INTEXP
	Progressive reduction		FS-FSC-PROGRED
	Islamic stock exchange		FS-FSC-ISLSTEX
	Need of revision		FS-FSC-NREV
FS	Future Research:	FS-FR	
	Static model to effect model		FS-FR-STMEFM
	More practical methodology		FS-FR-MPMETH
	Effect of netting		FS-FR-EFFNET

Table 5.2a Data analysis for interview questions 1

Interview question 1	*History of* Shari'a-compliant *screening methodologies and how and why they were introduced and rationale behind the use of the screening thresholds*	
Focused coding	*1st level coding*	*Subthemes/remarks*
1	HIST-SHA	*Shari'a* ruling on the stock market investments and companies deal in interest/*riba*: Ruling on Interest/*Riba* Quranic references on Interest/*Riba* OIC Fiqh Academy issued a Fatwa on investment in companies involved in mixed businesses *Shari'a* scholars agreed and issued a Fatwa *Shari'a* as a facilitator and not a hindrance for the humanity
2	HIST-PRC	Practice before the introduction of DJIMI: Use of private indexes by each firm Some of the discussions and debates at the time of DJIMI The screening practices prior to 1999 are rarely documented
3	HIST-SMI	Stock Market Investments—the need of screening methodologies: Islamic investments needed a benchmark The growth of internet and the access to stock market Business objective—the idea of access stock market for better returns There were no or very limited companies that were 100 per cent *Shari'a* compliant
4	HIST-MIX	Investment in mixed businesses: Rulings of *Shari'a* Scholars—Mixed views
5	HIST-THRSH	Use of thresholds: How did *Shari'a* scholars agree upon 33% How did *Shari'a* scholars agree upon 5%
6	HIST-CHNG	Changes to screening methodologies: The changes introduced in DJIMI since 1999

(continued)

Table 5.2a (continued)

Interview question 1	*History of* Shari'a-compliant *screening methodologies and how and why they were introduced and rationale behind the use of the screening thresholds*	
Focused coding	*1st level coding*	*Subthemes/remarks*
		The changes introduced at SEC Malaysia methodology in 2013
Concluding Theme	*Shari'a-compliant* stock market investments is a recent phenomenon, it evolved with the enhancement in technology and internet. OIC fiqh academy issued a fatwa, prohibiting investments in companies in mixed businesses (halal and haram). However, for the betterment of community and under *Maslahah Shari'a* scholars issued guidelines to invest in such companies (limiting the depth of involvement in *Shari'a* non-compliant activities) known as *Shari'a* screening methodologies—the first being Dow Jones Islamic Market Index methodology. Prior to this methodology, institutions used in-house screening methodology developed with the help of *Shari'a* advisors, which were rarely documented	

of interest-based transactions or revenue generated from *Shari'a* non-compliant businesses. Resultantly, a fatwa from the OIC fiqh academy allowing investments in companies that are in line with *Shari'a* while barring others that generate even a negligible amount from prohibited businesses. In essence, this meant that all the companies listed on the stock markets were not accessible to *Shari'a* sensitive investors as almost all of them directly or indirectly go through banking system and may deal in interest (incidentally). Hence, this issue started the planning process based on existing rules of *Shari'a* regarding the mixture of halal and haram. The process of planning started with the firm belief that *Shari'a* cannot be an impediment to growth and that it does not place restrictions on people where they cannot enjoin wealth, and hence it is a facilitator and not a barrier to growth.

Table 5.2c highlights the *Shari'a* screening practices before the introduction of DJIMI in 1999. Fund managers catering to the needs of *Shari'a* sensitive investors created private indexes using in-house methodologies which would be approved by a *Shari'a* advisor. Screening at the time was not documented as the industry was small and did not require a structured methodology. The existing screening methodologies evolved

Table 5.2b Focused coding no.1 for interview questions 1

Focused coding 1 *Sub-theme*	*Research Q1* Shari'a *ruling on the stock market investments and companies deal in interest/*riba*:*	
Interview no	*Pattern code*	*Remarks*
SI5	HIST-SHA-QVI	In the Quran Allah sbwt says "O Those who believe do not eat up *riba* doubled and redoubled" [Al -i-Imran 3:130]
SI2	HIST-SHA-FOIC	Resolution from Fiqh academy came which defined the publically traded company as a pool of funds. Impossible for any publicly traded company to refrain from dealing with banks—besides having liquidity. Final outcome Muslims cannot invest in the stock market
SI2	HIST-SHA-SOLF	Planning for existing rules in *Shari'a* about the mixture of halal and haram. Rule is based on the majority (not the minority)
SI1	HIST-SHA-SOLF	There were scholars who were against the companies involved in mixed activities (conservative opinion), while there were others who were in favour of it under the rule of exception and removing hardship
SI2	HIS-SHA-SHAFAC	*Shari'a* is not the imprisonment for Muslims and doesn't put restrictions on people that make them unable to enjoy life, enjoy wealth

from a lot of ideas, discussions, and trials and errors. Consequently, the end-result was a methodology that was widely accepted and hence gained prominence. Until this time, there were scholars who opined that trading in any equity that has any doubt was not allowed.

Table 5.2d focuses on the need for the *Shari'a* screening methodologies and the different users of it. *Shari'a* screening methodologies were needed to construct *Shari'a-compliant* portfolios, which would be used by funds and investment managers as a benchmark (not a best practice). In the past, Islamic fund managers were using conventional indexes or funds as a benchmark. Furthermore, with the growth of the internet, the accessibility of individuals to invest in the stock market was enhanced. Resultantly, these individuals were looking for advice; however, experts in

Table 5.2c Focused coding no.2 for research questions, 1

Focused coding 2 Sub-theme	*Research Q1 Practice before the introduction of DJIMI:*	
Interview no	*Pattern code*	*Remarks*
SI3	HIST-PRC-PRVIND	Dow Jones came 1996/7 but before that there were two attempts in Malaysia—RHB Islamic Index and BMB Islamic index
SI2	HIST-PRC-DISCS	- Tried various methodologies - Culmination of many trial and error and reached the one that gained more acceptance
SI3	HIST-PRC-NDSC	- Screening before DJIMI was not documented - Need for a book to be carried on to see how they worked
SI7,	HIST-PRC-NDSC	- Well, I think it is very much being done internally, internally they look at the activities because there was no specific methodology - Anyone who wanted to do Islamic even at that time would have their own sharia advices—case-by-case basis
SI1	HIST-PRC-NDSC	Scholars who use to say that trading in any equity in the international market, which has any doubt, any element of haram is haram

Islamic law were not able to offer a concrete advice at that time specifically for companies that generate part of their revenue (incidental) from *Shari'a* non-compliant activities. As a result of detailed discussions, it was realised that a mechanism is needed that will assist these individual investors and investment managers to invest in the stock markets in line with an industry benchmark.

Table 5.2e highlights the discussions that occurred in designing the first *Shari'a* screening methodology and the investment in the companies involved in mixed businesses. It was agreed in the discussions that as a rule a *Shari'a* sensitive investor should not invest in a venture that clearly states that part of its business activity is to generate revenue from *Shari'a* non-compliant activities. Furthermore, scholars also stated that

Table 5.2d Focused coding no.3 for interview question 1

Focused coding 3 *Sub-theme*	*Research Q1* *Stock Market Investments—the need for screening methodologies:*	
Interview no	*Pattern code*	*Remarks*
SI4	HIST-SMI-BENCH	Fund/asset managers with an Islamic equity investing mandate were using a social-ethical equity index or constructed an internal "Islamic equity" index so that can benchmark performance. There is a perceived conflict of interest which can undermine integrity of nascent equity investing among Muslims and compromise the benchmarked portfolio. Thus, to address the problem, an Islamic equity index by an independent index provider would not only provide transparency and accountability, and also establish the rules (initially) for screening
SI1	HIST-SMI-INTGR	– Late 1990s was the period of internet bubble and access to stock market was only a click away – Young generation was very active because they were pro-electronic and active in investments – Use to get lot of these questions
SI6	HIST-SMI-BUSOBJ	With a business objective, you will want to diversify your portfolios and access to *Shari'a-compliant* portfolio
SI6, SI9	HIST-SMI-BUSOBJ	– Reality on the ground is that 100% *Shari'a-compliant* were very limited – Very much individual in nature – As an investor I cannot just go and invest my money there so you have to find some other utility – Need big corporations—but they deal in multiple activities
SI6,	HIST-SMI-NMSHACC	– Large corporations that have zero haram element—impossible to find – Different types of activities even though it is halal activity but there might be some element which is doubtful or haram

these rulings are for existing companies that generate the revenue incidentally from the non-compliant businesses and hence does not apply to new businesses. Furthermore, it was also discussed that if they go for the most conservative opinion, then there will not be very many companies available for investment.

Table 5.2f highlights the thresholds introduced to obtain a solution for investment in companies involved in mixed businesses. *Shari'a* scholars started their research in trying to find a solution from the *Shari'a* and Islamic history in containing the revenue generated from *Shari'a* non-compliant businesses. There were two rulings needed quantitatively so

Table 5.2e Focused coding no.4 for interview question 1

Focused coding 4 *Sub-theme*	*Research Q1* *Investment in mixed businesses:*	
Interview no	*Pattern Code*	*Remarks*
SI5	HIST-MIX-ROSCH	– By choice a Muslim should never enter a venture or partnership, which at the outside is announced that it will seek interest-based financing – After deep discussions among the scholars for the interim period, there was slight majority in the board that we resolve to certain maxims that gives us some rule of thumb as to what is major and what is minor
SI6	HIST-MIX-ROSCH	– In a hotel everything is not haram—they are there to provide accommodation – Some elements in the hotel are haram – Ijtihad of the scholars particularly when it comes to mixed companies, so they come up with the criteria and developed it—with a view to enhance it
SI1	HIST-MIX-ROSCH	– Paper of Rushdi Siddiqui had a good and practical solution to issues we were facing – At least we reduce the haram element and these young guys trading so if we can reduce it to a minimal then we thought this was an achievement – If any Muslim country in the future wants to establish an Islamic equity market we cannot build on vacuum, we need to have experience

that fund managers and other users can apply it to their portfolios and remove the companies that do not fulfil the criteria. One ruling needed was for the capital structure of the company and to ensure that a company is not highly dependent on interest-based financing and investments. The other is with regard to the business line of the company. *Shari'a* scholars wanted to form their verdict based on a ruling that has some connection with Islamic history and as such they found a hadith of Prophet PBUH that asks to donate up to 33% of the wealth in charity. This ruling was used for the capital structure, while *Shari'a* scholars agreed on a 5% threshold to contain the revenue generated from *Shari'a* non-compliant activities by way of *Ijtehad*.

DJIMI was introduced in the year 1999; however, since then there have been certain changes that were introduced in line with the market conditions and need of the time. DJIMI started with allowing *Shari'a* non-compliant revenue of up to 5%; however, they reduced this particular threshold to 0%. Additionally, the ratios used to contain the interest-based financing and investments used total assets at the time but was soon changed to 12 months market capitalisation as it served the purpose better. This was followed by the change in market capitalisation to 24 months average market capitalisation during the financial crises (to ensure the volatility in prices of the stocks was neutralised). Furthermore, the Securities and Exchange Commission of Malaysia (SEC Malaysia) introduced their screening methodology with no thresholds on the capital structure (financial screening). However, in 2013 they revised their screening methodology to introduce the financial screening and to better align with the global practices—as shown in Table 5.2g.

To conclude, *Shari'a-compliant* screening methodologies were introduced as a need of the time—a result of the growing requirement of *Shari'a* sensitive investors to invest in the stock market. Furthermore, the fund managers and index providers needed a benchmark for the *Shari'a-compliant* portfolios. The fatwa issued by OIC fiqh academy barring any investment in companies that generate even a little income from *Shari'a* non-compliant sources was countered by a fatwa issued by a group of scholars implementing thresholds in containing the revenue generated by *Shari'a* non-compliant sources. Since the launch of DJIMI, a number of other screening methodologies have been introduced by SEC Malaysia, including FTSE, MSCI, and AAOIFI. DJIMI and SEC Malaysia underwent some changes as the whole process of enhancing the methodologies is ongoing, as and when necessary.

Table 5.2f Focused coding no.5 for interview questions 1

Focused coding 5 *Sub-theme*	*Research Q1* *Use of thresholds*	
Interview no	*Pattern code*	*Remarks*
SI1	HIST-THRSH-33	– Discussions among the scholars, – Used from the hadith of Thuluth – In books of law, fiqh, a third is considered the border between what is substantive and what is not,
SI8	HIST-THRSH-33	Yes, those who hold this opinion base it on the said Hadith even though there is no indication in the Hadith whatsoever to the issue in question
SI7	HIST-THRSH-33	Yes, one hadith can be used to derive multiple rulings on different topics. Perfectly acceptable for scholars to take the concept of "yes, but less is more" and apply to anything
SI2–SI6	HIST-THRSH-33	It is based on the thuluth hadith
SI2,	HIST-THRSH-5	– There is no basis for it from *Shari'a* point of view – What is the difference between 5%, 4% and 3%. I don't like it – Not serving the purpose
SI1, SI4, SI6 & SI7	HIST-THRSH-5	– Most arbitrary set. Zero is not possible; – Scholars cannot leave it as vague as "a lot is not good"; – Fund managers need a quantitative number and we needed to begin somewhere
SI3 & SI5	HIST-THRSH-5	– Yes it is very subjective – I don't allow in situations where I have a say in it. However, when we are working in the board and you have AAOIFI guidelines, you just work by them

How Is Shari'a *Screening Process Carried Out and What Are the Issues Facing the Screening Methodologies?*

This section analyses the responses related to the *Shari'a* screening process, the steps involved in conducting *Shari'a* screening for a portfolio and the different issues facing it (as highlighted in the literature). The coding analysis reveals that the responses can be categorised under three focused coding. These focused codes are business screening, financial

Table 5.2g Focused coding no.6 for interview questions 1

Focused coding 6 *Sub-theme*	*Research Q1* *Changes to screening methodologies*	
Interview no	*Pattern code*	*Remarks*
SI3	HIST-CHNG-DJIMI	Evolution of DJIMI has seen many changes 10%, 5% and one time during no cap for non-halal business revenue, now they are coming back to 5%
SI2	HIST-CHNG-DJIMI	- No 5% thresholds - Further they have their own preferences. After 2008 fund managers wanted to move from one year moving average to 24 months and *Shari'a* board including DJIMI supported it
SI1	HIST-CHNG-DJIMI	- Market capitalisation is more representative - No accounting of goodwill in total assets
SI3	HIST-CHNG-SECM	- To move big corporates to Islamic banking who are still working with conventional banks—so we have to do something as a national level - It helps the whole eco-system, the whole mentality was there and at the same time bring our screening closer to global practices
SI2	HIST-CHNG-SECM	Harmonising of activities taking place between Malaysia and the Gulf in many aspects and this is one of it

screening and other issues. The response on business screening and financial screening explains the process involved in undertaking the screening and the issues facing it. These include the ruling on industries like tobacco and arms manufacturers, derivatives exposure and trading, the use of various ratios, debt contract and trading in cash. Furthermore, views of the *Shari'a* scholars have also been analysed on the other issues facing the *Shari'a* screening and the screening on source of funds which have also been highlighted by other researchers in the academic literature. These include the issue of standardisation of different screening methodologies and the use of market capitalisation versus total assets as a denominator of financial ratios.

The coding analysis is summarised in Table 5.3a.

Table 5.3a Data analysis for interview question 2

Interview question 2	*How is* Shari'a *screening process carried out and what are the issues facing the screening methodologies?*	
Focused coding	*1st level coding*	*Subthemes/remarks*
1	SPI-BS	Business Screening: What does the 5% ratio mean The ruling on tobacco and arms is not clear Ghabn—the gain that exceeds market price The ruling on companies involved in derivatives products
2	SPI-FS	Financial Screening: What does the 33% rule mean and how was it agreed upon Ratios: Debt-to-market cap Liquidity Ratio Debt contract and its effects interest income to total revenue Trading in cash
3	SPI-OISS	Other issues: Standardisation The debate between market cap and total assets: which is better How can enterprise value as a denominator help Why interest expense is not captured the ill effects of a society heavily involved in debt
4	SOF-SOF SOF-FEAS SOF-ISS	Screening on source of funds: Possible on actual interest this was thought upon at the time of DJIMI Feasibility: The current practice is open for discussions Pilot test can be carried out to see what would have been the effect on portfolio combination Issues: Some companies carry out window dressing for tax purposes Netting effect: The interest income and interest expense may cancel each other

(continued)

Table 5.3a (continued)

Interview question 2	*How is* Shari'a *screening process carried out and what are the issues facing the screening methodologies?*	
Focused coding	*1st level coding*	*Subthemes/remarks*
Concluding Theme	The *Shari'a* screening methodologies consist of two parts, business screening and financial screening. Business screening avoids businesses involved in *Shari'a* non-compliant activities while financial screening ensures the company remains *Shari'a-compliant* in its capital structure. The existing screening methodologies were not an ideal solution and constructed under need of time and as a portfolio with fully *Shari'a-compliant* companies were not available or possible. Since DJIMI there are more than half a dozen methodologies issued by different institutions around the world. All of them are a variant of DJIMI and are equally *Shari'a* compliant. Yet the portfolio's constructed by following them are different from each other. There is a need of standardisation as argued in the academic literature. Other issues include use of thresholds based on the source of funds and the use of total assets and market capitalisation. Further, the existing screening methodologies screen stocks based on the source of the funds and not the prohibited element, i.e. interest. It is possible to screen stocks based on the actual interest element and as such the current practices are open for changes and enhancements, a pilot test can be carried out to screen stocks based on prohibited element and source of funds (as practised at the moment) and see the difference it makes to the portfolio combination	

Table 5.3b analyses the views of the respondents on the process of business screening. The question starts with understanding the views of the respondents on the 5% threshold being used for the revenue generated from *Shari'a* non-compliant sources. From the academic research, it is understood that the views on investment in tobacco and arms manufacturers are not clear and the analysis answers this in the next step. Almost all the respondents have given a detailed answer, stating that tobacco is not good for health and hence investment in a company that promotes this dangerous material should not be allowed. However, there are some mixed views on the investment in arms and defence-related companies, and it is suggested that it should be discussed on a case-by-case basis after understanding the purpose of the manufacturer. Clearly, arms used for violent purposes are not allowed at all. Furthermore,

derivative investments are not allowed in *Shari'a*; however, the *Shari'a* screening methodologies do not take them into account when undertaking the screening. The respondents are asked to assist in understanding if it should be part of the *Shari'a* screening process.

In Table 5.3c, the process of financial screening is analysed from the views of the respondents. To start with, the views were compiled on why the threshold of 33% was taken and their thoughts on this. This was followed by the important question, as highlighted in the literature, regarding the reasons for screening the capital structure of the company based on the source of funds (i.e. the debt-to-market capitalisation and not the actual interest that we pay on it). This is because, according to *Shari'a*, it is the interest that is impermissible and not the debt. The respondents discussed issues with a debt contract according to *Shari'a*. Respondents are of the view that an interest-based debt contract itself is not allowed and is classed as null and void. Screening based on the source of funds was discussed at the time but it was agreed that it is better to capture it at the source; that is, what causes the rise of interest (either payable or receivable), and also that companies can window dress and not publish this information. Furthermore, interest rates vary in different markets and hence debt amount is more identifiable and the net interest income might remove the effect of interest income and expense. Concurrently, few respondents suggested undertaking a back test to understand correlation between screening based on the source of funds and the actual interest amount.

Table 5.3d summarises the responses of the respondents on the liquidity ratio used in the financial screening. The view is that when you are buying the stock of the company that has a large sum of liquid assets, the assumption is that it will place its fund in the interest-bearing accounts and hence companies should not be allowed to do this. However, the alternative is that you are actually not buying into the cash of the company and hence it should not be part of the screening process. Furthermore, we can screen portfolios without this screen to identify the difference it makes to the portfolio composition.

Table 5.3e compiles the views on the use of ratio interest income to total revenue and whether it can be enhanced. The response suggests that in some countries like Malaysia and GCC, the ratio can perhaps be lowered to 3% as these markets are now developed and Islamic financing availability in these countries is at an acceptable level. There is a need to look at the ratios and see if they can be achieved.

Table 5.3b Focused coding no. 1 business screening for interview questions 2

Focused coding 1	*How is* Shari'a *screening process carried out and what are the issues facing the screening methodologies?*	
Business screening	*Company involved in mixed businesses, then an up to 5% threshold of the* Shari'a *non-compliant is tolerated*	
Interview no	*Pattern code*	*Remarks*
S1–S7	SPI-BS-5	Tolerated in the interim period, until a better measure is available and should be adjusted in line with developments
SI2	SPI-BS-TOBARM	Tobacco, No. But for arms manufacturers, it is better for me to do case by case
SI6	SPI-BS-TOBARM	– Tobacco should be unacceptable for investment; – Arms & defence: problematic; definitely WMD not allowed; if the arms are known to be used to oppress people then one should avoid investing in that manufacturer
SI7	SPI-BS-TOBARM	– Defence is a grey area as countries need to purchase "warfare" to protect against hostile enemies – But companies that make deadly offensive products should be prohibited – On tobacco, nothing withstanding the evidence of harmful effects – I suggest include them, and then put them on notice to spend more money on educating public on the harmful effects of their product
SI4,SI9	SPI-BS-TOBARM	– Of course the default position of AAOIFI is that we should not allow. But if we are talking about existing in globally multinational armaments companies—they are actually financing civil wars, etc. this is forbidden—even in Muslim area – The hadith is very clear that we shouldn't buy arms at the times of Fitna. So, this is Muslim area – Very serious issue in *Shari'a* and it is not allowed to invest in – For the local arms industry for our local needs—it will be allowed—we need to arm ourselves to defend ourselves

(continued)

Table 5.3b (continued)

Focused coding 1	*How is* Shari'a *screening process carried out and what are the issues facing the screening methodologies?*	
Business screening	*Company involved in mixed businesses, then an up to 5% threshold of the* Shari'a *non-compliant is tolerated*	
Interview no	*Pattern code*	*Remarks*
SI5	SPI-BS-TOBARM	- Tobacco I think we should avoid—now when you say investing—so you are talking about companies that are producing this poison. So this has no ethical or religious value - Arms and defence, we don't say that arms per se is haram because every country has defence—has this and that—it has to be studied case by case—it is difficult to give a verdict
SI2, SI6 & SI4	SPI-BS-DER	Should be included. If you have the capability then you must take it into account. Because that is also very controversial in nature. Sometimes people say that it is for unmanageable purposes, it is a very thin line. Because nowadays most of them use their own thing just to make money
SI7	SPI-BS-DER	No, as it would encourage the use of this product. It may be used for mitigating risk, but, with pressure on performance, could well be used for enhancing returns, and documentation buried in legalise language in a footnote in the addendum, may make it difficult to find
SI5	SPI-BS-DER	I mean it is possible but as you know it is difficult, takes more time plus it can reduce the universe to very few stocks, because derivatives are a huge market and everybody uses it in USA an Europe. What we say is derivatives trading is haram

The views on the standardisation of the *Shari'a* screening methodologies are presented in Table 5.3f. Almost all of the scholars agree that ideally one would aspire to have standardisation across these screening methodologies and it is also better for stability.

Tables 5.3g, h, i and j continue to capture the views of the respondents on other issues, these include the use of market capitalisation or total

Table 5.3c Focused coding no. 2 data analysis of financial screening for interview question 2

Focused coding 2 *Financial screening*	*Research Q2* *How is* Shari'a *screening process carried out and what are the issues facing the screening methodologies?*	
Interview no	*Pattern code*	*Remarks*
S1–S7	SPI-FS-33	We needed to begin somewhere. For scholars to answer, but it's a reference point and not etched in stone. It is an interim tolerance parameter solution, more book is required in the religious text and findings of scholars
SI2	SPI-FS-DMC	Debt contract itself is NULL and VOID from *Shari'a* point of view. So that's why it is haram source
SI6	SPI-FS-DMC	Debt equity ratio is important because then it will be considered when buying stock that you are buying the debt, hence you cannot gain from your buy
SI1	SPI-FS-DMC	This debate was there, first in the beginning this ratio was not like that, the ratio was looking at interest income. However, then we saw people can play with it by way of netting. So, now we thought to capture it at source. *So that was the idea behind the source of funds usage*
SI4	SPI-FS-DMC	Sales are more important, as companies can, via balance sheet cosmetology, can make income disappear for, say, tax purposes
SI3	SPI-FS-DMC	It's a good suggestion perhaps we can do some back testing to see the correlation between the actual amount and the capped (current practices) and understand it
SI5	SPI-FS-DMC	The resolution is how much is interest-based financing regardless of the amount of interest—whether the financing cost 1% or 10% doesn't matter—as long as it is interest based
SI7	SPI-FS-DMC	Interest expense would be different in different interest rate environments; debt is more identifiable as a number on the balance sheet

assets as a denominator. Respondents view that it is better to use market capitalisation as it captures not only the tangible assets but also intangibles like goodwill. However, one of the respondents is of the view that it may be better to use enterprise value as a denominator as it is more reflective of the company value. Furthermore, respondents agree that *Shari'a*

Table 5.3d Focused coding no. 3 data analysis liquidity ratio for interview question 2

Focused coding 3 *Liquidity ratio*	*Research Q2* *Other issues*	
Interview no	*Pattern code*	*Remarks*
SI3	SPI-FS-LIQR	I don't agree on the issue. Further refinement needed on the issue of liquidity ratio. We are putting 51:49 or 33% because the fact that when you buy a share of the company; you are not buying into the cash of the company but somehow scholars tend to make it very legalistic in approach
SI4,	SPI-FS-LIQR	Your assertion makes sense logically, but book the impact of removing this screen, does it increase the universe of companies? If it increases the universe of companies, then let us look at economic sectors most impacted, and companies in those sectors for insights
SI1	SPI-FS-LIQR	Of these cash is Islamic or not Islamic. If it is Islamic, then all Islamic banks are 90% liquid but it is allowed. Now if you are trading in a company which is only 30% tangible and 70% is liquid, where are they going to put it—conventionally, *Riba*. So the screen will be caught from the other side
SI2, SI9	SPI-FS-TRACSH	I don't think we need any limit for cash. What is the worst that can happen, if a company has 100% cash? Further the receivables are there because the company has provided them a facility to buy now and pay later and not to charge interest

screening methodologies already capture the interest expense element by using debt-to-market capitalisation or total assets ratio. Lastly, in allowing the debt screen, companies are in essence borrowing or raising funds from other OIC countries, while the companies themselves may be in non-OIC block. This may result in freight of capital from Muslim to non-Muslim countries, which is not ideal.

Tables 5.3k, l and m compile the responses under source of funds, feasibility and window dressing. Respondents are of the view that it is possible and we should perhaps undertake some back testing to see the effect on portfolio combination if we screen based on actual prohibited

Table 5.3e Focused coding no.4 data analysis for interest income for interview question 2

Focused coding 4 Sub-theme	*Research Q2 How is* Shari'a *screening process carried out and what are the issues facing the screening methodologies?*	
Interview no	*Pattern code*	*Remarks*
SI3, SI9	SPI-FS-ININCTR	We have to see the market trend—if the market trend for companies based in Malaysia and GCC, perhaps we can downgrade from 5 to 3% that may help the industry to grow but companies in UK and Europe 5% will be great
SI2	SPI-FS-ININCTR	I think this criterion is still involved—it can be subject to new ideas—everything can be subject to discussion—I am not saying this is wrong—but let's look at it, maybe it will serve the purpose of *Shari'a* in a more accurate manner

element. Concurrently, we have to be mindful of the fact that people can play with the interest element figures, which may result in offsetting interest income element with interest expense.

To conclude, *Shari'a* screening process is conducted in two steps: business screening followed by financial screening. The rule of 5% is based on the *ijtehad* of the scholars while the 33% rule for financial screening is based on the hadith of the Prophet Muhammad (PBUH). Within business screening, the ruling on investment in companies in tobacco business is not allowed while companies involved in arms business should be dealt with on a case-by-case basis. Arms used for terrorist activities are undoubtedly against the principles of *Shari'a*. Furthermore, derivative instruments should become part of the screening exercise as they are highly interest-based products; however, it may be difficult to capture. In the financial screening, the liquidity ratio should be avoided as it makes very little sense and ideal situation screening methodologies should be standardised as it will ease the process for the investors and investment managers. Lastly, tests can be implemented to screen stocks based comparing the results of existing practices with results of screening based on interest income and interest expense to analyse its viability and impact.

Table 5.3f Focused coding no.5 data analysis for standardisation for interview question 2

Focused coding 5 *Sub-theme*	*Research Q2* *How is* Shari'a *screening process carried out and what are the issues facing the screening methodologies?*	
Interview no	*Pattern code*	*Remarks*
SI2	SPI-OISS-STAN	Maybe we need that, we should be open to discuss and innovate
SI6	SPI-OISS-STAN	For me it is very much subjective in the sense that at the moment looking at the development in the industry, looking at the size of the industry, I think it is not the time yet. However, standardisation is the ideal situation
SI7	SPI-OISS-STAN	In a perfect world, there would be standardisation; and there wouldn't be multiple schools of thoughts either; at the end of the day, fund managers should be able to adapt to the clients' needs, be it total assets or market cap
SI5	SPI-OISS-STAN	I think standardisation should be there—you have to standardise your unit of measure—and sometimes what happens is that when they move from one jurisdiction to the other—they will change the methodology because it is more in their favour
SI1	SPI-OISS-STAN	Not necessary, from the main element (business screening) they are unified. Now if you ask me unifying the methodologies, standardisation, does it help Yes Of course it helps, it makes it better and easy for other people to understand. But is it necessary in this particular field, I don't think so
SI4	SPI-OISS-STAN	For stability it may be better

Is There a Need to Incorporate Socially Responsible Principles Promoted by Shari'a *Within Existing Screening Methodologies?*

Socially responsible industry has become a very important industry as people have improved their understanding of the ill social practices prevailing in the world and hence started raising their voices against it. Resultantly, a growing number of people would like to ensure that their investments are not directly or indirectly supporting the companies that violate these social norms. A number of initiatives have been

Table 5.3g Focused coding no. 6 data analysis for market cap to total assets for interview question 2

Focused coding 6 Sub-theme	*Research Q2 How is* Shari'a *screening process carried out and what are the issues facing the screening methodologies?*	
Interview no	*Pattern code*	*Remarks*
SI4	SPI-OISS-MKTTA	For stability it may be better to use debt/asset (asset heavy sectors) and for capture pulse of market sentiments, better to use debt/market cap (tech and service)
SI1	SPI-OISS-MKTTA	DJIMI started with total assets but then the scholar debated that it is not capturing the intangible assets of the company—hence we moved to market capitalisation

Table 5.3h Focused coding no. 7 data analysis for enterprise value for interview question 2

Focused Coding 7 Sub-theme	*Research Q2 How is* Shari'a *screening process carried out and what are the issues facing the screening methodologies?*	
Interview No	*Pattern Code*	*Remarks*
SI3	SPI-OISS-ENTVAL	"Enterprise value" is more reflective of the company. Perhaps when you want to buy a company you don't look at the market cap or total assets you look at the enterprise value of the company. Very consistent unlike market capitalisation

initiated by global multilateral institutions that limit a company's involvement in these socially irresponsible activities. The overall SRI industry has reached US$ 33 trillion according to Thomson Reuters Global Asset Management Report 2015 and as such when we look at the principles promoted by the SRI industry, it is interesting to note that all of them are equally or even more supported by the *Shari'a*, yet the *Shari'a* screening methodologies do not incorporate them as part of the screening practices. Through this question, the book understands from the scholars how important it is to incorporate these principles. Through the responses,

Table 5.3i Focused coding no. 8 data analysis for interest expense for interview question 2

Focused coding 8 *Sub-theme*	*Research Q2* *How is* Shari'a *screening process carried out and what are the issues facing the screening methodologies?*	
Interview no	*Pattern code*	*Remarks*
SI6	SPI-OISS-INTEXP	Company shouldn't take interest loan. That should forbid the general criteria
SI7	SPI-OISS-INTEXP	Interest expense would be different in different interest rate environments; debt is more identifiable as a number on the balance sheet

Table 5.3j Focused coding no.9 data analysis for debt culture for interview question 2

Focused coding 9 *Sub-theme*	*Research Q2* *How is* Shari'a *screening process carried out and what are the issues facing the screening methodologies?*	
Interview no	*Pattern code*	*Remarks*
SI4,	SPI-OISS-DEBCUL	The debt screen for Muslim countries, a debt culture exists in Muslim countries, has an adverse impact, hence, many companies, while passing primary business (no pork, alcohol or weapons producer) screens usually fail the debt screen. If money is sourced for Islamic equity funds from OIC investors, and underlying components in an Islamic equity index are from non-OIC, then contributing to *Shari'a-compliant* capital flight

the focused codes look at the Maqasid *Shari'a*; that is, the objectives of *Shari'a* and how it supports these principles. The concept of Tayeb is it required by *Shari'a* and whose responsibility is it to enforce it, i.e. state or the company. Furthermore, what are the investor preferences, can it be enforced and what benefits does it bring to the overall Islamic finance industry? (Table 5.4a).

Table 5.3k Focused coding no.10 data analysis for Source of Funds for interview question 2

Focused coding 10 *Sub-theme*	*Research Q2* *Why do the* Shari'a *screening methodologies screen based on the source of funds?*	
Interview no	*Pattern code*	*Remarks*
SI3	SOF-SOF-PAINT	It's a good suggestion perhaps we can do some back testing to see the correlation between the actual amount and the capped (current practices) and to see the changes in portfolio combination
SI1	SOF-SOF-BCONSA	But first of all we found the problem when using that people play with it, sometimes they off-set the interest income with interest expense. However, how much debt you have, you can't play with it and of course you have to disclose it as well

Table 5.3l Focused coding no. 11 data analysis for the feasibility of SOF for interview question 2

Focused coding 11 *Sub-theme*	*Research Q2* *Why do the* Shari'a *screening methodologies screen based on the source of funds?*	
Interview no	*Pattern code*	*Remarks*
SI2	SOF-FEAS-ONID	It is possible
SI3	SOF-FEAS-PTSD	Perhaps one can back test and see the difference in the portfolio construction

The data analysis of the responses received has been divided into three parts and under ten focused codes and four of them have been stated in Tables 5.4b, c, d and e under the Pattern code of "Tayeb and Preferred". Scholars believe that there should be options available to investors, including a preferred level of screening and most recommended. However, by recommending this, it does not mean that the stocks screened under current screening methodologies are not *Shari'a* compliant. Concurrently, there can be different levels of screening options available for investors. There can be a portfolio that is compliant based on

Table 5.3m Focused coding no. 12 data analysis for window dressing for interview question 2

Focused coding 12 *Sub-theme*	*Research Q2* *Why do the* Shari'a *screening methodologies screen based on the source of funds?*	
Interview no	*Pattern code*	*Remarks*
SI1	SOF-ISS-WIND	People play with it
SI1	SOF-ISS-NETEFF	But first of all we found the problem when using that people play with it, sometimes they off-set the interest income without showing it so they since I am receiving interest and I am giving interest, they off-set it

existing screening and then there can be another that is compliant based on socially responsible principles in addition to being *Shari'a* compliant.

Tables 5.4f, g, h, i, j and k analyse the responses regarding the investor preferences. It should be our agenda to enhance the practices of investments to better align with the objectives of *Shari'a*; however, it will only flourish if there is enough demand for it from the investors. Furthermore, the ethical principles vary in different markets and should be dealt with on a case to case basis. One of the respondent stated that social responsibility in a developed country cannot be compared with social responsibility in a developing country. The respondents again reiterated that it would not be wise to make it an absolute requirement for the *Shari'a* portfolio but making it available as an option is encouraged. The respondents further confirmed that Muslims are concerned about the ethical issues and as such these ethical issues are not only promoted by *Shari'a* but encouraged. They went on to state that if the *Shari'a* boards are made aware of the unethical practices, they themselves will not endorse the investments.

In the last Patterns code "Building bridges with the SRI industry", it is mentioned that the SRI industry has a lot of commonalities with the Islamic finance industry, yet they tend to operate independently of each other. There are studies in academic literature that state that the SRI industry can benefit from the Islamic finance industry in the market downturn; simultaneously, the integration of SRI in Islamic investments will result in an increase in the AUM of the industry. *Shari'a* screening has always forbidden the evil; however, the time has arrived where it should

Table 5.4a Data analysis for interview question 3

Interview question 3	*Is there a need to incorporate socially responsible principles promoted by* Shari'a *within existing screening methodologies? This will also assist in tapping into the SRI industry—US$33 trillion industry*	
Focused coding	*1st level coding*	*Subthemes/remarks*
	SRI-MAQS	Maqasid *Shari'a*: Tayeb & Preferred Different levels of SRI can be introduced SRI screening is not required by *Shari'a* Whose responsibility is it to enforce SRI?
	SRI-INVPREF	Investors Preference: Market needs and Investors demand Different SRI principles are there for different countries Muslims are concerned about SRI Cannot enforce on all *Shari'a-compliant* investments
	SRI-BBSRI	Build bridges with SRI industry: Investment opportunities for Islamic investments industry Increase in AUM if there is integration
Concluding Theme	There are a number of similarities between the Islamic investments industry and the SRI industry, yet they operate independent of each other. Moreover, a number of principles followed by SRI industry are principles promoted by Islam yet, the Islamic investments industry has not incorporated them in screening practices, as a result the ill social activities may go unnoticed and become part of a *Shari'a-compliant* portfolio. It is believed that different levels of SRI principles can be introduced in Islamic investments and can be offered to investors in line with their preferences. There is no exhaustive list of SRI principles followed by the industry. However, it is not possible to enforce SRI principles in the *Shari'a* portfolio. The integration of SRI and Islamic industry will provide diversification of portfolios and an increase in the AUM	

Table 5.4b Focused code 1 Tayeb and Preferred for interview question 3

Focused coding 1 *Sub-theme*	*Research Q3* *Is there a need to incorporate socially responsible principles promoted by* Shari'a *within existing screening methodologies?*	
Interview no	*Pattern code*	*Remarks*
SI6	SRI-MAQS-TAYP	It is good to have and clarify that you are not saying that others are non-complaint. I mean there can be different degrees of offerings. This is mubah level and it is allowed, etc. But this one is recommended is Tayeb

Table 5.4c Focused code 2 different levels of SRI for interview question 3

Focused coding 2 *Sub-theme*	*Research Q3* *Is there a need to incorporate socially responsible principles promoted by* Shari'a *within existing screening methodologies?*	
Interview no	*Pattern code*	*Remarks*
SI1	SRI-MAQS-DIFLSRI	I mean you can say that we have companies that pass and there are companies that double pass and then you have companies that triple pass and so on. You can say that these companies only comply with Islamic principles, these companies comply with both Islamic and SRI screening, etc. and investor can choose from

Table 5.4d Focused code 3 not required by *Shari'a* for interview question 3

Focused coding 3 *Sub-theme*	*Research Q3* *Is there a need to incorporate socially responsible principles promoted by* Shari'a *within existing screening methodologies?*	
Interview no	*Pattern code*	*Remarks*
SI2	SRI-MAQS-NRSHA	We should have investment opportunities and cannot say that everything else is haram

Table 5.4e Focused code 4 whose responsibility for interview question 3

Focused coding 4 Sub-theme	*Research Q3 Is there a need to incorporate socially responsible principles promoted by* Shari'a *within existing screening methodologies?*	
Interview no	*Pattern code*	*Remarks*
SI5	SRI-MAQS-WRES	But I believe it is unfair to make the responsibility of the institution to go and do further book regarding the negative spillover of the project in these areas. It is the obligation of the government and the regulators
SI6	SRI-MAQS-WRES	Yes, and this is very much regulatory in nature

Table 5.4f Focused code 5 market needs and investor demands for interview question 3

Focused coding 5 Sub-theme	*Research Q3 Is there a need to incorporate socially responsible principles promoted by* Shari'a *within existing screening methodologies?*	
Interview no	*Pattern code*	*Remarks*
SI6	SRI-INVPREF-MNID	As we develop, it should be in, again depending on the market the one we are using right now is very much the faiths criteria. So, as the market evolve, we should include wherever possible and put all the social issues so that we can enhance—of course it is very much dependent on the investors demand
SI2, SI9	SRI-INVPREF-MNID	I think it is quite necessary, and in the fund analysis, we all are servants of the end user or the investor and nothing will fly unless there is a demand

move to enjoining the good and moving from just negative screening to more positive screening.

To conclude, from the responses of the scholars and other experts, it is clear that *Shari'a* not only promotes the SRI principles but goes a step beyond and encourages it. The scholars are in agreement that

Table 5.4g Focused code 6 different SRI principles for different countries for interview question 3

Focused Coding 6 Sub-theme	*Research Q3 Is there a need to incorporate socially responsible principles promoted by* Shari'a *within existing screening methodologies?*	
Interview No	*Pattern Code*	*Remarks*
SI1	SRI-INVPREF-DIFDIFC	We don't want to say it is halal or haram because these people play with things. I mean human rights, they will go to Pakistan and they will see some children making footballs in Sialkot and they will say this is against human rights. Now these people are dying from hunger and if they get something to eat and in future they will learn or something. But they don't look at what they are doing to children in their countries and what pornography they are using

Table 5.4h Focused code 7 Muslims are concerned about SRI principles for interview question 3

Focused coding 7 Sub-theme	*Research Q3 Is there a need to incorporate socially responsible principles promoted by* Shari'a *within existing screening methodologies?*	
Interview no	*Pattern code*	*Remarks*
SI2,SI9	SRI-INVPREF-MCSRI	Muslims like other people have concerns about environment, human rights, corruption, status of women, etc. they want to be part of the social change. I firmly and strongly believe that these opportunities should be available
SI5,	SRI-INVPREF-MCSRI	*Shari'a* doesn't only promotes it (issues of justice, morality, etc.)—it enforces or requires them. These are recognised goals and aims of *Shari'a*. And I don't know of any scholar or board who would permit investing in project where they know of violence of human rights, labour rights, etc

Table 5.4i Focused code 8 not wise for all stocks for interview question 3

Focused coding 8 *Sub-theme*	*Research Q3* *Is there a need to incorporate socially responsible principles promoted by* Shari'a*within existing screening methodologies?*	
Interview no	*Pattern code*	*Remarks*
SI2	SRI-INVPREF-NWSTOC	I don't think it will be wise to say that all Islamic investments should include ethical criteria as well

Table 5.4j Focused code 9 investment opportunities for interview question 3

Focused coding 9 *Sub-theme*	*Research Q3* *Is there a need to incorporate socially responsible principles promoted by* Shari'a *within existing screening methodologies?*	
Interview no	*Pattern code*	*Remarks*
SI2	SRI-BBSRI-INVOPP	I believe Muslims, like other people, have concerns about environment, human rights, corruption, and status of women. They want to be part of the social change—these values are enhanced through investment. I firmly and strongly believe that these opportunities should be available

effort should be made in moving the portfolios from being just *Shari'a-compliant* to a more preferred portfolio of Tayeb; however, it cannot be made as an absolute necessity. There should be options available for the investors, and concurrently, there is a need to make the investors aware of the differences in the two portfolios. Furthermore, a move away from being just *Shari'a-compliant* (i.e. negative screening) to enjoining the good or positive screening can also result in increasing the AUM of the Islamic investments.

What Is the Preferred Way of Purification?

Purification is a very important component of *Shari'a* screening methodologies; without it, the current *Shari'a* investment will not be *Shari'a*

Table 5.4k Focused code 10 increase in AUM for interview question 3

Focused coding 10 *Sub-theme*	*Research Q3* *Is there a need to incorporate socially responsible principles promoted by* Shari'a *within existing screening methodologies?*	
Interview no	*Pattern code*	*Remarks*
SI7	SRI-BBSRI-INCAUM	Tapping into more money should not be a reason to include in *Shari'a* screens; *Shari'a* screens is to avoid haram, not market opportunity; that said, screening has always been about "forbidding the evil"; it is time we moved to "enjoining the good" but I don't know if it should screen. Encouragement or a preference to SRI
SI4	SRI-BBSRI-INCAUM	Yes, time has arrived. It is time we build bridges to SRI, ESG and CRS communities and funds, and explain that there is an alignment of values and orientation

compliant. Through this research, we aim to enhance the existing practices of *Shari'a* screening methodologies; there are a number of purification methods followed by the industry. Through this question, we ask the respondents their preferred methods of purification and whether there are any changes to the existing strategies that they would like to encourage (Table 5.5a).

The responses have been analysed in Tables 5.5b, c, d and e. The responses are diverse, with most scholars preferring that the most common method used in purifying is just the dividends purification as that is the profit that the investors receive from their investments, while some also stated that the ideal is to purify capital gains as well. As such, capital gains are not a direct result of the activities of the company; it is from the market. Opponents of *Shari'a* screening methodologies opine that it is not helpful to willingly and knowingly invest in haram investments and then purify the income. Purification only helps if the investor was not aware of the haram element. Lastly, there was also a suggestion to conduct a research book to examine the linkage of high purification to stock price and low purification and stock price.

To conclude, most of the scholars opined that the existing common method of purification is something that they support fully; as dividend is

Table 5.5a Data analysis for interview question 4

Interview question 4	*What is the preferred way of purification?*	
Focused coding	*1st level coding*	*Subthemes/remarks*
	PU-PU	Purification: Only capital gains should be purified Only dividend should be purified Purification does not make sense What is the preferred model and what changes to be introduced
Concluding Theme	Income in stocks of mixed business is possible with the condition that income generated from such investments is purified. There are different models of purification practised in the industry; purifying dividends only and purifying both dividends and capital gains	

Table 5.5b Focused code 1 capital gains for interview question 4

Focused coding 1 *Sub-theme*	*Research Q4* *What is the preferred way of purification?*	
Interview no	*Pattern code*	*Remarks*
SI5, SI9	PU-PU-CAPG	Ideally you would purify capital gains—but not a requirement and not the practice. The main thing is that the returns (dividends) should be purified

Table 5.5c Focused code 2 dividend purification for interview question 4

Focused coding 2 *Sub-theme*	*Research Q4* *What is the preferred way of purification?*	
Interview no	*Pattern code*	*Remarks*
SI2,SI8	PU-PU-DIVPU	Investment purification. Capital gains need not to be purified, because they are coming from the market and not from the business of the company
SI6	PU-PU-DIVPU	Prefer purification at the company level and only dividend. Capital gain need not to be purified
SI1 & SI7	PU-PU-DIVPU	Purify any impure income from the revenue side and my view is that capital gains do not need to be purified

Table 5.5d Focused code 3 purification does not make sense for interview question 4

Focused coding 3 Sub-theme	*Research Q4 What is the preferred way of purification?*	
Interview no	*Pattern code*	*Remarks*
SI8, SI9	PU-PU-DNOTSECN	It does not help at all to willingly and knowingly invest in the haram then to purify the income. Purification may help only in cases where the investor was not aware of the presences of haram elements in his investment

Table 5.5e Focused code 4 preferred model for interview question 4

Focused coding 4 Sub-theme	*Research Q4 What is the preferred way of purification?*	
Interview no	*Pattern code*	*Remarks*
SI4	PU-PU-PREFM	Scholars, academics, index providers and fund managers are better positioned to answer. I would be interested in looking at linkage (if any) between high purification amounts and stock performance to peers, and with lower purification amounts and stock price

the revenue generated from the operations of the company it should be subject to purification.

How Can the Existing Shari'a *Screening Methodologies Be Enhanced?*
After seeking opinions on the issues that the existing *Shari'a* screening methodologies are facing, this section analyses how they can be enhanced. The coding analysis reveals that the responses can be categorised under four focused codes, namely business screening changes, progressive reduction and future research. The coding analysis is summarised in Tables 5.6a to j.

Table 5.6b analyses the response to business screen changes, including having a more robust and clearer ruling on the treatment of companies involved in tobacco and arms manufacturers. Scholars believe that

Table 5.6a Data analysis for interview question 5

Interview question 5	*How can the existing* Shari'a *screening methodologies be enhanced?*	
Focused coding	*1st level coding*	*Subthemes/remarks*
	FS-BSC	Business Screening Changes: Different criteria for technology and mining sector
	FS-FSC	Financial Screening Changes: Changes to 33% Introduction of Interest expense Move towards progressive reduction The creation of an Islamic stock exchange Current screening methodologies revisions
	FS-PROGRED	Progressive reduction: How feasible is it and if possible Possible but not necessary Expanding the investible universe At the moment there is no need for it Yes that was the idea when the methodologies were introduced It was not discussed at the time
	FS-FR	Future Research: Static model to effect model More practical methodology Effect of netting Need for alternative model
Concluding Theme	There is a need to enhance the existing *Shari'a* screening methodologies in line with the development in the Islamic banking industry, i.e. progressive reduction of the ratios. It may also be possible to design a model that is more dynamic compared to the existing static model	

Table 5.6b Focused code 1 business screening changes for interview question 5

Focused Coding 1 Sub-theme	*Research Q5 How can the existing* Shari'a *screening methodologies be enhanced?*	
Interview no	*Pattern Code*	*Remarks*
SI1–SI7	FS-BSC-TA	Clear ruling on the tobacco and arms manufacturers

tobacco manufacturers are not allowed, while the companies involved in arms manufacturing needs to be dealt with on a case-by-case basis.

Tables 5.6a, b, c, d, e and f summarise the views of the respondents on how the financial screening should evolve in the future. The 33% thresholds used for the financial ratios can be lowered to ensure that there is continuous exercise of reaching the optimal threshold of 0 per cent tolerance. The existing screening methodologies are based on exceptions and we should renew them based on the developments in the IBF industry. Hence, it should be lowered depending on the market conditions and so long as the portfolio remains investible. With regard to placing interest expense as criteria, the respondents opined that there should be a research book regarding this factor and *Shari'a* scholars should impose a limit on this too. Furthermore, research should be carried out on developing an Islamic stock exchange where global stocks that are compliant with *Shari'a* are listed. This will be a step towards standardising the *Shari'a* screening methodologies as all securities listed will be screened based on the same agreed criteria.

Table 5.6g and h analyses the views of the respondents on the progressive reduction of the financial ratios and the enhancements in it. Most of the respondents support the idea of progressive reduction, yet they opine in different manners. There should be progressive reduction as long as we can ascertain that the Islamic financing availability is at an acceptable level, as without it the whole exercise can be counter-productive. Furthermore, this can encourage companies to borrow in a *Shari'a-compliant* manner and resultantly companies may start converting their conventional loan portfolio to a *Shari'a-compliant* portfolio. One can perhaps look at the developments in the Islamic finance industry in the country and quantify

Table 5.6c Focused code 2 changes to financial screening—33% for interview question 5

Focused coding 2 *Sub-theme*	*Research Q5* *How can the existing* Shari'a *screening methodologies be enhanced?*	
Interview no	*Pattern code*	*Remarks*
SI2-S17	FS-FSC-C33	Can be lowered in line with the developments in the Islamic finance industry and as long as the portfolio remains Investible
SI6	FS-FSC-C33	Actually, yes—should be lowered in line with the developments. Can be based on the industry and the country—if Islamic banking is accessible
SI1,	FS-FSC-C33	As long as it is investible portfolio you can lower it but this is more of a financial decision than a *Shari'a* decision

Table 5.6d Focused code 3 interest expense for interview question 5

Focused coding 3 *Sub-theme*	*Research Q5* *How can the existing* Shari'a *screening methodologies be enhanced?*	
Interview no	*Pattern code*	*Remarks*
SI6	FS-FSC-INTEXP	Actually, interest expense, should be looked upon while making the *Shari'a* compliancy decision because interest expense is as important as interest income

Table 5.6e Focused code 4 Islamic stock exchange for interview question 5

Focused coding 4 *Sub-theme*	*Research Q5* *How can the existing* Shari'a *screening methodologies be enhanced?*	
Interview no	*Pattern code*	*Remarks*
SI1	FS-FSC-ISLSTEX	I think what we need is a market which deals with globally *Shari'a-compliant* shares, using a standardised methodology—developed by a regulator or OIC

Table 5.6f Focused code 5 need for revision for interview question 5

Focused coding 5 Sub-theme	*Research Q5 How can the existing* Shari'a *screening methodologies be enhanced?*	
Interview no	*Pattern code*	*Remarks*
SI6,SI9	FS-FSC-NREV	The existing methodologies are based on exception. So we need to renew them from time to time based on the development in the industry but that has not happened. So, it is well recommended, at least to start with as an academic research
SI5,	FS-FSC-NREV	There has been no revision in this interim period and it is very much needed

it, based on that the financial criteria for the particular stock that should be set.

Tables 5.6i and j analyse the opinions of respondents on future research in this area. When asked if they would like to see a more dynamic model of *Shari'a* screening where the screening threshold should be dependent on the effect of the impure income on the total revenue of the company, the respondents suggested that there is a need to conduct a detailed research in the area to see if it is possible and how will it work. Furthermore, in terms of standardising the screening methodologies, they stated that perhaps a detailed research book can be undertaken to see which screening methodology is more conservative and which is more liberal. Furthermore, there is a need to include the SRI components in

Table 5.6g Focused code 6 different criteria for mining and service sector for interview question 5

Focused coding 6 Sub-theme	*Research Q5 How can the existing* Shari'a *screening methodologies be enhanced?*	
Interview no	*Pattern code*	*Remarks*
SI4, SI8	FS-BSC-SIFCTMS	Maybe we should also look into debt/asset for asset heavy sectors (manufacturing and mining) and debt/market cap for (tech and service) sectors as better captured by sentiments

Table 5.6h Focused code 7 progressive reduction for interview question 5

Focused coding 7 *Sub-theme*	*Research Q5* *How can the existing* Shari'a *screening methodologies be enhanced?*	
Interview no	*Pattern code*	*Remarks*
SI3	FS-FSC-PROGRED	Progressive reduction should be carried out
SI2	FS-FSC-PROGRED	From a theoretical point of view it is a good idea but from a practical point of view it is very difficult because we may have several Islamic banks in Bahrain but that might not translate into Islamic finance availability. Yes I support, if there is an accurate measure of availability
SI6,SI8	FS-FSC-PROGRED	From what I have gathered is that the idea of Securities Commission Malaysia is they wanted the industry to grow because if you use the financial ratio then you are limiting the number of companies that can come in supplier list
SI7	FS-FSC-PROGRED	The idea was perhaps make them progressively lower; but the aim was also that more companies would become compliant at lower levels with the demand from Islamic investors; this has not happened, so lowering levels arbitrarily would be counter-productive. So research in this area is well recommended
SI4	FS-FSC-PROGRED	Is the purpose stability or have more companies in the compliant universe? If you want more companies from the Muslim world, which makes sense for Islamic investing, then increase the debt ratio or have all companies (from OIC) in the universe and give them 3–5 years to reduce to one-third. It may encourage corporate sukuk, used to refinance conventional debt
SI5, SI9,	FS-FSC-PROGRED	Yes, they should be depending on the availability of alternatives. Of course and this is something that should be done. There is nothing hard and fast about this 33% ratio. It is just a very rough rule of thumb, the actual rule is that it should be zero. So of course we should be raising the bar and reducing the percentages to lower numbers

(continued)

Table 5.6h (continued)

Focused coding 7 Sub-theme	*Research Q5 How can the existing* Shari'a *screening methodologies be enhanced?*	
Interview no	*Pattern code*	*Remarks*
SI1	FS-FSC-PROGRED	Until we have 100% *Shari'a-compliant* companies reach a level, we need a lot of efforts, time, expertise, lot of wealth and money because you cannot develop markets from nothing

the *Shari'a* portfolio and analyse the returns of the portfolio compared to other same portfolio that is only Islamic or only SRI portfolios. Lastly, there is a need to look at how the interest income and interest expense thresholds can be used instead of the debt-to-market capitalisation or total assets ratio without netting the effects of income with expense.

To conclude, the financial screening thresholds can be lowered in the future as there is no definitive rule around them. However, the lowering of the thresholds should be based on a research piece to ensure that there is an investible portfolio as without this it will not be successful. Research should also be conducted in creating an Islamic stock exchange where stocks would be listed based on a set agreed methodology. This can be one of the ways to achieve standardisation of screening methodologies. Lastly, progressive reduction is the ultimate goal of the screening methodologies and, as such, work should be undertaken in reaching this goal. The Islamic financing availability has improved in different countries and

Table 5.6i Focused code 8 static model to effect model for interview question 5

Focused coding 8 Sub-theme	*Research Q5 How can the existing* Shari'a *screening methodologies be enhanced?*	
Interview no	*Pattern code*	*Remarks*
SI2	FS-FR-STMEFM	Difficult question to answer, it needs some thinking to move from the existing incident based model to effect based

Table 5.6j Focused code 9 more practical methodology for interview question 5

Focused coding 9 *Sub-theme*	*Research Q5* *How can the existing* Shari'a *screening methodologies be enhanced?*	
Interview no	*Pattern code*	*Remarks*
SI1, SI9	FS-FR-MPMETH	Somebody can carry out a book on these indices and tell us which is more practical, conservative. For example: which indices out of 160,000 companies will exclude 100,000 and which indices will exclude 130,000, etc. Now all these things are subject to empirical research and we can have funds now like the Arabesque fund which can take this index combine it with SRI, with green index, etc. (halal industry) and come out with a small fund which has a universe of few thousand companies but it is very good, etc., before you were not able to do this

resultantly these screening methodologies should take into account these developments and adjust accordingly. This will also increase the AUM of the Islamic finance industry as increasingly more companies will borrow in a *Shari'a-compliant* manner.

5.3 Results Discussion

This section provides a discussion on the findings obtained from the coding analysis. This results' discussion is based on five interview questions of the interview analysis and each discussion is accompanied by a diagram derived from the data mapping process to give a broader perspective of the issue and aligning the research analysis.

History of Shari'a-Compliant *Screening Methodologies, How and Why They Were Introduced; and Rationale Behind the Use of the Screening Thresholds*

The coding analysis has established the history of *Shari'a* screening methodologies: the motivation behind them, how they were introduced and the reasoning behind the use of the screening thresholds. There are three background reasons for the introduction of screening methodologies. Islamic banks never had any problems in attracting the deposits as the *Shari'a* sensitive depositors were always in high numbers trying to align their financial dealings with their religious beliefs. However, the real issue banks and other financial institutions faced was how to invest these deposits to generate returns for their shareholders in line with the *Shari'a*. Consequently, these banks and investors had limited investment options, like *murabaha* (cars and homes primarily), leasing, and real estate investments. With the increased access to stock markets and advancements in technology, an important investment industry identified for the investors and intermediaries was to invest in the equities listed on the stock markets. However, at the time the ruling on investment in the stock market was not clear. Concurrently, there were institutions like Saturna Capital in the USA and RHB Investment Management in Malaysia, who, with the help of *Shari'a* advisors or boards, designed conditions under which these institutions were able to invest in the stock markets. At the time, this did not receive a lot of significance, acceptance, prominence and consensus, until the OIC Fiqh Academy's fatwa, approving stock markets investments (provided the underlying business of the company is *Shari'a* compliant). Additionally, the 1990s was the time of dot-com or internet bubble, which changed the way investments in the stock markets were conducted. Resultantly, young generation who was active and had electronic know-how wanted to invest their family's wealth and were attracted to the trading and stock markets investments world. This young generation would come to the *Shari'a* scholars with their questions about the type of stocks they could invest in. However, *Shari'a* scholars were only able to give them some general guidelines as to what is compliant and what is non-compliant according to *Shari'a*; they could not look into individual companies as it required deep analysis, time and effort.

During this time, the investment managers managing the funds of *Shari'a* sensitive investors were facing another issue; that was the unavailability of a *Shari'a-compliant* benchmark to compare the performance against. As such, institutions were using an internally constructed index as a benchmark, which is not preferred by international standards and is not a best practice. This was perceived as a weakness and conflict of interest, which can undermine the integrity of equity investing among Muslims and compromise benchmark portfolio. Hence, to address these issues, a possible solution proposed was the development of an Islamic equity index by an independent body, which would provide accountability, transparency and additionally establish rules for screening in line with the international standards and *Shari'a*.

Mr Rushdi Siddiqui, an expert in the field and who at the time was working with Dow Jones on this issue, approached Sheikh Nedham Yaquby to establish an Islamic index, which would ultimately also help in designing standardised terms and conditions for investing in the stock market known as *Shari'a* screening methodology. Simultaneously, Dow Jones also wanted the index and methodology to be established in consultation with a global *Shari'a* board consisting of renowned *Shari'a* scholars from different geographical locations to ensure the index becomes a global *Shari'a* benchmark. These scholars included Justice Mufti Taqi Usmani (from Pakistan, who also helped in structuring a methodology for Amana Mutual Fund), Sheikh Nedham Yaquby (Bahrain), Dr Mohamed Ali Elgari (Saudi Arabia), Sheikh Yousuf Talal DeLorenzo (USA), Sheikh Abdul Sattar Abu Ghudda (Syria); the scholars will be collectively referred to as DJIMI *Shari'a* board for the rest of this document. By this time, there was a Fatwa by OIC fiqh academy that allows stock market investments provided the company's line of business and financial dealings are *Shari'a* compliant. However, the real issue was that almost all of the companies listed on the stock market had to directly or indirectly go through the conventional banking industry in the form of an overdraft facility, deposits or financing. Furthermore, the issue on the business side was how to treat companies who's main line of business is *Shari'a* compliant but occasionally receives revenue from *Shari'a* non-compliant businesses (grey businesses). Such companies were not allowed to be invested in by the *Shari'a* sensitive investors (as clearly stated by the OIC Fiqh academy).

DJIMI *Shari'a* board was handed the task of designing a solution to this problem, as without it a majority of the listed equities will not be available for *Shari'a* sensitive investors; this would have ultimately meant that Muslims would not have been able to benefit from the stock market returns, which was identified as an important investment sector. In doing so, the DJIMI *Shari'a* board started the assignment with a firm belief that *Shari'a* is not for the imprisonment of Muslims and does not impose restrictions on people, which make them unable to enjoy wealth and get involved in the practices of investments and economics. *"In doing so we came across the fatwa of OIC Fiqh Academy, which defines a publically traded company as a pool of funds, these finds contributed by the shareholders and also funds coming from other sources and as a pool, this pool can have halal and haram"*. This opened up planning for existing rules in *Shari'a* about the mixture of halal and haram and that the rule is dependent on the majority and not minority. The scholars thought that now that we have this concept in *Shari'a*, what should be defined as majority and minority. Through their research, they found that the dividing line between the majority and minority is one-third, also known as the rule of Ghalaba—the majority upon which the rule is based. However, it was equally important to apply the concept of purification, namely removing the impure income from the revenue.

It is important to stress that all the scholars are in agreement that, by choice, a *Shari'a* sensitive investor should not be involved in a venture, which states that it will seek interest-based financing or that part of its strategy includes an involvement with *Shari'a* non-compliant businesses. This rule (screening methodologies) also does not apply to companies newly established; it is in fact for existing established companies whose decisions cannot be influenced by the *Shari'a* sensitive investors being a minority shareholders. We further understand that there is nothing more repugnant to *Shari'a* than interest and *gharar*. However, keeping everything in mind, the idea was to incorporate something (an acceptable methodology) in the interim period until we develop a methodology achieving that is perfectly in line with the *Shari'a*. After deep thoughts and discussions among the scholars on the issue, there was a slight majority on the side that allows investment in the companies in grey areas as long as purification is applied. *"Hence, it was a practical solution to a problem that we are facing and at least in this way the haram element will be reduced from 100% to say 5% or less*. Furthermore, *it will be a good start and in future we can build on it and align the methodology perfectly with the Shari'a"*. However, in the interim period, it is important that efforts are applied and work is undertaken to reach a level where we have 100% Sharia compliant companies.

To date, there remained scholars and institutions like that OIC Fiqh academy that does not allow investment in companies involved in mixed activities. As discussed in the literature review in Chapter 3, there were contemporary scholars who did not agree with this ruling of screening methodology; however, the interview analysis in this book re-affirmed that some of these scholars later changed their opinion in support of *Shari'a* screening methodologies.

As a result of these discussions, Dow Jones Islamic Market Index (DJIMI) was launched after the fatwa of the DJIMI board in 1998 with the launch of the index in February 1999 in Bahrain (Al Amine, n.d). The first regulating *Shari'a* screening methodology was also established at the same time and is comprised of a two-stage process, commonly known as business screening and financial screening.

1. **Business screening** avoids business involved in impermissible activities, namely consumption, buying and selling of alcohol, pork-related products, selling and manufacturing of tobacco, adult entertainment, conventional banking and financial institutions, casino and gambling.
2. **Financial screening** aims to capture and contain the involvement of *riba* (interest) in the company. This is undertaken by applying accounting-based criteria through testing the debt (leverage), cash and interest-bearing securities and accounts receivables weight against the thresholds determined by the *Shari'a* board. The ratios for DJIMI are as below:

    a. Total debt divided by 24-month average market capitalisation should be less than 33%
    b. Sum of cash and interest-bearing securities divided by 24-month average market capitalisation should be less than 33%
    c. Accounts receivables divided by 24-month average market capitalisation should be less than 33% (this was 45% until 2011).

The denominator was changed from 12-month average market capitalisation to 24-month average market capitalisation in 2011 to even out the effects and volatility in prices caused by the financial crises.

Further, achieving this result was a learning curve for the *Shari'a* board and all those involved as it was not achieved in a short time. For example, the denominator was initially agreed to be total assets as the idea was to capture the total value of the company. However, total assets did not reflect the true value of the company as it would not include the intangible assets like goodwill. Resultantly, it was agreed to use market capitalisation as it is more representative of the true value of the company.

The next issue concerned the threshold for the revenue generated from the *Shari'a* non-compliant businesses, in order to contain the reliance of the underlying company on interest-based transactions. The ratio of 33% used for the financial screening is derived from the Hadith "Al thuluth

Kathir", which means "One-third is a lot"; this was a comment made by the Prophet Muhammad (PBUH) when Saad ibn Abi Waqqas wanted to make a bequest (wasiyyah). Further, in many books of fiqh, a third is considered the border between what is substantive (majority) and what is not (minority). With regard to the threshold of 5%, it was based upon the consensus of the scholars and consequently there is no historical *Shari'a* reference for it. Interestingly, there is a difference of opinion among the scholars on the use of the 5% threshold as some scholars when individually advising an institution would not allow investment in a company with even a minimal percentage of impure business; however, when collectively sitting on the board, they agree to the majority. This is interesting as the scholars also agree that both these thresholds are for an interim period only and as soon as a better measure is available the idea is to switch to them. Nevertheless, it was also agreed that efforts should be continued in making these thresholds more conservative as the Islamic finance industry grows. Hence, this explains the decision of DJIMI board to move from total assets to market capitalisation, 12-month market capitalisation to 24-month average market capitalisation, and 5% business screen to no business screen.

After the DJIMI methodology, a number of other methodologies were launched by Kuala Lumpur *Shari'a* Index in April 1999 and the FTSE Islamic Index in October 1999. Some of the other *Shari'a* screening methodologies issued were by MSCI, AAOIFI, SEC Malaysia, Meezan Investments, and Al Rajhi Bank. The SEC Malaysia's screening methodology has undergone changes recently in 2013; it moved from having only business screening to including financial screening and aligning it with global practices to enhance the screening practices, thereby reemphasising the aim of enhancing the screening methodologies on a regular basis. The reason why SEC Malaysia enhanced its methodology was to motivate big banks and big companies towards Islamic banking, as they cannot now borrow more than 33% conventionally (compared to unlimited earlier) and if they need to raise debt they can do through *Shari'a*-compliant instruments like sukuk; resultantly, the whole Islamic banking industry will benefit and grow. Figure 5.1 shows a map to present a broader perspective on the historical development of the screening methodologies.

In the following question, the research shall examine the *Shari'a* screening process and the issues facing it. Some of these have been highlighted in the literature. It will discuss the responses received by the scholars on these criticisms and the way forward.

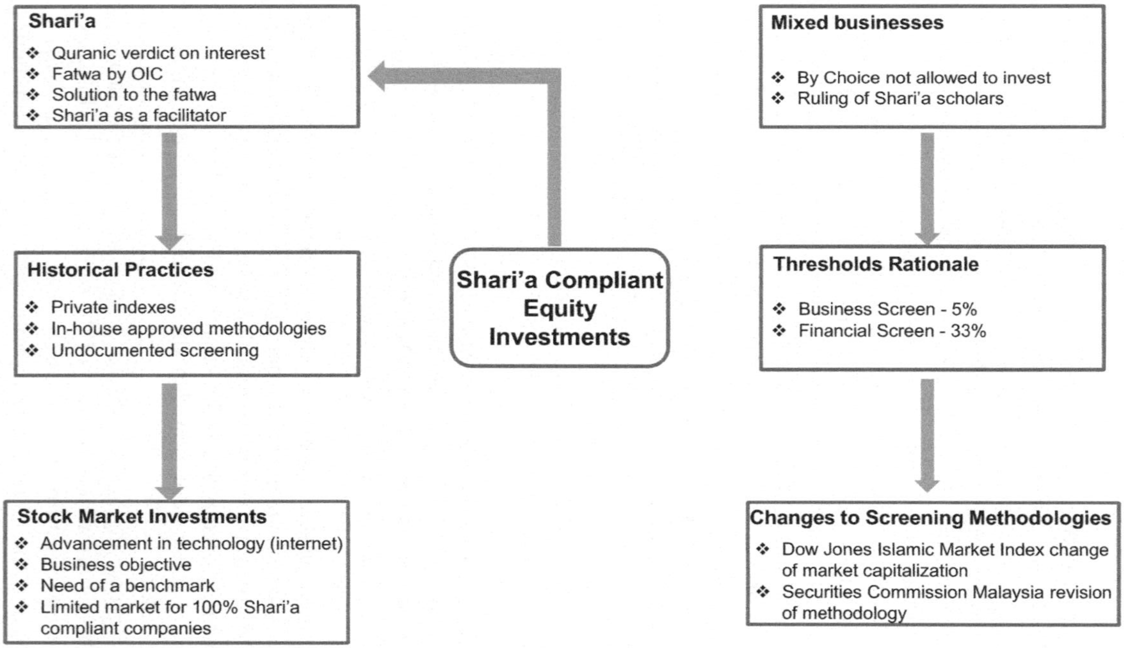

Fig. 5.1 Historical background of *Shari'a* screening methodologies (*Source* Malik, R., Dar, H. and Muneeza, A. (2024), "Reforms required for Shariah screening of equities using the case study of Dow Jones Islamic market index (DJIMI)", *International Journal of Law and Management*, Vol. ahead-of-print No. ahead-of-print. https://doi.org/10.1108/IJLMA-08-2023-0171)

How Is Shari'a *Screening Process Carried Out and What Are the Issues Facing the Screening Methodologies?*

This section discusses how the *Shari'a* screening process is conducted, exploring and discussing different issues facing it. The coding analysis has analysed the thoughts of the scholars in how they address these issues and has been presented in Fig. 5.3. In doing so, it has been revealed that the academic literature has already highlighted some of the issues in both business screening and financial screening, while some other issues were highlighted during this research (as discussed in the literature review in Chapter 3). Hence, it is important to look at this first broadly and then the issues specifically.

The *Shari'a* process and the coding analysis are shown in Table 5.2 (a) to (m). As stated in the previous section and earlier chapters, the *Shari'a* screening process is made of two parts—business screening followed by financial screening as shown in Fig. 5.2 while Fig. 5.3 represents the overall map. Additionally, as discussed in the earlier section, the limit of 5% for companies involved in mixed activities that is majority *Shari'a-compliant* with some incidental *Shari'a* non-compliant revenue is based on the consensus of the scholars and, as such, does not have any concrete backing. *Shari'a* scholars are of the view that since it has no foundation, it is quite problematic and that is why it has been removed from the DJIMI. Furthermore, a number of *Shari'a* scholars do not support this threshold individually, however; when sitting on a *Shari'a* board along with other scholars, they agree to the majority and industry guidelines like that of AAOIFI. The view of such scholars is that it is not permissible to invest in a company where from the outset you know that it will generate income from *Shari'a* non-compliant sources. Furthermore, one of the scholar opined that "*this maxim is not serving any purpose and does not have any historical reference to Shari'a*".

Further, another scholar opined that there is no legal maxim to allow even a negligible amount of *Shari'a* non-compliant revenue. He stated that an argument that proponents of tolerating the *Shari'a* non-compliant revenue if below a certain threshold applies to cases where the *Shari'a* non-compliant has been accidentally mixed with *Shari'a-compliant* and it became inseparable: for example, the meat of a non-slaughtered animal mixed with that of a slaughtered animal.

Since this maxim has been explained as problematic and that has no backing, the researcher asked if the maxim can be removed or reduced to 3% or 2%. The analysis of the responses state that the key issue is stability

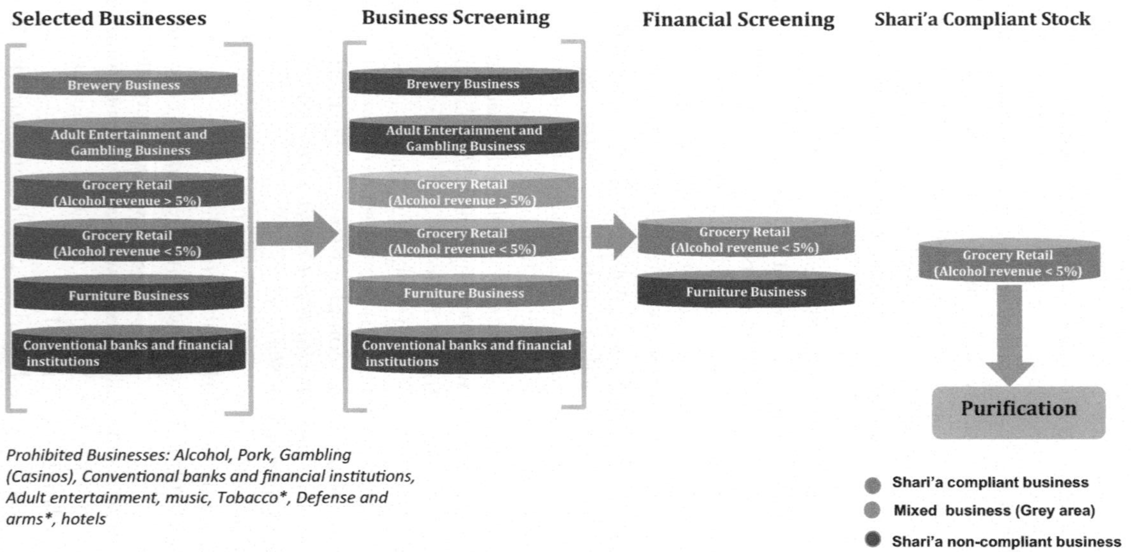

Fig. 5.2 *Shari'a-compliant* screening process (*Source* Malik, R., Dar, H. and Muneeza, A. (2024), "Reforms required for Shariah screening of equities using the case study of Dow Jones Islamic market index (DJIMI)", *International Journal of Law and Management*, Vol. ahead-of-print No. ahead-of-print. https://doi.org/10.1108/IJLMA-08-2023-0171)

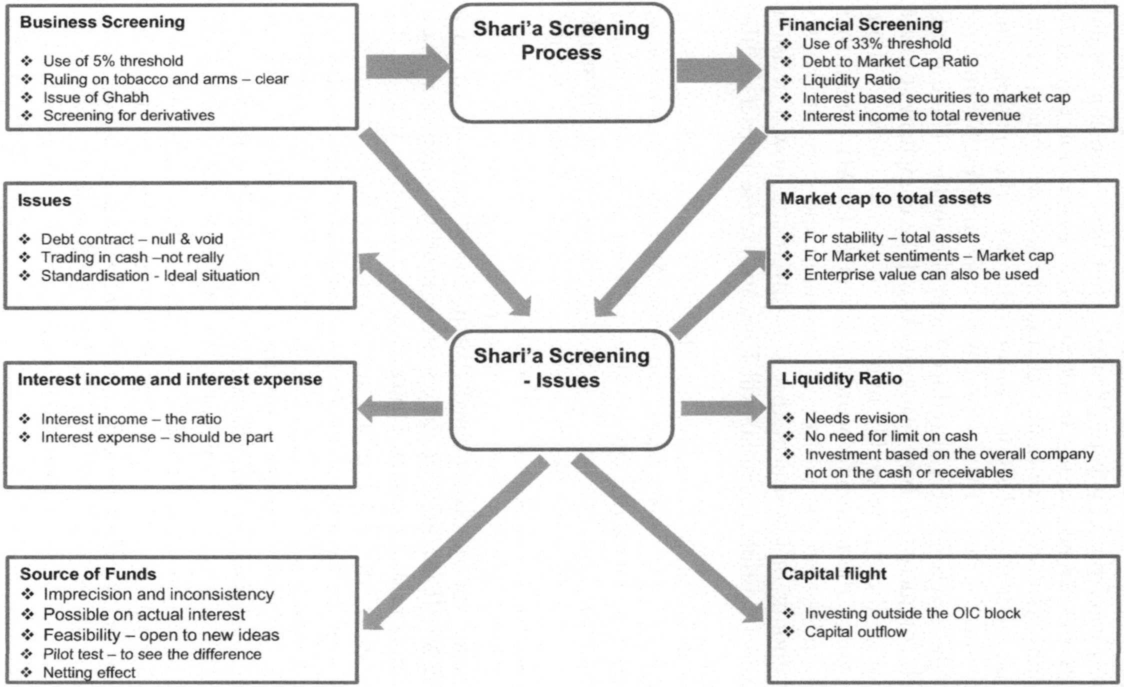

Fig. 5.3 *Shari'a* Screening Process and issues (*Source* Malik, R., Dar, H. and Muneeza, A. (2024), "Reforms required for Shariah screening of equities using the case study of Dow Jones Islamic market index (DJIMI)", *International Journal of Law and Management*, Vol. ahead-of-print No. ahead-of-print. https://doi.org/10.1108/IJLMA-08-2023-0171)

and that we should indeed try and eliminate it. A majority of scholars stated that there is no distinctive rule about this 5%, and since it has no historical *Shari'a* reference, it is problematic, and hence the aim should be to eradicate this screen and not to tolerate any *Shari'a* non-compliant business revenue. However, we cannot change the screens without extensive book and internal analysis in conjunction with the market. The underlying reason for this is that as long as there is an investible universe available for the investors we can reduce these thresholds. There needs to be research conducted on how many stocks will be compliant at lower thresholds and if there is investible universe we should move to those thresholds. One of the founding board members of DJIMI opined that you need to understand the underlying reasoning and have the know-how of the amount of investment that is involved and how a decision of reduction in investible portfolio will have an adverse impact on the investors.

The academic literature also states that there is no solid backing from a *Shari'a* perspective that bans tobacco and arms. All the scholars involved in this research unanimously agreed that tobacco should be banned as it is harmful to the humanity. They stated that nothing withstands the evidence of the harmful effects it causes to human beings. Consequently, investment in tobacco manufacturing and selling companies is not allowed. With regard to investing in companies involved in buying and selling arms, the scholars opined that it should be reviewed on a case-by-case basis. It is a grey area as countries need to purchase warfare to protect against hostile enemies. However, companies that make deadly offensive products should be prohibited. Hence, it is important that careful analysis of the underlying company is undertaken before allowing or prohibiting investment in it as both can have adverse effect upon the investor. If not looked at properly, the former can take away an investment opportunity from the investor, while the latter will make him part of something that is *Shari'a* non-compliant. Concurrently, one of the leading scholars suggested that companies selling their technology and other software to defence companies are allowed to be invested in.

On the issue of including derivatives in *Shari'a* screening process, most of the scholars stated that it should be part of the *Shari'a* screening process as it is not allowed to be traded in by *Shari'a*. However, they are also mindful of the fact that it may not be possible to receive the detailed information about a company's involvement on a regular basis.

Nevertheless, efforts should be put in to generate as much information as possible and consult the *Shari'a* scholars on a case-by-case basis.

With regard to the limit of 33% threshold, it has some reference to *Shari'a* that is the Hadith of Thuluth. Opponents of this argue that there is no link of the hadith to purification and it is used out of context, with no indication that one-third is a valid benchmark for what is excessive. At the most, the hadith is indicating that one-third is more than enough in bequest and the attempt to drive a general benchmark from this hadith is an out of context interpretation of the hadith and resultantly it should be regarded as wrong. On the other hand, the proponents of using this as the threshold argue that they needed to begin somewhere and that it is a reference point for an interim period only, which can be changed as and when a better measure is available. Furthermore, scholars argue that it is better to have some indirect relevance, validity and precedence to hadith or Quran than to use the consensus of the scholars; where available, we should do that. Simultaneously, when it was mentioned that the ratio of 33% introduced for the interim period has not been revised in the last 17 years, the scholars provided a mixed response. Most of them stated that the thresholds should indeed be adjusted in line with the developments in the industry and re-affirmed that the actual threshold should be 0 per cent. However, detailed research should be undertaken before doing so, in order to ensure that there remains an investible universe for the investors. Another opinion was that if the idea is to have more companies from the Muslim world for Islamic investing, then one way would be to increase the debt ratio or have all companies from the Muslim world and allow them 3–5 years to reduce to one-third. This may encourage these companies to borrow in a *Shari'a-compliant* manner (sukuk) instead of the conventional debt.

The next section covers the underlying ratios used in the financial screening, to understand the purpose of them, and also analyse the responses of the scholars on the critics of it.

i. **Debt-to-Market Capitalisation**
 Through this ratio, the aim is to capture the interest that is involved as a result of borrowing funds: liabilities. The idea is to ensure that the underlying company is not heavily indebted (or heavily involved in interest-based transactions); if this is the case, and the equity portion of a company is small, then it will be considered as if an investor is buying the debt of the company. Resultantly,

when you are buying a stock of the company, it will be as if you are lending the company and hence one cannot benefit from the gain as it will be considered that the debt of the company has changed in value. This view has been criticised in the literature to the effect that basing the assumption on the debt and not the actual interest expense of the company generates imprecision. The scholars responded with mixed opinions, with most saying that there is a need to undertake research on a portfolio comparing the composition of the stocks with the existing debt-to-market capitalisation with the interest expense as a measure of total expenses. If the result gives us a better measure with actual interest expense value then we should switch to it. However, other scholars explained that this was discussed at the beginning but they found that analysts and the underlying companies can window dress (balance sheet cosmetology) and make the interest expense disappear from the balance sheet. Additionally, companies may at times not even report the interest expense figure and instead just mention the net interest income or expense or even include it in the total expense figures. To tackle this issue, scholars, coupled with the researchers, examined what causes interest expense; they found that it is debt (short-term plus long-term debt) and hence they decided to capture it at source. Furthermore, interest rates will differ in different markets; debt is more identifiable as a number on the balance sheet. Scholars also stated another reason of using this ratio is through the Hanafi view, that the interest-based debt contract between the borrower and the lender is null and void and there is no *Shari'a* credibility of it. However, since the funds have been borrowed, it is the duty of the borrower to return them.

On another note, this debt screen is not required as long as the interest expense can be captured through another ratio. The debt screen is generally used by businesses to understand the gearing ratio of the company, which is also a variable representing the riskiness of the company. However, in the *Shari'a* screening methodologies, it is used to make a *Shari'a* opinion on a company, which may not be best use of it. This screen should be left to the individual businesses or analysts to show the risk involved in the capital structure of the company and not to make a *Shari'a* opinion on it.

On another note, an important point has been highlighted on the debt culture "*The debt screen for Muslim countries, a debt culture exists in Muslim countries, has an adverse impact, hence, many companies, while passing primary business (no pork, alcohol or weapons producer) screens usually fail the debt screen. If money is sourced for Islamic equity funds from OIC investors, and underlying components in an Islamic equity index are from non-OIC, then contributing to Shari'a-compliant capital flight*". Restrictions can be imposed by the regulators on the capital invested overseas and, as such, the same capital can be used to develop the local businesses.

ii. **Liquidity Ratio (Cash and Receivables to Market Capitalisation) and Interest-Bearing Securities**
AAOIFI and Shari'a scholars have included a benchmark on how much cash, near cash items and receivables a company can have on its balance sheet to qualify as a *Shari'a-compliant* stock. For example, AAOIFI has a restriction of having at least 30% tangible assets, so intangibles can be up to 70%, while other screening methodologies have contained it with different limits. From the analysis of the interviews, it is ascertained that there is no need for such a screen because of the fact that when you are buying a share of the company you are not buying into the cash of the company. An investor does not invest in a company because it is cash rich, but invests keeping in mind the overall performance, management, and the returns in can generate. As such, there should not be a limit on the cash of the company as this can be the strategy of the company due to the business cycle or economic conditions—and that the company is not in the business of earning interest on the cash. It is just incidental and strategical in nature. Additionally, there should not be any restriction on the receivables as this may not be interest based, as long as the company is not in the financing business. A scholar further stated that "*In most countries receivables is an amount that a buyer owes the seller against the items bought and a large number of companies sell on a deferred payment basis. This deferred payment is regarded as profit and not interest – interest is only cash for cash. However, if there is a factory producing goods, and they have merchants buying from them, the factory has to give them some time, 30 or 90 days to make payment - this give rise to receivables*". Further, suppose there is a company that has 100% receivables, for these receivables the principle is 100 and the profit

on it is 15 and the total market capitalisation for this company is 115; some scholars say that it is haram to trade at 115 and that you have to trade at 100 because that is the principle—otherwise you will be trading in debt. However, this is not the case as there is no trading in debt neither there is an interest being charged. The increase in market capitalisation and value of the company is due to the fundamental business of the company and hence has no link to the receivables. Another scholar stated that "*if the company is sitting on more than 33 percent cash & receivables, one must question if they have either changed their business or cannot collect their invoices on time, only the former is problematic; the latter is a business issue*". Finally, another scholar supported the idea, stating that it is a logical concept; however, it will be wise to conduct research on a portfolio after removing this liquidity screen and analyse how it changes the portfolio composition compared to the existing practices.

The other ratio generally used is the interest-bearing securities to total assets or market capitalisation to capture the interest income. The opinions of *Shari'a* scholars in capturing the interest income based on the source of funds (interest-bearing securities) is same as that of debt to total assets or market capitalisation. They stated that research can be undertaken to analyse if a decision can be made based on the actual interest income only and as such a comparison should be made with the existing practices to understand the difference it makes to the portfolio combination.

iii. **Interest Income to Total Revenue**

This ratio is not used by many screening methodologies and captures the interest income that has been received by a company to total revenue. When the scholars were asked if this ratio should be adjusted in line with the developments in the industry, they were of the view that this is possible as long as research is conducted to identify if there is enough availability of Islamic financing in the local market. This may assist the overall growth in the Islamic banking and finance as companies will be pushed to deposit their funds in a *Shari'a-compliant* manner.

The next section examines some of the other issues facing the current practices of *Shari'a* screening methodologies. There is extensive discussion in the academic literature on the topic of standardisation; that is, having different screening methodologies with little differences and all of them being equally *Shari'a-compliant* yet one investor may be better off in terms of the performance of his portfolio by following a particular methodology while the other may suffer. One of the major differences among the screens is using market capitalisation or total assets as a denominator. Scholars gave a mixed response when asked about this, with a majority agreeing that in the perfect model standardisation would be the case and there would not be multiple methodologies; this would provide stability. Hence, we should be open for innovation. A scholar opined that "*for stability it may be better to use debt to total assets for asset heavy sectors (manufacturing and mining) and debt to market capitalization for (tech and service) sectors*".

However, some scholars were of the view that it may not be the right time yet as "*different jurisdictions may have different constraints in developing the industry and if they follow a stricter criteria that might affect the development in the industry as we grow*".

Fund managers should be able to adapt to the clients' needs and the choice should be left to the investors. However, this research suggests that this may not be practical as in an investment portfolio if the choice is left to the investors then one may want to have total assets while the other may prefer market capitalisation. Hence, this may not be ideal and will cause various issues. Another scholar shared his opinion that from the main element, i.e. avoiding *Shari'a* non-compliant businesses, we are unified and that standardising the methodologies help, however it is not necessary. "*I think we should leave people to innovate, the main element is to have screening standards, you have to purify, you have to exclude haram element, percentages or other things can be left for ijtihad*". He further stated that the problem will be caused when a fund manager changes his underlying screening methodology as the conditions suit him; hence, as long as we stick to one methodology in both the good and bad times, there is no issue.

One scholar stated that both the total assets and market capitalisation used to value the overall business are not reflective of the true value of the company and that it should be replaced with enterprise value. He further stated that when you want to buy a company, you look at the enterprise value of the company rather than the market capitalisation or total assets. Furthermore, research needs to be conducted on this recommendation to understand the difference it will make to the portfolio. For the industry to move forward efficiently; standardisation is key as Shari'a sensitive investors in general care about the investment portfolio to be Shari'a compliant without getting into the details of their preference on the use of ratios. Hence, it is critical that as the industry matures standardisation of the underlying base variables is achieved.

Is There a Need to Incorporate Socially Responsible Principles Promoted by Shari'a *Within Existing Screening Methodologies? This Will also Assist in Tapping into the SRI Industry—US$33 Trillion Industry*

Shari'a-compliant screening methodologies were introduced to reflect the contemporary need in 1999; however, they have remained virtually the same since then. It started with having exclusionary criteria (negative screening), which filters companies that are involved in *Shari'a* non-compliant businesses and a ceiling on the interest involvement in the capital structure of the company and have remained the same. However, the objective of *Shari'a* is not only prohibiting evil but also promoting good as stated in the Ayat (3.110*) "You are (the) best (of) people raised for the mankind - enjoining the right and forbidding [from] the wrong and believing in Allah"*. As such, the *Shari'a* screening methodologies have served part of it, which is prohibiting evil, and has made very little progress in enjoining and promoting good. In terms of investments, the promotion of the good can be done by supporting the companies that are putting a lot of efforts in to ensuring that their dealings are in line with good conduct, ethical standards and add value to the environment and the surroundings that they operate in and avoiding companies that are violating the ethical principles, which are also supported by Shari'a. Resultantly, this question aims to understand how the scholars perceive this topic and if the emphasis on this is justifiable and how the inclusion of SRI principles in screening methodologies can be achieved practically.

The scholars unanimously agreed that the time has arrived to align *Shari'a-compliant* investments to the values and objectives of *Shari'a* (Maqasid *Shari'a*), "*Shari'a screening has always been about forbidding the evil; it is time we move to enjoining the good*" opined a scholar. One of the ways this can be done is through encouragement or preference to SRI compared to a portfolio that is just *Shari'a-compliant* portfolio. The SRI industry is built on the principles that align with *Shari'a* but *Shari'a* goes a step further in enforcing them. Yet, the *Shari'a-compliant* industry has not included it as criteria for an investment to be Shari's compliant, resulting in unethical companies being part of Shari'a compliant portfolio. On the other hand, the SRI industry has developed a large portfolio and investor base who would like to invest following the SRI principles. *"The time has arrived that we build bridges with the SRI, ESG and CSR industries, this will not only bring diversification but also increase the AUM of the industry*" said a scholar. Another scholar stated that "*Muslims like other people have concerns about environment, human rights, corruption, status of women* etc. *they want to be part of the social change – these values are enhanced through investment and I firmly and strongly believe that these opportunities should be available*". The criteria that we are using at the moment are faith-based, and hence efforts should be made to move from the faith-based criteria to the one based on Maqasid *Shari'a*. As the market develops, we should include all the issues that oppose the welfare of the society. Yet the scholars are of the view that it would not be wise to say that all investments should include ethical criteria as well, but there should be investment opportunities that take into account these considerations. Hence, the investment does not become haram if it does not include the social criteria. Scholars were also mindful of different social norms practised in different cultures and countries and, as such, something like child labour may not be seen as a violation of human rights in some developing countries because that is the only way they can earn their livelihood. However, the developed world will call it child labour and thus it violates their norms. Concurrently, abortion may not be regarded as something that is against social norms in some developed countries, while it is a sin in the Muslim world. Hence, these issues should be looked at on a case-by-case basis. Figure 5.4 presents the links identified through coding analysis regarding the need of including SRI principles in the screening methodologies.

A scholar opined that the best approach would be to have different portfolios based on different levels of *Shari'a* and social compliancy. Another scholar expressed a similar view, stating that one can have different levels of investment opportunities available and can be coloured as yellow, green, or blue, for instance, based on the levels of *Shari'a* and social compliancy, and, as such, investors can pick the portfolio based on their personal values, beliefs and norms.

A scholar clarified the position of *Shari'a* scholars by stating that none of the *Shari'a* scholars will allow investment in a company where from

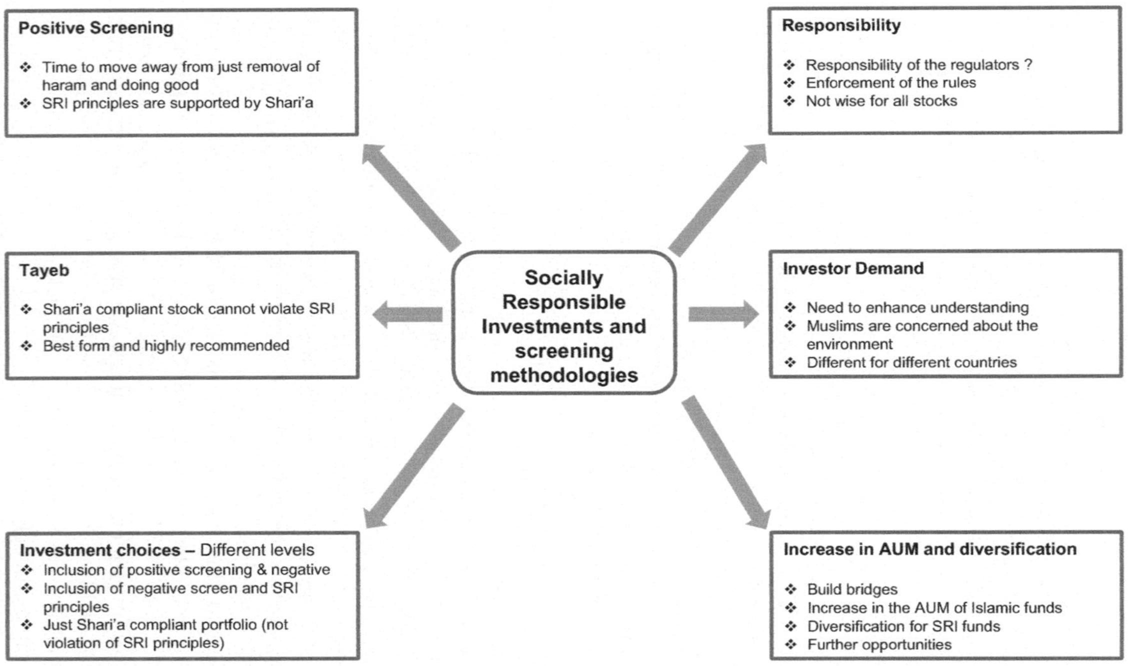

Fig. 5.4 Socially responsible investments and *Shari'a* screening methodologies (*Source* Malik, R., Dar, H. and Muneeza, A. (2024), "Reforms required for Shariah screening of equities using the case study of Dow Jones Islamic market index (DJIMI)", *International Journal of Law and Management*, Vol. ahead-of-print No. ahead-of-print. https://doi.org/10.1108/IJLMA-08-2023-0171)

the outset it is known that the company violates human rights or any other social issues. However, if it is not disclosed, then the *Shari'a* board cannot be held responsible. It is the duty of the investment management company to ensure that it does not invest in a company that violates these social rules. *"We at the Shari'a board understand the company will not present the case to us in the first instance, if they are aware of it violating the social rules". Furthermore,* on the issue of whose responsibility is to ensure that social norms are followed, he stated *that "it is unfair to make it the responsibility of the institution because at the end of the day it is the responsibility of the government and the regulators to ensure social norms are followed"*. For example, on the issue of labour rights, if the weather is as such that it is intolerable for anyone to work then even the law will not allow it. Additionally, it is very subjective in nature as to what happens to a company if it is *Shari'a-compliant* but the company contributed to the detriment of the environment to the extent that the negative effects are greater than the benefits. How should this company be treated? Such cases should be looked at on a case-by-case basis to ensure a correct decision is made.

To conclude, after analysing the above opinions, it is clear that an investment cannot be *Shari'a-compliant* if it violates any of the social criteria; as such the Shari's screening methodologies should include an additional screen as "social screen", which screen stocks based on the SRI principles to ensure it does not violate any underlying SRI principles. Further, there should be different options available for the Shari'a sensitive investors; best would be to have something that is fully *Shari'a-compliant* and promotes social issues—positive screening; this can be referred to as Tayeb (the best form) or Mustahab (recommended) and as such is highly recommended; the next layer can be Mubah (permitted), a portfolio that is *Shari'a-compliant* and takes into account social issues (but not positive screening as Mustahab), followed by Wajib (obligatory) that is *Shari'a-compliant* only, Makruh (disliked)—a portfolio that is *Shari'a-compliant* but violates social issues and haram (forbidden) that is not *Shari'a* compliant. In this way, we can have different levels of Shari'a compliancy, so at one time an investor might be at one particular level (Mubah), he has the option of moving to the higher level of Shari'a compliance (Tayeb). One should also be mindful that the awareness of SRI principles is at a basic level among the Shari'a sensitive investors; hence efforts should be made by the Shari'a scholars, regulators and government bodies to enhance their understanding and awareness.

Further, a detailed research book needs to be conducted—as suggested by some scholars—regarding how these social responsible principles can be included in the screening methodologies ensuring that they align to the *Shari'a* principles as well.

What Is the Preferred Way of Purification?

Purification (Zakat) is an important concept in Islam; it is considered as one of its five pillars and is a duty of each Muslim in line with specific conditions. It is a pivotal component of the existing *Shari'a* screening methodologies as it is used to allow *Shari'a* sensitive investors to access the stock market (precisely, the companies involved in mix activities and interest earnings). Investing in companies involved in mixed activities is based on the rule of exception and hence does not make an impermissible transaction permissible (Gamaleldin, 2015). Screening methodologies use this principle of purification to remove the contribution of impermissible income to the total income of the company. According to the permissibility and absence of prohibition principle, all transactions are permissible unless there is a proof for prohibiting them. Some of the things are absolutely prohibited such as pork and alcohol, which cannot be bought or sold, while some are prohibited as a result of impermissible transactions (as one has no control over it) and purification of such income is by way of purging the impermissible revenue.

All the scholars who support the *Shari'a* screening methodologies unanimously agree that impermissible income included in the assets of the company must be purified by giving it to charitable activities without expecting any reward in return. However, there are differences of opinions on how to determine such income and when it should be purified. Furthermore, estimating the impure income itself is a formidable task as a company is a living entity with far-reaching enterprise and widely stretched activities. Hence, it is a task that needs excellent knowledge of accounting, corporate finance, and an outstanding ability to handle *Shari'a* issues. Figure 5.5 maps the coding process and the opinions of *Shari'a* scholars and other experts.

Through this question, the scholars were asked for their opinions on what the best model of purification is and how it should be undertaken. One of the scholars who opposed the idea of the *Shari'a* screening methodologies stated that "*it does not help at all to willingly and knowingly invest in companies involved in haram activities and then to purify the income. Purification only helps in cases where the investor was not aware of*

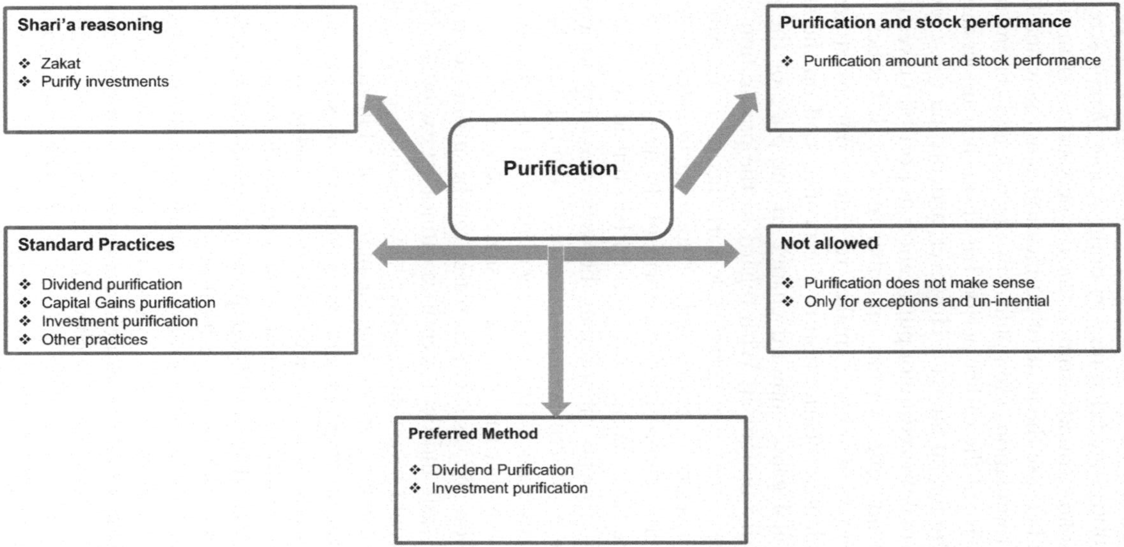

Fig. 5.5 Purification (*Source* Malik, R., Dar, H. and Muneeza, A. (2024), "Reforms required for Shariah screening of equities using the case study of Dow Jones Islamic market index (DJIMI)", *International Journal of Law and Management*, Vol. ahead-of-print No. ahead-of-print. https://doi.org/10.1108/IJLMA-08-2023-0171)

the presence of haram element". There are other scholars who oppose the idea and say that the *Shari'a* basis for such a programme is speculative. However, Elgari (2000) stated that no part of the whole *Shari'a* screening process has more solid grounds from a *Shari'a* perspective than that of purification. This is because the issue of purification is not new and hence finds clear *Shari'a* foundation, exemplified in the fiqh and statements of major learned scholars of the earlier period based on their understanding of the texts from Quran and Sunnah. However, articulating these *Shari'a* principles into a formal procedure of purification in portfolio investments is quite a brave task and one that has a number of unsettled issues.

There are two ways an investor makes revenue from investment in the shares, (1) dividends—distribution of the profit based on the shares owned and (2) capital gains—upward change in the price of the share compared to the price bought at. With regard to the purification, there are those who believe that non-permissible earnings of a company will transpire into the investor's returns only if such an investor collects a direct receipt from the company in the form of dividends. Hence, it is only that part of the total revenue that should be purified. On the other hand, there are others who differentiate between investing in a single company and being a subscriber in an investment fund. Here, the fund itself is treated as a company, where investment units are like the company shares. Another view is that the increase in share prices in the market is a complex phenomenon and, as such, increases can be attributed to many factors from which cash and debt securities cannot be excluded. Hence, even capital gain should be purified. Other views include company liabilities to be purified because of the *Shari'a* maxim of "Lilkatheer Hukm Alkull" (rule is based on majority and not minority). As such, since the majority of the sources of funds derive from permissible sources, then the minority source is ignored and not subject to purification. However, there are others who say that this maxim permits investments and that the composition of liability side needs purification.

Of these, the most common purification method is dividends purification where only dividends revenue is purified. Of the total, about 80% stated that purification should be done from dividends, namely from the revenue distributed among the shareholders. As such, the capital gains should not be purified as it is more of a result of market sentiment and the overall business, while one of the scholars stated that "*ideally capital gains should be purified but it is not a requirement nor practice, the main thing is that the returns should be purified*".

However, there remains an issue as to what happens for a company that does not distribute dividends in a particular year or is not a dividend-paying company. Through this research, we propose using investment purification. This view is also shared by a scholar who stated that the best solution is to purify investments "*My methodology has always been to purify any impure income from the revenue side and that capital gains do not need to be purified*". In essence, what this means is that if the impure revenue of a company is GBP 1000 in a particular year, we divide this by the total number of shares outstanding, for example 10,000. The outcome is GBP 0.1 per share. Multiply this by the shares owned; if it is 100 shares, then the amount for purification is GBP 10 for the year. However, if the share is held for only 5 months then the GBP 10 should be divided by 12 and multiplied by 5 months, then only GBP 4.17 needs to be disposed-off out of the total investment in the company. This method aims at purifying investment itself; the company in which a *Shari'a* sensitive investor owns a share has attained income which needs to be purified even if the company has made a loss during the year. This method in fact allows companies to purify their impure income without having to delve into the issue of dividend-paying company or not, or either the investment made capital gain or loss; the formula is applied to total investments.

How Can the Shari'a *Screening Methodologies Be Enhanced Going Forward?*

After holding the discussions with the *Shari'a* scholars on various issues within *Shari'a* screening methodologies, this section aims to tackle the strategic concept of enhancement of the overall methodologies. The coding analysis has examined different areas for the enhancement of the *Shari'a* screening methodologies including the overall business screens, clear ruling on tobacco and arms, financial ratios and the changes desired, progressive reduction of the ratio thresholds, and also some ideas on the future research in the area. Figure 5.6 represents a map for the way forward. Hence, this section analyses the recommendations of *Shari'a* scholars on progressive reduction, enhancement to business and financial screens, and the need for an Islamic stock exchange and suggests areas of future research.

Business Screens

The coding analysis has revealed that there is a clear understanding and a unanimous view among the scholars restricting investment in a tobacco

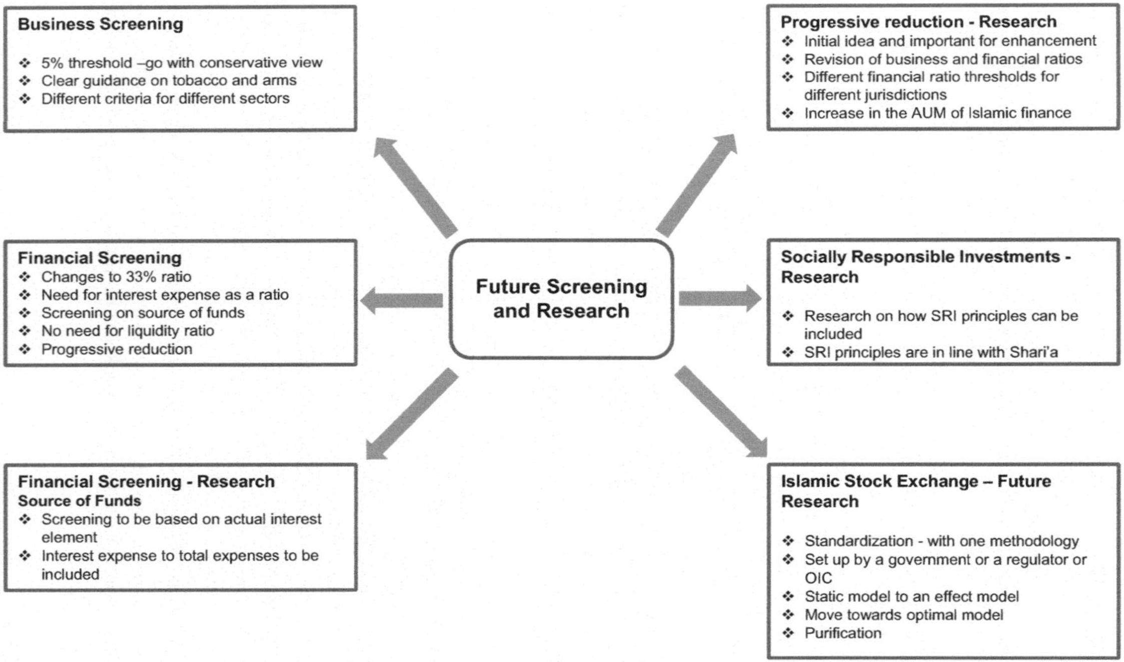

Fig. 5.6 Future screening and research (*Source* Malik, R., Dar, H. and Muneeza, A. (2024), "Reforms required for Shariah screening of equities using the case study of Dow Jones Islamic market index (DJIMI)", *International Journal of Law and Management*, Vol. ahead-of-print No. ahead-of-print. https://doi.org/10.1108/IJLMA-08-2023-0171)

manufacturing and selling company. This is due to the fact that tobacco is injurious to health and nothing is more important than the health of mankind. Hence, a clear ruling should be made as part of *Shari'a* screening methodologies and inform the stakeholders accordingly. This ruling can be generalised and used for all products that assist in the deterioration of the human health.

The issue of investment in arm manufacturers should be treated on a case-by-case basis. This is because a general ruling of allowing all arms and other related items may risk in allowing investment in some of the companies that are contributing to the terrorism and violent activities. On the other hand, a strict and conservative view, such as not allowing investments in such companies, may not do justice to the investors as well as the company. The investors may not be able to benefit from an investment opportunity and the company may not be able to access the capital that would have been available to them otherwise. However, investments in companies that produce defence material for the governments in the peaceful region and for their own defence purposes are allowed to be invested in. Yet the companies producing the arms and selling it to the local government for export purposes need to be scrutinised on a case-by-case basis. Finally, the companies that are producing arms and selling to regimes that are using it against the Muslims should not be allowed to invest in.

With regard to the 5 per cent thresholds used for companies involved in mixed businesses, it should be studied in detail and should be based on a case-by-case basis to ascertain that the Shari'a non-compliant income is purely incidental. As this particular ratio has no historical Shari'a reference and is very subjective in nature; efforts should be made to replace it with a better measure or remove it completely, hence not allowing investments in companies involved in mixed businesses. In this way, the companies will only be left with incidental *Shari'a* non-compliant revenue in the capital structure of the company. Furthermore, this threshold has remained static since the introduction of the Shari'a screening methodologies, research can be carried to analyse how the removal of this screen affects the *Shari'a-compliant* portfolio. If the underlying portfolio has a large impact, then another way of removing this threshold would be to have a three to five-year plan of removing this threshold slowly and steadily. Having said this, the latter is a less preferred route as it is very much a market-driven ideology and as such a *Shari'a-compliant* investment should not be allowed to receive even a small amount of *Shari'a* non-compliant revenue.

5.4 Conclusion

This chapter has reviewed the *Shari'a* screening methodologies using qualitative face-to-face interviews involving nine *Shari'a* scholars and experts in the field globally. The analysis is intended to assist the Islamic equity investments industry in enhancing the practices of *Shari'a* screening methodologies. Furthermore, the aim was to enhance the understanding behind the introduction of the methodologies with the help of primary data.

The analysis found that *Shari'a* screening methodologies were introduced to fulfil a contemporary need and as an alternative to the most conservative *Shari'a* opinion with regard to investing in the companies involved in mixed activities. The growth in technology and the internet eased the access to stock markets, which further increased the need for a mechanism for Shari'a sensitive investors access the stock market. The aim was to create some basic parameters, which define clearly the boundaries for an investment to qualify as *Shari'a-compliant*. These basic parameters aimed to filter the companies whose main line of business was *Shari'a* non-compliant; further the aim was to contain the *Shari'a* non-compliant element for a company that generates revenue from both *Shari'a-compliant* and *Shari'a* non-compliant. It is clear from the review and analysis that had the scholars waited for the perfect moment where *Shari'a* sensitive investors were only allowed to invest in a company, which generates 100 per cent of its revenue from *Shari'a-compliant* business and has no direct or in direct dealing with a conventional bank then for the last 20 years *Shari'a* sensitive investors would not have been able to invest in a large number of listed equities. Without this facilitation and barring of stock market investments, it is believed that Muslims would not have been able to benefit from the opportunity that would have been otherwise available to non-Muslims. The scholars and other experts wisely opted with an approach to have basic parameters that contains the *Shari'a* non-compliant element and slowly and steadily develop them to achieve a zero tolerance level. Dow Jones launched the first official *Shari'a* screening methodology in line with international standards in the year

1999 and became the first *Shari'a-compliant* index to be used as a benchmark. Subsequently, a number of other methodologies were introduced, which were based on similar principles. Before DJIMI, institutions were using methodologies and indexes that were established by the institutions themselves with the help of their *Shari'a* advisors or were using a conventional index as a benchmark—a practice that is not preferred. Further, investments in organisations with mixed activities are allowed as long as it passes the business and financial screen thresholds. The threshold for business screening of 5% is based on the *ijtihad* of the scholars and has no solid historical *Shari'a* reference and as such it is not liked by a number of scholars; hence, it should be completely removed from the business screening. This is because a *Shari'a* sensitive investor cannot own a company where from the outset it is mentioned that part of its revenue will be generated from *Shari'a* non-compliant businesses. In this way, investments will be only left with *Shari'a* non-compliant revenue on the financial side, which is purely incidental in nature. Financial screening as part of screening methodologies contains the interest involvement in the capital structure of the company. The current financial ratios are best described as imprecise and lead to inconsistency as they are not based on the actual prohibited element, namely the interest income and interest expense. They are based on the source of funds, including debt, cash and receivables, interest-based securities to market capitalisation or total assets. One of the important outcomes from the discussions with the Shari'a scholars and other experts through the interviews has been the willingness of moving from the existing methodology to the one based on more precise measures such the interest income and interest expense. An exploratory book comparing the portfolio results based on the existing filters and based on actual interest element was suggested to understand and analyse the difference it makes to the portfolio combination. Furthermore, the financial ratios were introduced as the IBF industry was not developed and as such Islamic financing availability was limited. However, since the introduction in 1999 (for DJIMI), the IBF industry has evolved to develop *Shari'a-compliant* alternatives to conventional financial products, resulting in increase in the Islamic financing availability; yet, the *Shari'a* screening ratios have remained the same. It is time for the existing screening methodologies to be adjusted in line with the development in the IBF industry; such that the screening filters are dependent on the country where the underlying company is domiciled or have major operations. This enhancement of the screening ratios is a continuous process and should be adjusted on an ongoing basis until the optimum 0 per cent is achieved. As stated earlier, this may be seen as a market-driven strategy; however, it should be understood that without having the opportunity to invest in the stock market, the *Shari'a* sensitive investors will be worse-off and at a disadvantage. Hence, the aim is to slowly and steadily develop the screening methodology linked with the IBF development in the country such that a level where 0 per cent *Shari'a* non-compliance tolerance level is achieved.

The liquidity ratio (cash and receivables to total assets or market capitalisation) should not be part of *Shari'a* screening methodologies as there is no rationale to limit how much cash and receivables (assets) a company can hold at any given time. Hence, this ratio should be removed from the screening methodologies.

Furthermore, on the issue of standardisation there are a number of *Shari'a* screening methodologies, all of them are equally *Shari'a* compliant, yet each of them gives a different portfolio combination. There is a need for the development of a global *Shari'a-compliant* stock exchange by the OIC countries or a government of Muslim majority country, which has a universally accepted screening methodology. For institutions to be listed on this exchange and enhance their visibility to attract investments from *Shari'a* sensitive investors, they will have to abide by the screening methodology followed by the exchange. This will assist in standardising the screening methodologies.

With regard to the issues of purification, a common method used is dividend purification, which removes the impure income from any returns received from the stock. However, for non-paying dividends this will not be possible as the returns will be invested back into the company. Hence, the author suggests that the best method would be to use the investment purification method, which removes impure income from the invested income even if the company has made a loss. In this way, the retained earnings and the dividend will be pure from the *Shari'a* non-compliant revenue.

Socially responsible industry has received a lot of prominence in the recent past, and as such is based on the principles of ethics, which are otherwise in line with the principles of *Shari'a*. Yet, the *Shari'a* screening methodologies do not take them into account and resultantly a *Shari'a-compliant* portfolio may be socially irresponsible. It has been concluded from the data analysis that it is now time that such principles are included in the *Shari'a* screening methodologies to offer investors different investment choices in line with their preferences and thus move towards positive screening. There can be different kinds of portfolio; that is, a portfolio with positive and negative screening (most preferred), portfolio with negative screening and socially neutral, and a portfolio that is just *Shari'a* compliant. Hence, the *Shari'a-compliant* screening methodologies need to include this as an additional screening criteria "social screening" to existing business and financial screening. This additional social screen can be based on universally accepted principles such as United National Global Compact or Principles for Responsible Investments. However, before following these universally accepted principles, it is important that a detailed book is carried out to ensure that these principles are in compliance with *Shari'a*. Once achieved and followed by *Shari'a-compliant* screening methodologies it will make the *Shari'a-compliant* investments socially responsible and open to investment from the conventional SRI industry. Resultantly, the SRI companies may be able to invest in the *Shari'a-compliant* companies and indexes for diversification purposes, thus increasing the AUM of Islamic equity investments. Furthermore, there is enough research on the positive element that SRI brings and hence to make a stronger business case, the research can further review the performance of the SRI portfolio once the *Shari'a* principles are embedded in it to analyse how a *Shari'a-compliant* portfolio brings value to a conventional ethical portfolio.

Lastly, further research can be undertaken to see how the increase in purification affects the returns of the stock and vice versa. Research also can be conducted to analyse how the existing static model can be changed to a more dynamic (effect) model that analyses the effects of impure income on the revenue of the company.

In line with the conclusions of the interview analysis conducted with *Shari'a* scholars and other experts, there are a number of suggestions proposed. Accordingly, this research book has selected two important suggestions, which will be further studied in detail in the next chapter (Chapter 6). These suggestions are: (1) research on the comparison of portfolio combination screened on the actual interest income and interest expense compared to the existing methodologies. This will assist in answering an important criticism in the academic literature, where the existing practices are referred as imprecise. (2) Research on enhancing and developing screening methodologies in line with the growth and development in the IBF industry. As such, an important contribution will be constructing a gauge that quantifies the development in the IBF industry in an accurate and objective manner. Based on it, the book will propose screening thresholds to be adjusted in line with the developments in the IBF industry in an individual country where the underlying company is domiciled.

References

Al Amine, M. B. M. (2002). *Comments of Muhammad Al Bashir Muhammad Al Amine on Reviewing the Concept of Shares: Towards a Dynamic Legal*. Perspective by Faisal Ahmed Manjoo [online]. http://www.kantakji.com/media/163527/file521.pdf. Accessed on 14 December 2013.

Elgari, M. A. (2000). Purification of Islamic Equity Funds: Methodology and *Shari'a* Foundation. In *Proceedings of the Fourth Harvard University Forum on Islamic Finance*. Harvard University.

Gamaleldin, F. (2015). *Shariah-Compliant Stocks Screening and Purification* (MSc Dissertation). University of Liverpool.

CHAPTER 6

Enhancing the *Shari'a* Screening Methodologies: An Empirical Analysis

6.1 Introduction

This chapter provides the discussions and results of the quantitative analysis undertaken in this book. The primary objective of the quantitative analysis is to propose and examine enhancements to the existing *Shari'a* screening methodologies and, as such, it is the direct outcome of the qualitative part and thus based on the recommendations of the *Shari'a* scholars and other experts interviewed (as discussed in Chapter 5). The *Shari'a* scholars endorsed in particular two proposed methods of enhancing the existing *Shari'a* screening methodologies and suggested that both should be examined and studied using different portfolios to analyse the difference they make to the portfolio combinations compared to the existing methodologies.

In line with two proposed methods, the analysis in this chapter is divided into two parts;

(1) Research Analysis 1: This is based on the analysis of screening stocks based on more precise measures of *Shari'a* compliancy, such as interest income and interest expense. The interest income and interest expense are something that the existing practices measure, however in an indirect method (based on the source of funds) of having debt to market capitalisation or total assets ratio to capture interest expense, while interest income element

R. Malik, *Shari'a Compliant Equity Investments*,
https://doi.org/10.1007/978-3-031-70822-0_6

is captured using cash, receivables and interest-based securities to market capitalisation or total assets.

(2) Research Analysis 2: This is based on the analysis of setting screening thresholds for stocks based on an IBF index that analyses and quantifies the growth and development in IBF industry in a particular country. The intelligence behind this is the fact that the IBF industry has grown manifold since the introduction of *Shari'a-compliant* equity indices in 1999, yet the screening thresholds have remained stagnant. Hence, through this analysis, the book propose that stocks domiciled in a country with a developed IBF industry should have different screening thresholds compared to countries where IBF industry is in developing stage. In doing so, the research selected different portfolios to analyse the effects. The construction and composition of the portfolios is explained in Chapter 4.

This chapter is organised as follows. First, Research Analysis 1 is outlined, where the descriptive analysis of the data is undertaken, before analysing the portfolio combination based on the proposed more precise measures compared to existing practices. The chapter then continues with Research Analysis 2, where a descriptive analysis is conducted on the characteristics of underlying variables that assist in the construction of an IBF index. It then discusses the growth and development of IBF in various countries and in line with it screen portfolios based on newly proposed thresholds for different countries (in line with the developments). After the empirical analysis and results' discussion sections, the chapter ends with a conclusion.

6.2 Research Analysis 1

As discussed in Chapter 4, this section focuses on the empirical analysis of three selected portfolios, in terms of existing *Shari'a* screening compared to the newly proposed more precise approach. This section will be divided into three parts; each of the three portfolios selected will be discussed separately.

Nasdaq 100

In our portfolio of Nasdaq 100 stocks, there were 105 stocks. These were screened based on both financial screening and business screening issued by AAOIFI. As discussed in the literature review, business screening filters organisations that are involved in *Shari'a* non-compliant activities, while financial screening contains the involvement of interest in the capital structure of a company. Although Nasdaq 100 is a non-financial index and thus will not have any banks or financial institutions, there will be others stocks whose underlying operations are not in compliance with *Shari'a*. Hence, business screening was applied to the Nasdaq portfolio, which reduced the available stocks to 97, so businesses of 8 stocks were in contradiction with *Shari'a*.

Financial screening was applied to the remaining 97 stocks, which resulted in the *Shari'a-compliant* portfolio being reduced to 59 and thereby available to construct a *Shari'a-compliant* portfolio or to invest in by *Shari'a* sensitive investors. In total, 38 stocks were filtered out based on the financial screening thresholds. In general, information was available for all the stocks except two, which had missing information for cash and receivables to total assets. However, there was enough information available on other filters to reach a conclusion for these two stocks.

On the other hand, we applied the newly proposed filters; interest income to revenue and interest expense to total expenses, with the same threshold of 5%, otherwise used to limit impermissible revenue. The business screening outcome is the same as existing methodology as the stocks would be *Shari'a* non-compliant according to both methodologies. With regard to the financial screening, the information was missing on quite a lot of stocks. For example, for 49 stocks, information was missing on interest income to revenue, while information was missing on 29 stock based on interest expense to total expenses filter. In total, based on the newly proposed methodology, only 23 stocks are *Shari'a* non-compliant while based on the existing methodology it is 38. In total, there was no information available for 26 stocks based on both filters.

We further analysed the two sets of portfolio combinations to discuss the commonalities and differences of the screening outcome. Through the analysis, we found that there are 24 stocks that are compliant based on both the existing methodology and newly proposed, while there are 19 stocks in common that are *Shari'a* non-compliant based on both methodologies, as presented in Tables 6.1 and 6.2.

At the same time, there are 14 stocks that are non-compliant based on existing filters but are compliant under the interest income and expense filters; this means is that if we are to base our decisions on the new filters

Table 6.1 *Shari'a-compliant* based on both methodologies

Stocks Compliant based on both Methodologies		
1	ADBE US Equity	ADOBE SYS INC
2	ADI US Equity	ANALOG DEVICES
3	ADP US Equity	AUTOMATIC DATA
4	AKAM US Equity	AKAMAI TECHNOLOG
5	AMZN US Equity	AMAZON.COM INC
6	BIIB US Equity	BIOGEN INC
7	BMRN US Equity	BIOMARIN PHARMAC
8	CTSH US Equity	COGNIZANT TECH-A
9	CTXS US Equity	CITRIX SYSTEMS
10	EXPE US Equity	EXPEDIA INC
11	FAST US Equity	FASTENAL CO
12	HSIC US Equity	HENRY SCHEIN INC
13	INTC US Equity	INTEL CORP
14	INTU US Equity	INTUIT INC
15	JD US Equity	JD.COM INC-ADR
16	MAT US Equity	MATTEL INC
17	MCHP US Equity	MICROCHIP TECH
18	ORLY US Equity	O'REILLY AUTOMOT
19	PCLN US Equity	PRICELINE GROUP
20	ROST US Equity	ROSS STORES INC
21	SYMC US Equity	SYMANTEC CORP
22	XLNX US Equity	XILINX INC
23	YHOO US Equity	YAHOO! INC
24	XRAY US Equity	DENTSPLY SIRONA

then there will be stocks that will pass through the filters, which otherwise would have been regarded *Shari'a* non-compliant under the existing filters.

Interestingly, there are also 4 stocks that pass through the existing filters but are regarded *Shari'a* non-compliant based on the new filters; in total, there are 18 stocks where the decision based on the two types of filters would have been different. This raises the *Shari'a* governance risk, where a stock which is *Shari'a* non-compliant is regarded as *Shari'a-compliant* and vice versa. These stocks are presented in Tables 6.3 and 6.4. Most importantly, there are stocks on which information is missing based on new filters and are either *Shari'a-compliant* or non-compliant. In the practical world, this would raise a lot of issues for the fund

Table 6.2 Stocks non-compliant based on both methodologies

Stocks non-compliant based on both methodologies		
1	CMCSA US Equity	COMCAST CORP-A
2	COST US Equity	COSTCO WHOLESALE
3	DISCA US Equity	DISCOVERY COMM-A
4	DISCK US Equity	DISCOVERY COMM-C
5	DISH US Equity	DISH NETWORK-A
6	KHC US Equity	KRAFT HEINZ CO/T
7	LBTYA US Equity	LIBERTY GLOBAL-A
8	LBTYK US Equity	LIBERTY GLOBAL-C
9	LRCX US Equity	LAM RESEARCH
10	LVNTA US Equity	LIBERTY VENTUR-A
11	NFLX US Equity	NETFLIX INC
12	SBAC US Equity	SBA COMM CORP-A
13	TMUS US Equity	T-MOBILE US INC
14	VIAB US Equity	VIACOM INC-B
15	FOX US Equity	TWENTY-FIRST - B
16	FOXA US Equity	TWENTY-FIRST C-A
17	AAPL US Equity	APPLE INC
18	GOOG US Equity	ALPHABET INC-C
19	GOOGL US Equity	ALPHABET INC-A

managers, *Shari'a* sensitive investors and auditors as there is no information for them to base their decision upon; such stocks are presented in Tables 6.5 and 6.6.

S&P 500

In the S&P 500 portfolio, there are 505 stocks; these were screened based on the existing filters stated in Chapter 4. When business screening was applied to the overall portfolio, there are 34 stocks that were screened out based on both the existing as well as proposed methodology. These stocks are from banks, financial institutions and entertainment organisations (including casinos). With regard to the financial screening, complete data were available, based on all the variables, except for interest-based receivables (15 stocks). This is only one filter among the three filters and as such there is enough information available to form our conclusion on the overall portfolio for the purpose of this research.

Table 6.3 Stocks non-compliant based on existing methodology but compliant based on interest income and expense

Stocks Non-Compliant Based on Existing methodology but Compliant based on Interest income and expense		
1	BIDU US Equity	BAIDU INC-SP ADR
2	CSCO US Equity	CISCO SYSTEMS
3	CTRP US Equity	CTRIP.COM-ADR
4	MAR US Equity	MARRIOTT INTL-A
5	MU US Equity	MICRON TECH
6	NTAP US Equity	NETAPP INC
7	NVDA US Equity	NVIDIA CORP
8	PAYX US Equity	PAYCHEX INC
9	QCOM US Equity	QUALCOMM INC
10	SHPG US Equity	SHIRE PLC-ADR
11	SRCL US Equity	STERICYCLE INC
12	STX US Equity	SEAGATE TECHNOLO
13	TSLA US Equity	TESLA MOTORS
14	WBA US Equity	WALGREENS BOOTS

Table 6.4 Stocks compliant based on existing methodology but non-compliant based on interest income and expense

Stocks Compliant Based on Existing methodology but Non-Compliant based on Interest income and expense		
1	CELG US Equity	CELGENE CORP
2	GILD US Equity	GILEAD SCIENCES
3	SIRI US Equity	SIRIUS XM HOLDIN
4	VRSK US Equity	VERISK ANALYT

In total, there are 267 stocks that are *Shari'a-compliant* based on both business and financial screening; resultantly, there are 238 stocks that are *Shari'a* non-compliant. When we screened the stocks based on the new filters, it was discovered that there were about 100 stocks for which information is missing completely (for both interest income and interest expense filters). Hence, making a decision on them becomes very difficult for the *Shari'a* sensitive investors and fund managers. Furthermore, there are 229 stocks for which the data on interest income to total revenue are missing, while for 176 the information is missing on interest expense. This makes a total of 405 stocks on which complete data are not available based on the proposed filters. For the purpose of our analysis, we have included the stocks in the analysis even if information is available on only one filter. Furthermore, for the purpose of this research, the

Table 6.5 Information missing and are *Shari'a* compliant

Information on Interest missing and are compliant based on existing methodology		
1	ADSK US Equity	AUTODESK INC
2	BBBY US Equity	BED BATH & BEYOND
3	CERN US Equity	CERNER CORP
4	CHKP US Equity	CHECK POINT SOFT
5	EBAY US Equity	EBAY INC
6	FB US Equity	FACEBOOK INC-A
7	ISRG US Equity	INTUITIVE SURGIC
8	MNST US Equity	MONSTER BEVERAGE
9	MNST US Equity	MONSTER BEVERAGE
10	NXPI US Equity	NXP SEMICONDUCTO
11	PYPL US Equity	PAYPAL HOLDINGS
12	REGN US Equity	REGENERON PHARM
13	TSCO US Equity	TRACTOR SUPPLY
14	ULTA US Equity	ULTA SALON COSME
15	VRTX US Equity	VERTEX PHARM

Table 6.6 Information on interest missing and are non-compliant

Information on Interest missing and are non-compliant based on existing methodology		
1	AAL US Equity	AMERICAN AIRLINE
2	AMGN US Equity	AMGEN INC
3	CA US Equity	CA INC
4	CHTR US Equity	CHARTER COMMUN-A
5	CSX US Equity	CSX CORP
6	DLTR US Equity	DOLLAR TREE INC
7	NCLH US Equity	NORWEGIAN CRUISE
8	PCAR US Equity	PACCAR INC
9	VIAB US Equity	VIACOM INC-B
10	VOD US Equity	VODAFONE GRP-ADR
11	WDC US Equity	WESTERN DIGITAL

stocks (for comparison) on which financial information is not available completely are regarded *Shari'a* compliant. There are 394 stocks that are *Shari'a-compliant* based on the proposed filters; this includes 100 stocks on which complete information was not available, hence making the actual *Shari'a-compliant* stocks 294.

The research then analysed the treatment of stocks under the two methodologies and concluded that there are 198 stocks that are *Shari'a-compliant* based on both existing and new filters, while there are 99 stocks that are *Shari'a* non-compliant based on both filters as presented in Tables 6.7 and 6.8.

Further, there are 128 stocks on which information is missing; of these 73 are non-compliant while 55 are *Shari'a-compliant* compared to existing thresholds. This missing information makes them difficult and unattractive for *Shari'a* sensitive investments. These portfolios are presented in Tables 6.9 and 6.10.

Lastly, there are 79 stocks which will receive different treatment based on both types of filters; as such, there are 66 stocks that are *Shari'a* non-compliant and would have been concluded as *Shari'a-compliant* based on the new filters. Equally, there are 13 stocks that are considered *Shari'a-compliant* but would be *Shari'a* non-compliant based on the new filters. These stocks are presented in Tables 6.11 and 6.12.

FTSE 100

After analysing the US based indices (Nasdaq 100 and S&P 500), we move to the UK index FTSE 100, which hosts the top 100 companies based on the market capitalisation. When the business screening was applied to the FTSE 100, 12 stocks were filtered out as being involved in *Shari'a* non-compliant activities (including financial institutions). The stocks filtered out based on the basis of business screens are the same for both methodologies. When we applied the existing financial FTSE *Shari'a* screening methodology to the portfolio, only 57 stocks were classified as *Shari'a* compliant; the other 31 stocks did not fulfil the financial screens criteria, thus making the total *Shari'a-compliant* portfolio 57% of the total portfolio.

There are a total of 52 stocks for which information for cash and receivables as well as interest income to revenue was missing. Although in practice the fund managers would manually try and get the information, for the purpose of this research it was beyond the scope. Concurrently, there was complete information available on the two other filters, which assisted in making the conclusions from the analysis. When we screened the stocks based on the new filters, we found that there are completely missing data for 53 stocks, while looking separately information on interest income was missing for 60 stocks and interest expense

Table 6.7 S&P non-compliant based on both filters

Stock Non-compliant based on both					
1	ABBV US Equity	ABBVIE INC	50	KHC US Equity	KRAFT HEINZ CO/T
2	ACN US Equity	ACCENTURE PLC-A	51	KMI US Equity	KINDER MORGAN IN
3	AEE US Equity	AMEREN CORP	52	LUK US Equity	LEUCADIA NATL
4	AEP US Equity	AMERICAN ELECTRI	53	LVLT US Equity	LEVEL 3 COMM INC
5	AES US Equity	AES CORP	54	MA US Equity	MASTERCARD INC-A
6	AFLAC INC	Non-Compliant	55	MET US Equity	METLIFE INC
7	AMP US Equity	AMERIPRISE FINAN	56	MNK US Equity	MALLINCKRODT
8	APC US Equity	ANADARKO PETROLE	57	MS US Equity	MORGAN STANLEY
9	AWK US Equity	AMERICAN WATER W	58	MTB US Equity	M&T BANK CORP
10	AXP US Equity	AMERICAN EXPRESS	59	NAVI US Equity	NAVIENT CORP
11	BAC US Equity	BANK OF AMERICA	60	NBL US Equity	NOBLE ENERGY INC
12	BBT US Equity	BB & T CORP	61	NEE US Equity	NEXTERA ENERGY
13	BDX US Equity	BECTON DICKINSON	62	NFLX US Equity	NETFLIX INC
14	BK US Equity	BANK NY MELLON	63	NLSN US Equity	NIELSEN HOLDINGS
15	CUS Equity	CITIGROUP INC	64	NI US Equity	NISOURCE INC
16	BLK US Equity	BLACKROCK INC	65	NRG US Equity	NRG ENERGY
17	CFG US Equity	CITIZENS FINANCI	66	NTRS US Equity	NORTHERN TRUST
18	CI US Equity	CIGNA CORP	67	OKE US Equity	ONEOK INC
19	CMA US Equity	COMERICA INC	68	ORCL US Equity	ORACLE CORP
20	CMS US Equity	CMS ENERGY CORP	69	PBCT US Equity	PEOPLE'S UNITED
21	EIX US Equity	EDISON INTL	70	PEG US Equity	PUB SERV ENTERP

(continued)

Table 6.7 (continued)

Stock Non-compliant based on both					
22	CNP US Equity	CENTERPOINT ENER	71	PPL US Equity	PPL CORP
23	COF US Equity	CAPITAL ONE FINA	72	PCG US Equity	PG&E CORP
24	COG US Equity	CABOT OIL & GAS	73	PNC US Equity	PNC FINANCIAL SE
25	CTL US Equity	CENTURY LINK INC	74	PRU US Equity	PRUDENTL FINL
26	D US Equity	DOMINION RES/VA	75	PNW US Equity	PINNACLE WEST
27	ED US Equity	CONS EDISON INC	76	RF US Equity	REGIONS FINANCIA
28	DFS US Equity	DISCOVER FINANCI	77	RIG US Equity	TRANSOCEAN LTD
29	DISKA US Equity	DISCOVERY COMM-A	78	RRC US Equity	RANGE RESOURCES
30	DISCK US Equity	DISCOVERY COMM-C	79	SCG US Equity	SCANA CORP
31	DTE US Equity	DTE ENERGY CO	80	SCHW US Equity	SCHWAB (CHARLES)
32	DUK US Equity	DUKE ENERGY CORP	81	SE US Equity	SPECTRA ENERG
33	ENDP US Equity	ENDO INTERNATION	82	STT US Equity	STATE ST CORP
34	ES US Equity	EVERSOURCE ENERG	83	SO US Equity	SOUTHERN CO
35	EQIX US Equity	EQUINIX INC	84	SRE US Equity	SEMPRA ENERGY
36	ETFC US Equity	E*TRADE FINANCIA	85	STI US Equity	SUNTRUST BANKS
37	ETR US Equity	ENTERGY CORP	86	TGNA US Equity	TEGNA INC
38	EXC US Equity	EXELON CORP	87	SYF US Equity	SYNCHRONY FINANC
39	FE US Equity	FIRSTENERGY CORP	88	V US Equity	VISA INC-CLASS A
40	FITB US Equity	FIFTH THIRD BANC	89	USB US Equity	US BANCORP
41	FOX US Equity	TWENTY-FIRST-B	90	TWX US Equity	TIME WARNER INC
42	FOXA US Equity	TWENTY-FIRST C-A	91	WU US Equity	WESTERN UNION

(continued)

Table 6.7 (continued)

Stock Non-compliant based on both

43	FTR US Equity	FRONTIER COMMUNI	92	WEC US Equity	WEC ENERGY GROUP
44	GS US Equity	GOLDMAN SACHS GP	93	WFC US Equity	WELLS FARCO & CO
45	HBAN US Equity	HUNTINGTON BANC	94	WMB US Equity	WILLIAMS COS INC
46	IRM US Equity	IRON MOUNTAIN	95	WY US Equity	WEYERHAEUSER CO
47	IVZ US Equity	INVESCO LTD	96	WYNN US Equity	WYNN RESORTS LTD
48	JPM US Equity	JPMORGAN CHASE	97	XEL US Equity	XCEL ENERGY INC
49	KEY US Equity	KEYCORP	98	ZBH US Equity	ZIMMER BIOMET HO
			99	ZION US Equity	ZIONS BANCORP

information was missing for 71 stocks. In terms of the commonality between the two screens, there were 42 stocks that had similar treatments, namely 21 stocks were regarded *Shari'a* non-compliant and another 21 were regarded *Shari'a-compliant* based on both filters. These stocks are presented in Tables 6.13 and 6.14.

Like Nasdaq 100 and S&P 500, there are stocks that have missing data, so the number of stocks that are *Shari'a-compliant* based on existing filters and those that are *Shari'a* non-compliant but their data are missing based on new filters are 30 and 13, as presented in Tables 6.15 and 6.16. Simultaneously, there are 13 stocks that are non-compliant based on existing methodology but are *Shari'a-compliant* according to new filters. Furthermore, there are 5 stocks that are *Shari'a-compliant* based on existing methodology but violate the interest expense to total expenses threshold of 5%, as shown in Tables 6.17 and 6.18, and thus creating *Shari'a* governance risk.

To conclude, although the existing screening filters are not precise, in that they base their thresholds on the source of prohibited income (i.e. interest-based debt and not the prohibited element of interest itself), there is not enough data available on the newly proposed filters to make a conclusion on. There are two predominant reasons for the missing information: (1) there is no regulatory requirement from the authorities to

Table 6.8 S&P *Shari'a-compliant* based on both filters

Stocks Compliant on both					
1	A US Equity	AGILENT TECH INC	101	IR US Equity	INGERSOLL-RAND
2	AAP US Equity	ADVANCE AUTO PAR	102	LOW US Equity	LOWE'S COS INC
3	ABC US Equity	AMERISOURCEBERGE	103	ITW US Equity	ILLINOIS TOOL WO
4	ABT US Equity	ABBOTT LABS	104	JEC US Equity	JACOBS ENGIN GRP
5	ADBE US Equity	ADOBE SYS INC	105	JNJ US Equity	JOHNSON&JOHNSON
6	ADI US Equity	ANALOG DEVICES	106	JNPR US Equity	JUNIPER NETWORKS
7	ADM US Equity	ARCHER-DANIELS	107	LUV US Equity	SOUTHWEST AIR
8	ADP US Equity	AUTOMATIC DATA	108	K US Equity	KELLOGG CO
9	AKAM US Equity	AKAMAI TECHNOLOG	109	KO US Equity	COCA-COLA CO/THE
10	ALXN US Equity	ALEXION PHARM	110	LB US Equity	L BRANDS INC
11	AMAT US Equity	APPLIED MATERIAL	111	LEG US Equity	LEGGETT & PLATT
12	AME US Equity	AMETEK INC	112	LLL US Equity	L-3 COMM HLDGS
13	AMZN US Equity	AMAZON.COM INC	113	LLTC US Equity	LINEAR TECH CORP
14	AON US Equity	AON PLC	114	LLY US Equity	ELI LILLY & CO
15	APD US Equity	AIR PRODS & CHEM	115	LYB US Equity	LYONDELLBASELL-A

(continued)

Table 6.8 (continued)

Stocks Compliant on both					
16	APH US Equity	AMPHENOL CORP-A	116	MAS US Equity	MASCO CORP
17	ATVI US Equity	ACTIVISION BLIZZ	117	MAT US Equity	MATTEL INC
18	AVGO US Equity	BROADCOM LTD	118	MCD US Equity	MCDONALDS CORP
19	AVY US Equity	AVERY DENNISON	119	MCHP US Equity	MICROCHIP TECH
20	AYI US Equity	ACUITY BRANDS	120	MCK US Equity	MCKESSON CORP
21	AZO US Equity	AUTOZONE INC	121	MCO US Equity	MOODY'S CORP
22	BA US Equity	BOEING CO/THE	122	MDLZ US Equity	MONDELEZ INTER-A
23	BAX US Equity	BAXTER INTL INC	123	MHK US Equity	MOHAWK INDS
24	BBY US Equity	BEST BUY CO INC	124	MJN US Equity	MEAD JOHNSON
25	BCR US Equity	CR BARD INC	125	MKC US Equity	MCCORMICK-N/V
26	BF/B US Equity	BROWN-FORMAN -B	126	MLM US Equity	MARTIN MAR MTLS
27	BIIB US Equity	BIOGEN INC	127	MMC US Equity	MARSH & MCLENNAN
28	BMY US Equity	BRISTOL-MYER SQB	128	MMM US Equity	3 M CO
29	BSX US Equity	BOSTON SCIENTIFC	129	MNST US Equity	MONSTER BEVERAGE

(continued)

Table 6.8 (continued)

Stocks Compliant on both					
30	BWA US Equity	BORGWARNER INC	130	MRK US Equity	MERCK & CO
31	CAG US Equity	CONAGRA FOODS	131	MON US Equity	MONSANTO CO
32	CHD US Equity	CHURCH & DWIGHT	132	MOS US Equity	MOSAIC CO/THE
33	CI US Equity	CIGNA CORP	133	MTD US Equity	METTLER-TOLEDO
34	CLX US Equity	CLOROX CO	134	NKE US Equity	NIKE INC -CL B
35	CMG US Equity	CHIPOTLE MEXICAN	135	NOC US Equity	NORTHROP GRUMMAN
36	CMI US Equity	CUMMINS INC	136	NOV US Equity	NATL OILWELL VAR
37	COH US Equity	COACH INC	137	NUE US Equity	NUCOR CORP
38	COL US Equity	ROCKWELL COLLINS	138	NVDA US Equity	NVIDIA CORP
39	COO US Equity	COOPER COS INC	139	OMC US Equity	OMNICOM GROUP
40	COST US Equity	COSTCO WHOLESALE	140	ORLY US Equity	O'REILLY AUTOMOT
41	CPB US Equity	CAMPBELL SOUP CO	141	OXY US Equity	OCCIDENTAL PETE
42	CRM US Equity	SALESFORCE.COM	142	PAYX US Equity	PAYCHEX INC
43	CTAS US Equity	CINTAS CORP	143	PCLN US Equity	PRICELINE GROUP

(continued)

Table 6.8 (continued)

Stocks Compliant on both					
44	CTSH US Equity	COGNIZANT TECH-A	144	PDCO US Equity	PATTERSON COS
45	CTXS US Equity	CITRIX SYSTEMS	145	PEP US Equity	PEPSICO INC
46	CVS US Equity	CVS HEALTH CORP	146	PFE US Equity	PFIZER INC
47	CVX US Equity	CHEVRON CORP	147	PG US Equity	PROCTER & GAMBLE
48	DAL US Equity	DELTA AIR LI	148	PH US Equity	PARKER HANNIFIN
49	DD US Equity	DU PONT (EI)	149	PKI US Equity	PERKINELMER INC
50	DG US Equity	DOLLAR GENERAL C	150	PPG US Equity	PPG INDS INC
51	DHI US Equity	DR HORTON INC	151	S LB US Equity	SCHLUMBERGER LTD
52	DHR US Equity	DANAHER CORP	152	PSX US Equity	PHILLIPS 66
53	DIS US Equity	WALT DISNEY CO	153	PWR US Equity	QUANTA SERVICES
54	DLPH US Equity	DELPHI AUTOMOTIV	154	SNA US Equity	SNAP-ON INC
55	DOV US Equity	DOVER CORP	155	PXD US Equity	PIONEER NATURAL
56	DPS US Equity	DR PEPPER SNAPPL	156	PYPL US Equity	PAYPAL HOLDINGS
57	EA US Equity	ELECTRONIC ARTS	157	STJ US Equity	ST JUDE MEDICAL
58	EFX US Equity	EQUIFAX INC	158	QRVO US Equity	QORVO INC
59	ECL US Equity	ECOLAB INC	159	RHI US Equity	ROBERT HALF INTL

(continued)

Table 6.8 (continued)

Stocks Compliant on both					
60	EL US Equity	ESTEE LAUDER	160	RHT US Equity	RED HAT INC
61	EMR US Equity	EMERSON ELEC CO	161	RL US Equity	RALPH LAUREN COR
62	EQR US Equity	EQUITY RESIDENTI	162	ROK US Equity	ROCKWELL AUTOMAT
63	ESRX US Equity	EXPRESS SCRIPTS	163	ROP US Equity	ROPER TECHNOLOGI
64	ETN US Equity	EATON CORP PLC	164	ROST US Equity	ROSS STORES INC
65	EW US Equity	EDWARDS LIFE	165	RTN US Equity	RAYTHEON CO
66	EXPD US Equity	EXPEDITORS INTL	166	SBUX US Equity	STARBUCKS CORP
67	EXPE US Equity	EXPEDIA INC	167	SYY US Equity	SYSCO CORP
68	FAST US Equity	FASTENAL CO	168	SIG US Equity	SIGNET JEWELERS
69	FB US Equity	FACEBOOK INC-A	169	TDC US Equity	TERADATA CORP
70	FBHS US Equity	FORTUNE BRANDS H	170	SPLS US Equity	STAPLES INC
71	FDX US Equity	FEDEX CORP	171	SRCL US Equity	STERICYCLE INC
72	FFIV US Equity	F5 NETWORKS	172	STX US Equity	SEAGATE TECHNOLO
73	FISV US Equity	FISERV INC	173	TEL US Equity	TE CONNECTIVITY
74	FL US Equity	FOOT LOCKER INC	174	SWK US Equity	STANLEY BLACK &

(continued)

Table 6.8 (continued)

Stocks Compliant on both					
75	FLIR US Equity	FLIR SYSTEMS	175	SWKS US Equity	SKYWORKS SOLUTIO
76	FLR US Equity	FLUOR CORP	176	TRIP US Equity	TRIPADVISOR INC
77	FLS US Equity	FLOWSERVE CORP	177	TXN US Equity	TEXAS INSTRUMENT
78	FRT US Equity	FED REALTY INVS	178	TJX US Equity	TJX COS INC
79	GOOG US Equity	ALPHABET INC-C	179	UTX US Equity	UNITED TECH CORP
80	GOOGL US Equity	ALPHABET INC-A	180	TSN US Equity	TYSON FOODS-A
81	GPC US Equity	GENUINE PARTS CO	181	UHS US Equity	UNIVERSAL HLTH-B
82	GPS US Equity	GAP INC/THE	182	WFM US Equity	WHOLE FOODS MKT
83	GRMN US Equity	GARMIN LTD	183	UNH US Equity	UNITEDHEALTH GRP
84	GWW US Equity	WW GRAINGER INC	184	UNP US Equity	UNION PAC CORP
85	HD US Equity	HOME DEPOT INC	185	UPS US Equity	UNITED PARCEL-B
86	HAS US Equity	HASBRO INC	186	VAR US Equity	VARIAN MEDICAL S
87	HON US Equity	HONEYWELL INTL	187	VFC US Equity	VF CORP
88	HP US Equity	HELMERICH & PAY N	188	VLO US Equity	VALERO ENERGY

(continued)

Table 6.8 (continued)

Stocks Compliant on both					
89	HRB US Equity	H&R BLOCK INC	189	WAT US Equity	WATERS CORP
90	HRL US Equity	HORMEL FOODS CRP	190	WBA US Equity	WALGREENS BOOTS
91	HSIC US Equity	HENRY SCHEIN INC	191	WMT US Equity	WAL-MART STORES
92	KMB US Equity	KIMBERLY-CLARK	192	XEC US Equity	CIMAREX ENERGY C
93	HSY US Equity	HERSHEY CO/THE	193	XLNX US Equity	XILINX INC
94	IBM US Equity	IBM	194	XOM US Equity	EXXON MOBIL CORP
95	LMT US Equity	LOCKHEED MARTIN	195	XRAY US Equity	DENTSPLY SIRONA
96	IFF US Equity	INTL FLVR & FRAG	196	XYL US Equity	XYLEM INC
97	ILMN US Equity	ILLUMINA INC	197	YHOO US Equity	YAHOO! INC
98	INTC US Equity	INTEL CORP	198	ZTS US Equity	ZOETIS INC
99	INTU US Equity	INTUIT INC			
100	IPG US Equity	INTERPUBLIC GRP			

disclose this information (interest expense and interest income separately); resultantly, the underlying companies present the figure of net interest income or expense or present a consolidated income or revenue figures in the annual reports. (2) The information may be available but is not captured by the secondary source, Bloomberg in our case, which has not collected information on these particular variables. If the latter is true,

Table 6.9 S&P information missing and *Shari'a* non-compliant

Information on Interest missing and are non- on existing methodology compliant based		
1	AAL US Equity	AMERICAN AIRLINE
2	ADS US Equity	ALLIANCE DATA
3	AMERICAN INTE	Compliant
4	AIV US Equity	APARTMENT INVEST
5	AIZ US Equity	ASSURANT INC
6	ALL US Equity	ALLSTATE CORP
7	AMT US Equity	AMERICAN TOWER C
8	AN US Equity	AUTONATION INC
9	BEN US Equity	FRANKLIN RES INC
10	BXP US Equity	BOSTON PROPERTIE
11	CB US Equity	CHUBB LTD
12	CCI US Equity	CROWN CASTLE INT
13	CHTR US Equity	CHARTER COMMUN-A
14	CSRA US Equity	CSRA INC
15	CSX US Equity	CSX CORP
16	DLTR US Equity	DOLLAR TREE INC
17	ESS US Equity	ESSEX PROPERTY
18	FIS US Equity	FIDELITY NATIONA
19	GGP US Equity	GENERAL GROWTH P
20	GM US Equity	GENERAL MOTORS C
21	GPN US Equity	GLOBAL PAYMENTS
22	GT US Equity	GOODYEAR TIRE
23	HAL US Equity	HALLIBURTON CO
24	HBI US Equity	HANESBRANDS INC
25	HCA US Equity	HCA HOLDINGS INC
26	HCN US Equity	WELLTOWER INC
27	HCP US Equity	HCP INC
28	HES US Equity	HESS CORP
29	HIG US Equity	HARTFORD FINL SV
30	HOG US Equity	HARLEY-DAVIDSON
31	HOLX US Equity	HOLOGIC INC
32	HPE US Equity	HEWLETT PACKA
33	HRS US Equity	HARRIS CORP
34	IP US Equity	INTL PAPER CO
35	JCI US Equity	JOHNSON CONTROLS
36	KIM US Equity	KIMCO REALTY
37	KMX US Equity	CARMAX INC
38	LKQ US Equity	LKQ CORP
39	KSS US Equity	KOHLS CORP
40	LM US Equity	LEGG MASON INC
41	LNT US Equity	ALLIANT ENERGY

(continued)

Table 6.9 (continued)

Information on Interest missing and are non- on existing methodology compliant based		
42	LRCX US Equity	LAM RESEARCH
43	M US Equity	MACY'S INC
44	MRO US Equity	MARATHON OIL
45	MSFT US Equity	MICROSOFT CORP
46	MSI US Equity	MOTOROLA SOLUTIO
47	NEM US Equity	NEWMONT MINING
48	NSC US Equity	NORFOLK SOUTHERN
49	NWL US Equity	NEWELL BRANDS IN
50	O US Equity	REALTY INCOME
51	PBI US Equity	PITNEY BOWES INC
52	PCAR US Equity	PACCAR INC
53	PFG US Equity	PRINCIPAL FINL
54	PGR US Equity	PROGRESSIVE CORP
55	PLD US Equity	PROLOGIS INC
56	PNR US Equity	PENTAIR PLC
57	RSG US Equity	REPUBLIC SVCS
58	SLG US Equity	SL GREEN REALTY
59	SNI US Equity	SCRIPPS NET-CL A
60	SPG US Equity	SIMON PROPERTY
61	SWN US Equity	SOUTHWESTRN ENGY
62	TAP US Equity	MOLSON COORS-B
63	TDG US Equity	TRANSDIGM GROUP
64	TMK US Equity	TORCHMARK CORP
65	TRV US Equity	TRAVELERS COS IN
66	TSO US Equity	TESORO CORP
67	UNM US Equity	UNUM GROUP
68	URI US Equity	UNITED RENTALS
69	VIAB US Equity	VIACOM INC-B
70	VNO US Equity	VORNADO RLTY TST
71	WDC US Equity	WESTERN DIGITAL
72	WM US Equity	WASTE MANAGEMENT
73	XL US Equity	XL GROUP LTD

then there is a need to collect this information and make it available on the portals to be used by the fund managers and researchers to analyse the portfolio combination in more detail.

Some of the screening methodologies (like FTSE) already include interest income to revenue as a filter; however, none of the screens have paid attention to the interest expense to total expenses filter. Although it is difficult to make a precise conclusion, we have found from our analysis

Table 6.10 S&P information missing and *Shari'a* compliant

Information on Interest missing and are compliant based on existing methodology		
1	ADSK US Equity	AUTODESK INC
2	AMG US Equity	AFFIL MANAGERS
3	AMGN US Equity	AMGEN INC
4	AVB US Equity	AVALONBAY COMMUN
5	BBBY US Equity	BED BATH &BEYOND
6	BHI US Equity	BAKER HUGHES INC
7	CA US Equity	CA INC
8	CERN US Equity	CERNER CORP
9	CAH US Equity	CARDINAL HEALTH
10	CHRW US Equity	CH ROBINSON
11	CL US Equity	COLGATE-PALMOLIV
12	CME US Equity	CME GROUP INC
13	DRI US Equity	DARDEN RESTAURAN
14	EBAY US Equity	EBAY INC
15	EOG US Equity	EOG RESOURCES
16	FB US Equity	FACEBOOK INC-A
17	FMC US Equity	FMC CORP
18	FTI US Equity	FMC TECHNOLOGIES
19	FTV US Equity	FORTIVE CORP
20	GD US Equity	GENERAL DYNAMICS
21	GIS US Equity	GENERAL MILLS IN
22	GLW US Equity	CORNING INC
23	HAR US Equity	HARMAN INTL
24	HPQ US Equity	HP INC
25	HST US Equity	HOST HOTELS & RE
26	ICE US Equity	INTERCONTINENTAL
27	ISRG US Equity	INTUITIVE SURGIC
28	JBHT US Equity	HUNT (JB) TRANS
29	JWN US Equity	NORDSTROM INC
30	KORS US Equity	MICHAEL KORS HOL
31	KSU US Equity	KANSAS CITY SOUT
32	MO US Equity	ALTRIA GROUP INC
33	NWS US Equity	NEWS CORP-CL B
34	NWSA US Equity	NEWS CORP-CL A
35	PM US Equity	PHILIP MORRIS IN
36	PRGO US Equity	PERRIGO CO PLC
37	PSA US Equity	PUBLIC STORAGE
38	PX US Equity	PRAXAIR INC
39	QCOM US Equity	QUALCOMM INC
40	REGN US Equity	REGENERON PHARM
41	SHW US Equity	SHERWIN-WILLIAMS

(continued)

Table 6.10 (continued)

Information on Interest missing and are compliant based on existing methodology		
42	SPGI US Equity	S&P GLOBAL INC
43	SYK US Equity	STRYKER CORP
44	TGT US Equity	TARGET CORP
45	TIF US Equity	TIFFANY & CO
46	TROW US Equity	T ROWE PRICE GRP
47	TSCO US Equity	TRACTOR SUPPLY
48	UA US Equity	UNDER ARMOUR-A
49	UA/C US Equity	UNDER ARMO-C
50	ULTA US Equity	ULTA SALON COSME
51	VMC US Equity	VULCAN MATERIALS
52	VRTX US Equity	VERTEX PHARM
53	URBN US Equity	URBAN OUTFITTER
54	WLTW US Equity	WILLIS TOWERS WA
55	YUM US Equity	YUM! BRANDS INC

that the new filters can play an important role in ensuring that the portfolio is *Shari'a-compliant* (particularly the interest expense). This is due to the fact that there are in total 22 stocks among the three portfolios, which are considered *Shari'a-compliant* but violate the interest expense to total expenses threshold. In light of the conclusion and analysis of this research, the book propose that for the time being and on the side of caution all screening methodologies should include this filter of interest expense to total expenses to screen the stocks in addition to the existing methodology. This will ensure that all of the portfolios remain within the thresholds and, furthermore, it will be a step towards using more precise filters for *Shari'a* compliancy.

6.3 Research Analysis 2

This section focuses on the empirical analysis conducted on creating an IBF index, which quantifies the growth and development in Islamic banking and finance in various countries based on different sets of data using a multivariate analysis technique of factor analysis using PCA. A univariate analysis based on different variables is also undertaken to highlight the difference when variables are analysed in isolation compared to using a holistic method of creating an indicator or index using statistical measures without subjectively assigning weights to the variables.

Table 6.11 *Shari'a* non-compliant based on existing methodology but *Shari'a-compliant* based on new

Stocks Non-Compliant Based on Existing methodology but Compliant based on Interest income and expense		
1	AJG US Equity	ARTHUR J GALLAGH
2	ALB US Equity	ALBEMARLE CORP
3	ALK US Equity	ALASKA AIR GROUP
4	ANTM US Equity	ANTHEM INC
5	APA US Equity	APACHE CORP
6	ARNC US Equity	ARCONIC INC
7	BLL US Equity	BALL CORP
8	BRK/B US Equity	BERKSHIRE HATH-B
9	CAT US Equity	CATERPILLAR INC
10	CF US Equity	CF INDUSTRIES HO
11	CBG US Equity	CBRE GROUP INC-A
12	CBS US Equity	CBS CORP-B
13	CHK US Equity	CHESAPEAKE ENERG
14	CMCSA US Equity	COMCAST CORP-A
15	CNC US Equity	CENTENE CORP
16	COP US Equity	CONOCOPHILLIPS
17	COTY US Equity	COTY INC-CL A
18	CSCO US Equity	CISCO SYSTEMS
19	DE US Equity	DEERE & CO
20	DGX US Equity	QUEST DIAGNOSTIC
21	DLR US Equity	DIGITAL REALTY
22	DOW US Equity	DOW CHEMICAL CO
23	DNB US Equity	DUN & BRADSTREET
24	DVA US Equity	DAVITA INC
25	DVN US Equity	DEVON ENERGY CO
26	EMN US Equity	EASTMAN CHEMICAL
27	EXR US Equity	EXTRA SPACE STOR
28	F US Equity	FORD MOTOR CO
29	FCX US Equity	FREEPORT-MCMORAN
30	FSLR US Equity	FIRST SOLAR INC
31	GE US Equity	GENERAL ELECTRIC
32	HUM US Equity	HUMANA INC
33	KR US Equity	KROGER CO
34	L US Equity	LOEWS CORP
35	LEN US Equity	LENNAR CORP-A
36	LH US Equity	LABORATORY CP
37	LNC US Equity	LINCOLN NATL CRP
38	MAC US Equity	MACERICH CO

(continued)

Table 6.11 (continued)

Stocks Non-Compliant Based on Existing methodology but Compliant based on Interest income and expense		
39	MAR US Equity	MARRIOTT INTL-A
40	MPC US Equity	MARATHON PETROLE
41	MU US Equity	MICRON TECH
42	MUR US Equity	MURPHY OIL CORP
43	MYL US Equity	MYLAN NV
44	NDAQ US Equity	NASDAQ INC
45	NFX US Equity	NEWFIELD EXPLORA
46	NTAP US Equity	NETAPP INC
47	OI US Equity	OWENS-ILLINOIS
48	PHM US Equity	PULTEGROUP INC
49	PVH US Equity	PVH CORP
50	R US Equity	RYDER SYSTEM INC
51	RCL US Equity	ROYAL CARIBBEAN
52	SEE US Equity	SEALED AIR CORP
53	SJM US Equity	JM SMUCKER CO
54	SYMC US Equity	SYMANTEC CORP
55	T US Equity	AT&T INC
56	TMO US Equity	THERMO FISHER
57	TSS US Equity	TOTAL SYS SERVS
58	TXT US Equity	TEXTRON INC
59	UAL US Equity	UNITED CONTINENT
60	UDR US Equity	UDR INC
61	VTR US Equity	VENTAS INC
62	VZ US Equity	VERIZON COMMUNIC
63	WHR US Equity	WHIRLPOOL CORP
64	WRK US Equity	WESTROCK CO
65	WYN US Equity	WYNDHAM WORLDWID
66	XRX US Equity	XEROX CORP

Furthermore, after the creation of the index, different equity portfolios are analysed against the proposed thresholds for filters based on the development and growth of the IBF in a country.

Data Analysis

The IBF industry has witnessed a tremendous growth in last 15 years with an average annual growth of 11% per year to reach a value of US$

Table 6.12 *Shari'a-compliant* based on existing methodology but *Shari'a* non-compliant based on new

Stocks Compliant Based on Existing methodology but Non-Compliant based on Interest income and expense		
1	AGN US Equity	ALLERGAN PLC
2	ALLE US Equity	ALLEGION PLC
3	CELG US Equity	CELGENE CORP
4	COG US Equity	CABOT OIL & GAS
5	CXO US Equity	CONCHO RESOURCES
6	EQT US Equity	EQT CORP
7	GILD US Equity	GILEAD SCIENCES
8	KLAC US Equity	KLA-TENCOR CORP
9	MDT US Equity	MEDTRONIC PLC
10	RAI US Equity	REYNOLDS AMERICA
11	STZ US Equity	CONSTELLAT1ON-A
12	VRSK US Equity	VERISK ANALYTI
13	VRSN US Equity	VERISIGN INC

Table 6.13 FTSE *Shari'a-compliant* based on both filters

Stocks Compliant on both		
1	ANTO LN Equity	ANTOFAGASTA PLC
2	BDEV LN Equity	BARRATT DEV
3	BLT LN Equity	BHP BILLITON PLC
4	CCH LN Equity	COCA-COLA HBC AG
5	CCL LN Equity	CARNIVAL PLC
6	CRH LN Equity	CRH PLC
7	KGF LN Equity	KINGFISHER PLC
8	MDC LN Equity	MEDICLINIC INTER
9	MNDI LN Equity	MONDI PLC
10	MRW LN Equity	WM MORRISON SUP
11	RMG LN Equity	ROYAL MAIL
12	RR/ LN Equity	ROLLS-ROYCE HOLD
13	SBRY LN Equity	SAINSBURY PLC
14	SGE LN Equity	SAGE GROUP
15	SMIN LN Equity	SMITHS GRP PLC
16	SN/ LN Equity	SMITH & NEPHEW
17	SSE LN Equity	SSE PLC
18	TSCO LN Equity	TESCO PLC
19	TUI LN Equity	TUI AG-DI
20	TW/ LN Equity	TAYLOR WIMPEY PL
21	WOS LN Equity	WOLSELEY PLC

Table 6.14 FTSE stocks non-compliant based on both filters

Stocks Non-Compllant based on both		
1	BARC LN Equity	BARCLAYS PLC
2	HSBA LN Equity	HSBC HOLDINGS PL
3	LLOY LN Equity	LLOYDS BANKING
4	OML LN Equity	OLD MUTUAL PLC
5	PFG LN Equity	PROVIDENT FIN
6	PRU LN Equity	PRUDENTIAL PLC
7	RBS LN Equity	ROYAL BK SCOTLAN
8	SDR LN Equity	SCHRODERS PLC
9	STAN LN Equity	STANDARD CHARTER
10	BATS LN Equity	BRIT AMER TOBACC
11	III LN Equity	3I GROUP PLC
12	POLY LN Equity	POLYMETAL
13	DLG LN Equity	DIRECT LINE INSU
14	GKN LN Equity	GKN PLC
15	GLEN LN Equity	GLENCORE PLC
16	LGEN LN Equity	LEGAL & GEN GRP
17	POLY LN Equity	POLYMETAL
18	RSA LN Equity	RSA INSURANCE G
19	SL/ LN Equity	STANDARD LIFE
20	WPP LN Equity	WPP PLC
21	WTB LN Equity	WHITBREAD PLC

4.9 trillion (IFDI 2024). It is projected to increase to US$ 7.5 trillion by 2028.

Figure 6.1 presents the IBF actual growth between 2017 and 2023, while forecasting growth until 2028. The past two decades have witnessed a substantial increase in the number of Islamic banks and financial institutions (IBFIs) in different parts of the world. Even if sizes of IBFIs are relatively small compared to international standards, it has to be noted that the prospects for growth and expansion in both Muslim and non-Muslim countries are strong. There are now more than one thousand institutions involved in IBFIs worldwide; these include commercial, investment and offshore banks, takaful companies, fund management companies and micro-finance organisations. When we conduct a univariate analysis based on the top five countries with the highest number of IBFIs, these are Indonesia, Iran, Saudi Arabia, Kuwait and UAE, with a total of 582 institutions among them. Thus, if we were to make a decision on the most developed IBF industry based on this one variable then we would

Table 6.15 FTSE information missing but *Shari'a-compliant*

Information on Interest missing and are compliant based on existing methodology		
1	AAL LN Equity	ANGLO AMER PLC
2	ABF LN Equity	ASSOC BRIT FOODS
3	AZN LN Equity	ASTRAZENECA PLC
4	BA/ LN Equity	BAE SYSTEMS PLC
5	BAB LN Equity	BABCOCK INTL GRP
6	BLND LN Equity	BRIT LAND CO PLC
7	BP/ LN Equity	BP PLC
8	BRBY LN Equity	BURBERRY GROUP
9	BT/A LN Equity	BT GROUP PLC
10	DC/ LN Equity	DIXONS CARPHONE
11	DCC LN Equity	DCC PLC
12	EZJ LN Equity	EASYJET PLC
13	FRES LN Equity	FRESNILLO PLC
14	GSK LN Equity	GLAXOSMITHKLINE
15	HIK LN Equity	HIKMA PHARMACEUT
16	IAG LN Equity	INTL CONS AIRLIN
17	ITV LN Equity	ITV PLC
18	JMAT LN Equity	JOHNSON MATTHEY
19	LAND LN Equity	LAND SECURITIES
20	MKS LN Equity	MARKS & SPENCER
21	PPB LN Equity	PADDY POWER BETF
22	PSN LN Equity	PERSIMMON
23	RB/ LN Equity	RECKITT BENCKISE
24	RDSA LN Equity	ROYAL DUTCH SH-A
25	RDSB LN Equity	ROYAL DUTCH SH-B
26	RIO LN Equity	RIO TINTO PLC
27	RRS LN Equity	RANDGOLD RES LTD
28	STJ LN Equity	ST JAMES'S PLACE
29	TPK LN Equity	TRAVIS PERKINS
30	ULVR LN Equity	UNILEVER PLC

conclude that Indonesia ranks number one, followed by Iran, Saudi Arabia and so on. However, when we look at the size of the Islamic financial assets (IFAs) in different countries, we find that Iran leads the Islamic financial assets with USD 1.7 trillion followed by Saudi Arabia with US$ 1.1 trillion, followed by Malaysia (US$682bn), UAE (US$371bn), Kuwait (US$371bn) and Indonesia (US$162bn). Hence, if we are to base our decision on this variable, then the ranking will change to Iran, Saudi Arabia, Malaysia, UAE and Kuwait, while Indonesia will not appear in the

Table 6.16 FTSE information missing and are non-compliant

Information on Interest missing and are non-compliant based on existing methodology		
1	ADM LN Equity	ADMIRAL GROUP
2	AHT LN Equity	ASHTEAD GROUP
3	AV/ LN Equity	AVIVA PLC
4	HL/ LN Equity	HARGREAVES LANSD
5	HMSO LN Equity	HAMMERSON PLC
6	IHG LN Equity	INTERCONTINENTAL
7	INF LN Equity	INFORMA PLC
8	INTU LN Equity	INTU PROPERTIES
9	ITRK LN Equity	INTERTEK GROUP
10	NXT LN Equity	NEXT PLC
11	REL LN Equity	RELX PLC
12	UU/ LN Equity	UNITED UTILITIES
13	VOD LN Equity	VODAFONE GROUP

Table 6.17 Non-compliant based on existing but compliant on new

Stocks Non-Compliant Based on Existing methodology but Compliant based on Interest income and expense		
1	BNZL LN Equity	BUNZL PLC
2	CNA LN Equity	CENTRICA PLC
3	CPG LN Equity	COMPASS GROUP
4	CPI LN Equity	CAPITA PLC
5	CRDA LN Equity	CRODA INTL
6	DGE LN Equity	DIAGEO PLC
7	EXPN LN Equity	EXPERIAN PLC
8	IMB LN Equity	IMPERIAL BRANDS
9	MCRO LN Equity	MICRO FOCUS INTL
10	MERL LN Equity	MERLIN
11	SHP LN Equity	SHIRE PLC
12	SKY LN Equity	SKY PLC
13	SVT LN Equity	SEVERN TRENT

Table 6.18 *Shari'a-compliant* based on existing but non-compliant based on new

Stocks Compliant Based on Existing methodology but Non- Compliant based on Interest income and expense		
1	LSE LN Equity	LONDON STOCK EX
2	WPG LN Equity	WORLDPAY GRP
3	LSE LN Equity	LONDON STOCK EX
4	NG/ LN Equity	NATIONAL GRID PL
5	WPG LN Equity	WORLDPAY GRP

top 5 countries. Figure 6.2 presents data on the top 14 countries in terms of IFA and the number of institutions involved in IBF, based on the data collected from secondary sources.

Further, when the research analysed the Islamic banking data, the results were again interesting as the ranking of the countries would be different based on the number of banks involved in Islamic finance (both fully-fledged and Islamic windows) than above. In terms of Islamic banking assets, Iran ranks number one as its banking assets of US$1.43 trillion are far more than others; Saudi Arabia follows Iran with US$794bn, followed by Malaysia, which has only US$275bn. It is also interesting to note that the Islamic finance industry in both the top two countries is highly dependent on the Islamic banking assets; 88% for Iran, 78% for Saudi Arabia, 79% for UAE, 84% for Qatar, while it is only 39% for Malaysia. This explains that Malaysia has a well-developed non-banking Islamic finance sector, which contributes heavily to the overall IFA's in the country. Figure 6.3 presents the top 10 countries in terms of Islamic banking assets and the number of Islamic banks involved in Islamic finance.

Figure 6.4 represents the contribution of takaful industry to the overall IBF industry; although the segment of IBF industry has not developed to its potential yet, there are countries that are leading and are ahead of others. Saudi Arabia, Iran and Malaysia collectively represent 84% of the

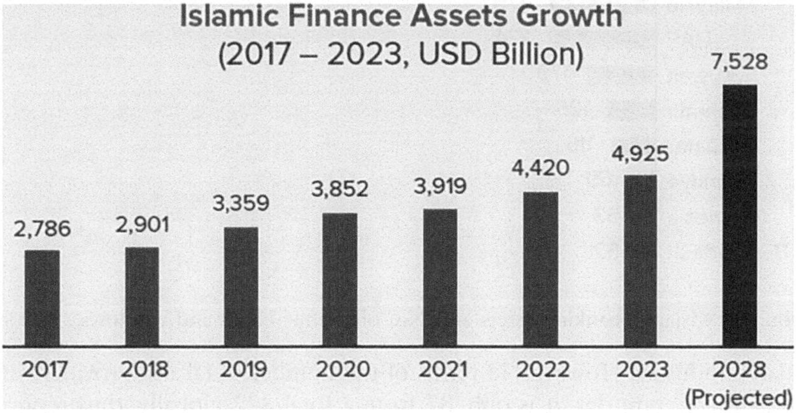

Fig. 6.1 Islamic finance growth projection (*Source* Islamic Finance Development Indicator Report 2024)

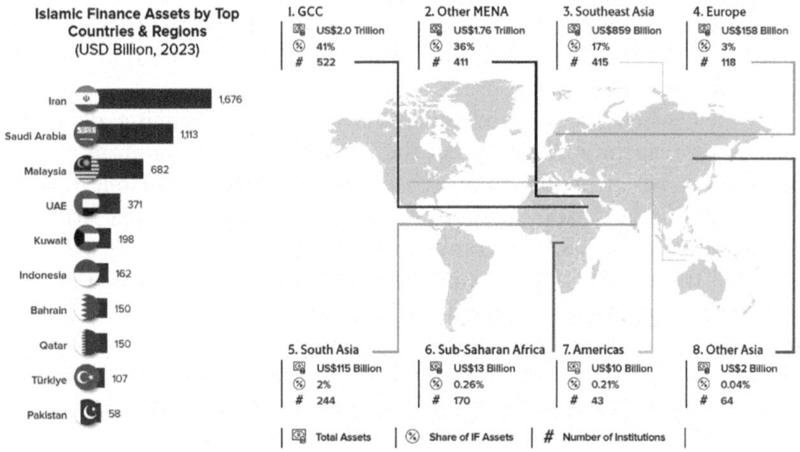

Fig. 6.2 Islamic financial assets and No. of IFIs (*Source* Islamic Finance Development Indicator Report 2024)

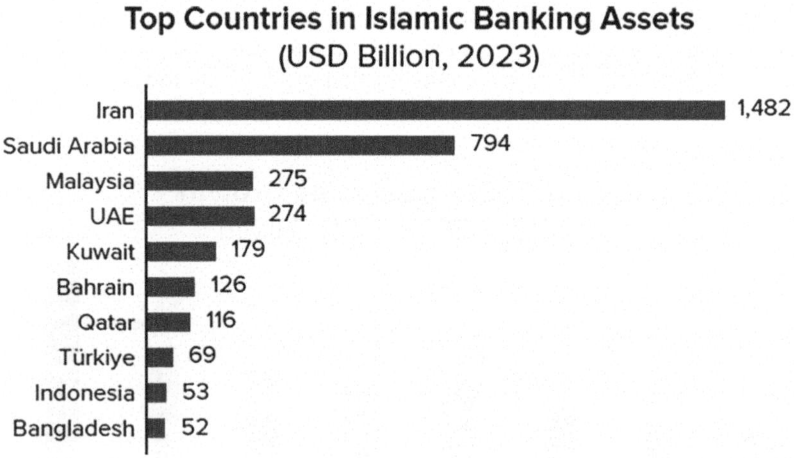

Fig. 6.3 Islamic banking assets and No. of Islamic banks and windows

takaful industry. However, in terms of the number of takaful providers in these three countries, it is only 87 from a total 322 globally, thus representing only 27% of the market share. Furthermore, Indonesia has the most number of takaful providers at 57, although it only has US$ 1.27bn takaful assets representing only 3% of the global takaful assets.

As discussed earlier, Malaysia has a well-developed IBF industry compared to other countries that are highly dependent on banking assets. This can be further evidenced by analysing Figs. 6.5 and 6.6, where Malaysia has the largest portion of sukuk outstanding with US$313bn, while the second country in terms of sukuk issuance is Saudi Arabia with only US$245bn. Iran, which for all other indicators was among the top five, is number seven in terms of the total sukuk amount outstanding. Hence, if we were to rank and analyse countries based only on sukuk issuance, then clearly Malaysia was the winner and other countries would have been lagging behind. The total sukuk outstanding is US$863bn, of which the top 10 countries represent 98%.

With regard to other non-quantitative variables like regulatory environment, this data has ranked countries according to the number of regulations issued for the Islamic finance industry and in general how supportive the regulatory system of a country is towards the development of IBF. For example, Malaysia has received 6 points as it has the best

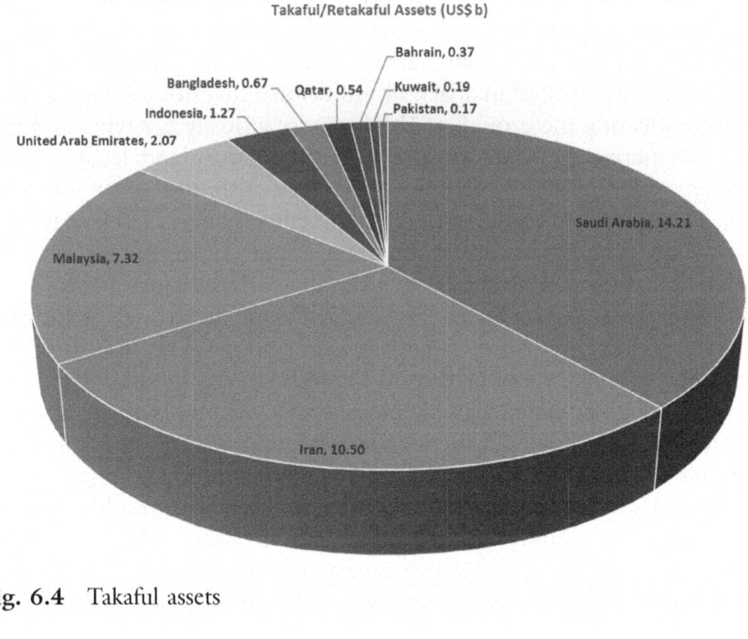

Fig. 6.4 Takaful assets

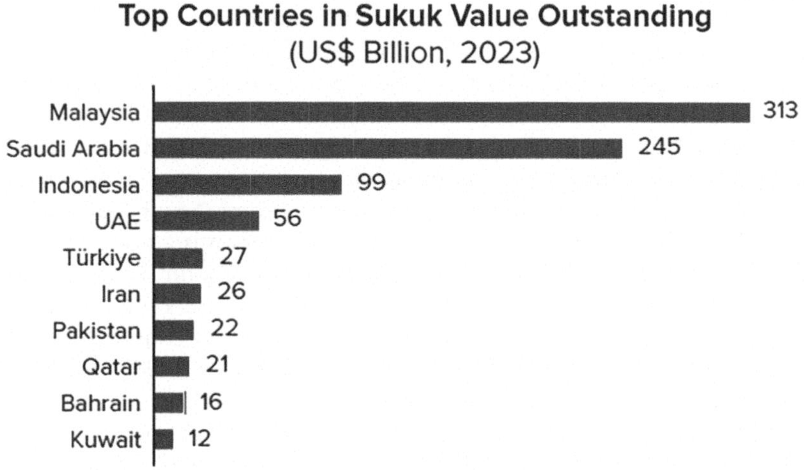

Fig. 6.5 Sukuk outstanding

and supportive regulatory system in IBF industry. On the other hand, Saudi Arabia has received 2 points as it is lagging behind in terms of issuing common regulation, such as Islamic banking regulation. However, it provides a uniform treatment across Islamic banks and conventional banks, which has resulted in a lack of uniformity, investor confidence and ultimately affecting the growth of IBF industry globally as a whole (IFDI, 2016). Furthermore, other indicators like regulatory and legal system, education and centralised *Shari'a* supervisory authority cover information if a country has these resources; for education, this refers to if a particular country has an education programme, university or institute offering IBF courses. Furthermore, a number of regulatory bodies have set-up centralised *Shari'a* supervisory, which assist the growth of the IBF industry and preparing rules, which should be adopted by all institutions and thereby assisting in the growth of the industry. As such, to date there are seven countries which have implemented a central *Shari'a* supervisory authority. This includes one of the latest entrants to Islamic finance, Oman, while Bahrain has also recently put this requirement in place.

After analysing all the variables above, it is difficult to reach a conclusion as to which country is leading or has the most developed IBF industry. The analysis above does suggest that Malaysia, Iran and Saudi Arabia have somewhat more developed IBF industries compared to

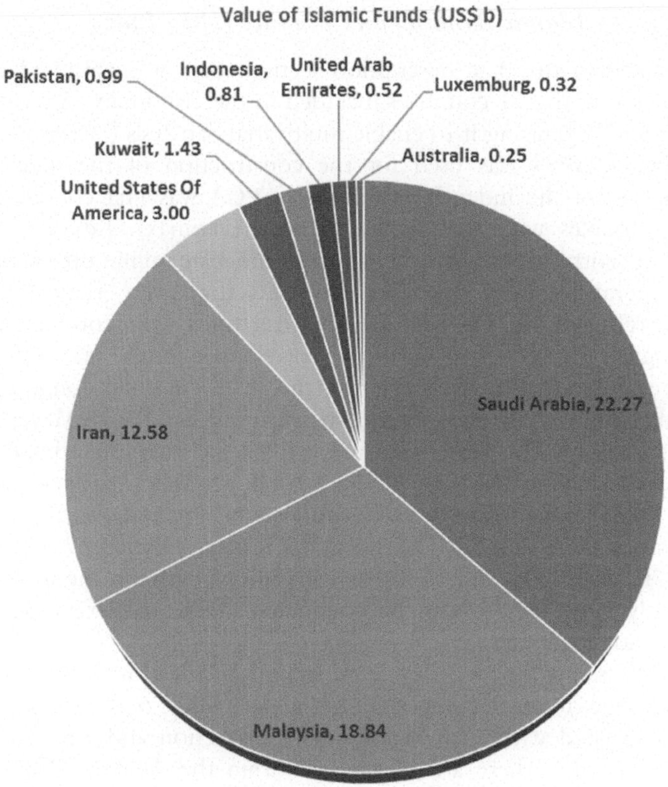

Fig. 6.6 Value of Islamic funds

others. However, we will not be able to state with authority based on all the different variables that a particular country is ranked number 1. Furthermore, it will not be possible to assess the development of other countries in a holistic manner. Hence, this is where the difference occurs in terms of analysing countries in isolation or undertaking a univariate analysis compared to using statistical techniques that assist in analysing the data in a collective manner objectively. As discussed in the Methodology and Data (Chapter 4), an IBF index needs to be created; this is outlined in the following sections.

Islamic Banking and Finance (IBF) Index

As discussed in the data description section, data was gathered on 25 variables for all the 41 countries included in the IBF index. After coding the data and organising it to enable multivariate analysis (factor analysing using PCA), SPSS was used for the construction of the index. The construction of the index is as follows: a PCA was first conducted on the 25 variables with orthogonal rotation (varimax). Resultantly, the anti-image correlations were lower than the bare minimum suggested in the literature for 7 variables and thus they were removed from the research analysis. The anti-image correlations were conducted after removing the 7 variables to ensure the correlations for the remaining variables are at acceptable levels. Hence, the PCA was then conducted on the remaining 18 variables which also enhanced the Kaiser-Meyer-Olkin (KMO) measure. The KMO measure verified the sampling adequacy for the research analysis, KMO = 0.732 ('good' according to Field, 2011), and all KMO values for the individual items were above the acceptable limit of 0.5 (Field, 2011). Bartlett's test of sphericity X^2 (153) = 1428.270, $p < 0.001$ indicated that correlations between the items were sufficiently large for PCA to be conducted. Table 6.19 represents the sampling adequacy test.

After the sampling adequacy tests, an initial analysis was run to obtain the eigenvalues for each component in the data. Table 6.20 lists the eigenvalues associated with each factor before extraction and after rotation. Before extraction, there are 18 factors within the data set. The eigenvalues associated with each factor represent the variance explained by that particular factor and the results also display the eigenvalues in terms of the percentage of variance explained (so, factor 1 explains 57.99% of the total variance) whereas the remaining factors explain only small amounts of variance. The first few factors (especially Factor 1) generally explains relatively large amount of variance whereas the subsequent factors explains only explain small amount of variance (Field, 2005).

Table 6.19 KMO and Bartlett's test

Kaiser-Meyer-Olkin measure of sampling adequacy		0.732
Bartlett's Test of Sphericity	Approx.	1428.270
	Df	153
	Sig.	0.000

The extraction method employed—PCA- generated 4 significant factors, which have eigenvalues more than 1 and explain 83.4% of the variance. The screen plot is slightly ambiguous and would justify retaining 4 and 5 components—Fig. 6.7. However, following the Kaiser's criteria also supported by the screen plot above, 4 components were retained. In the next part of the table (labelled Rotation Sums of Squared Loadings), the eigenvalues of the factors after rotation are displayed. Rotation has the effect of optimising the factor structure and one of the consequence for these data is that the relative importance of the four factors is equalised. Before rotation, factor 1 accounted for considerably more variance than the remaining three (57.99%, compared to 11.7%, 8% and 5.7%) while after extraction and rotation it accounts for only 30.687% of variance (compared to 24.050%, 15.795% and 12.906%, respectively). Based on the common variance explained by the underlying factors, weights of these factors have been calculated.

Table 6.20 After extraction four factors with eigenvalues > 1

Component	*Initial Eigenval ues*			*Rotation Sums of Squared Loadings*			
	Total	*Variance*	*e %*	*Total*	*Variance*	*e %*	*Weights*
1	10.438	57.990	57.990	5.524	30.687	30.687	36.78%
2	2.107	11.703	69.693	4.329	24.050	54.737	28.82%
3	1.443	8.017	77.710	2.843	15.795	70.532	18.93%
4	1.031	5.729	83.438	2.323	12.906	83.438	15.47%
5	0.951	5.282	88.720				
6	0.476	2.647	91.367				
7	0.455	2.525	93.893				
8	0.415	2.304	96.197				
9	0.301	1.674	97.870				
10	0.205	1.139	99.010				
11	0.079	0.439	99.448				
12	0.039	0.218	99.667				
13	0.036	0.199	99.866				
14	0.013	0.073	99.938				
15	0.007	0.037	99.975				
16	0.002	0.013	99.988				
17	0.002	0.011	100.000				
18	2.404E-05	0.000	100.000				

Extraction Method: Principal Component Analysis

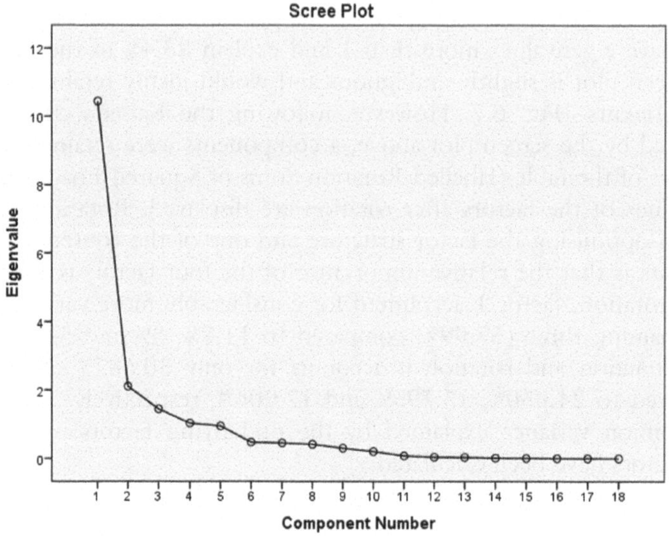

Fig. 6.7 Screen plot—PCA

Table 6.21 shows the factor loadings after rotation. The variables that cluster together on the same component suggest that component 1 represents the non-bank Islamic finance sector development, component 2 the number of Islamic financial institutions (non-bank), component 3 the banking sector development and component 4 as Islamic finance infrastructure development (see Fig. 6.8).

After identifying the four factors, the variance of the rotated component matrix was used after normalising to show how individual underlying variables are weighted in a particular factor. Once this was done, the IBF index was constructed using the below method.

$$\text{IBF Index}(C_i) = \sum_{i=1}^{4} \alpha i . Xi.$$

where α_i are the weights given to different factors Xi. More specifically, the IBF index can be written as: IBF Index $= 0.367.X_1 + 0.2882.X_2 + 0.1893.X_3 + 0.1547.X_4$, where X_1 is Non-Bank IF sector Development, X_2 is Number of IFIs (non-bank), X_3 is Banking sector development and X_4 is Islamic finance infrastructure development.

Table 6.21 Rotated component matrix[a]

	Component			
	1	*2*	*3*	*4*
No.of.IFIs.involved.in.IF		0.798	0.420	
Islamic.Financial.Assets	0.807	0.492		
Islamic.Banks.Windows		0.456	0.729	
Sukuk	0.836			
IF.Regulations.and.legal.infr Astructure			0.408	0.542
Central.Sharia.Supervisory. Board			0.873	
Education				0.549
Islamic.banking.assets	0.645	0.646		
Takaful.Retakaful.Assets	0.768	0.550		
No.of.Takaful.Retakaful.Operators		0.759		
Other.IFIAs	0.828			
No.of.other.IFIs		0.838		
Value.of.Islamic.Funds	0.884			
No.of.Islamic.Funds	0.861			
Regulatory.Environment			0.739	
No.of.IF.transactions				0.775
Value.of.IF.transactions	0.506			0.720
Liquid.Assets		0.770		

Extraction Method: Principal Component Analysis
Rotation Method: Varimax with Kaiser Normalization
[a]Rotation converged in 9 iterations

After the construction of the index, all the countries were ranked in terms of their growth and development in Islamic finance as shown in Fig. 6.9. The above IBF index has concluded the rankings based on all the variables under book and using the most objective methodology, as it does not rely on a single variable and even when we were able to estimate the relative importance of each of the underlying variables, they were employed together in a multivariate manner to derive the final ranking. As presented in Fig. 6.9, Saudi Arabia has appeared as number 1, followed by Malaysia and Iran. It is also clear from the above index that most of the developed countries are based in the GCC (Saudi Arabia, UAE, Kuwait, Qatar and Bahrain), Malaysia and Indonesia, as they have appeared among the top 10 countries according to the IBF index. As discussed earlier, it is important to note that on the basis of univariate analysis if a view was taken on the amount of sukuk issuance by a country then Iran would

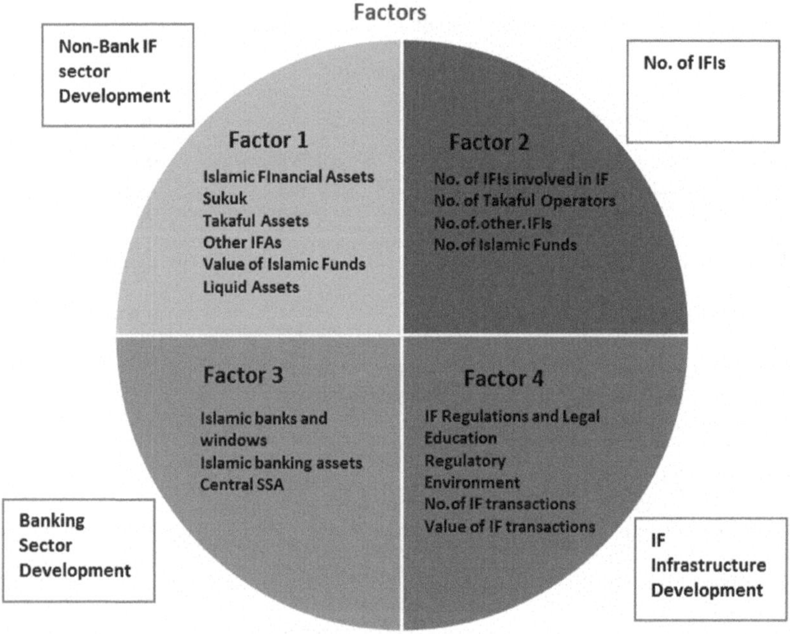

Fig. 6.8 Grouping of variables into four factors

have ranked number 8; however, based on a multivariate analysis Iran has appeared as number 3. Similarly, if an analysis was conducted on the basis of the value of Islamic banking assets, then Malaysia would have been ranked lower than Iran and close to UAE; however, according to the index, Malaysia is the second most developed Islamic finance market in the world. This clearly presents the difference between a univariate and multivariate analysis, collectively looking at different variables.

Pakistan and Turkey are two other countries that have appeared in the top 10. Both countries have taken IBF very seriously and made strides in developing IBF as an important alternative to a conventional financial system. As such, with a Muslim population of about 200 m, the government of Pakistan has undertaken a number of important initiatives in developing the IBF industry domestically as well as running awareness campaigns to ensure IBF is well understood by the masses, thereby enhancing the IBF growth potential in the country.

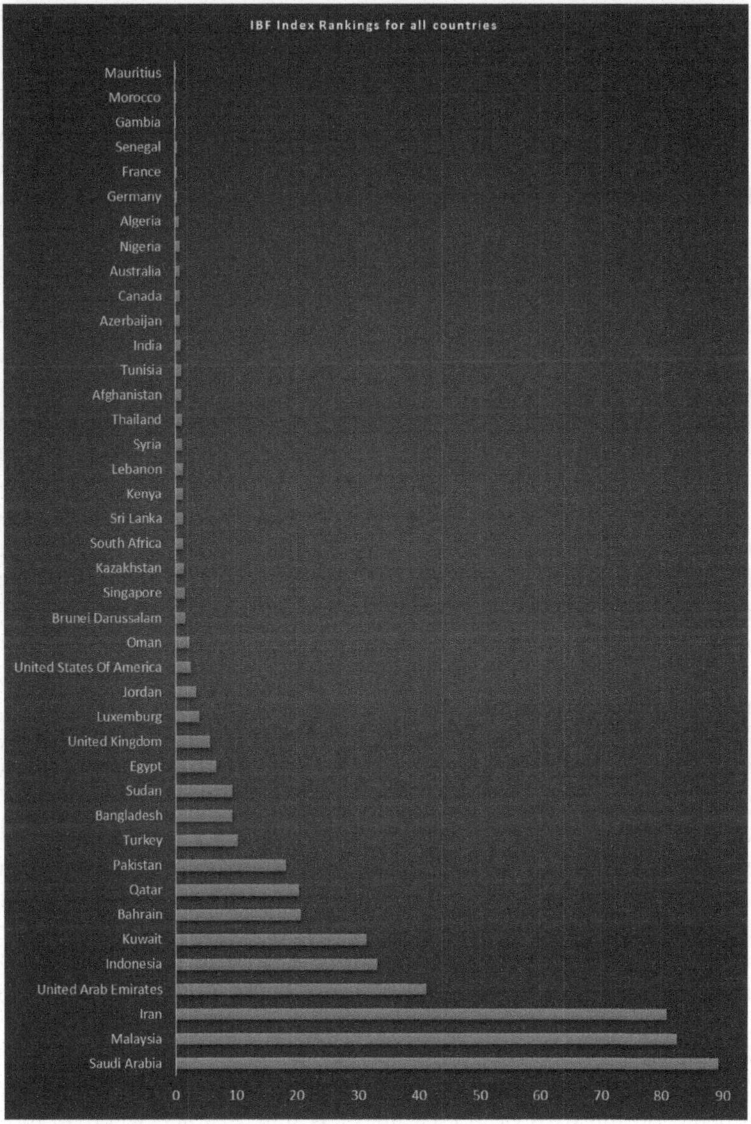

Fig. 6.9 Rankings of countries based on IBF index

Shari'a *Screening and Development in IBF*

After developing the IBF index, we return to our research purpose of how this index can be used to enhance the *Shari'a* screening methodologies. For the purpose of adjusting the *Shari'a* screening thresholds, we have divided the countries into five different groups based on the IBF index rankings and index values. The top 10 countries represent about 90% of the index values (see index groupings in Table 6.22). Concurrently, these countries represent about 94% of the global Islamic financial assets and as such more focus has been placed on these countries.

The Table 6.22 presents the five groups in which we have placed all the countries included in the IBF index. As discussed in the analysis of IBF index, Saudi Arabia, Malaysia and Iran have appeared the most developed Islamic financial markets based on their index values of 89.36, 82.56 and 81 and we have classified them as "Leaders" or "Advanced Countries". Among the three, Saudi Arabia and Malaysia have the most developed Islamic financial industry with well-developed infrastructures (particularly Malaysia), which has advanced and developed all the components of IBF industry (including the infrastructure). Furthermore, the share of Islamic banking assets of Saudi Arabia is 51% compared to the total banking assets, while it is 21% for Malaysia. For the purpose of our equity screening methodologies, we have not included Iran in the analysis as it attracts mixed views on the *Shari'a* authenticity of its practices.

After Iran, the next most developed Islamic finance market is UAE with an index value of almost half of Iran at 41; hence this is where we start our second group. Other countries in this group are Indonesia (33), Kuwait (31), Bahrain (21), Qatar (20) and Pakistan (18). These countries are grouped together as "Developed Countries". These countries are not the leaders in IBF but have developed strong domestic Islamic financial markets. The share of Islamic banking assets compared to the total overall banking assets in these countries are as follows: Kuwait—45%, Bahrain—29.3%, Qatar—26%, UAE—22%, Indonesia—3.7% and Pakistan—12%. The above countries also represent about 90% of the global Islamic banking assets.

As mentioned above, the grouping of these countries has been conducted on the basis of index values. As stated earlier, when an index value for a country drops by almost a half then it has been moved to the next group. For example; the value of Iran as the last country in "Leaders" group is 81, while the next country after it is UAE with an index value

Table 6.22 Index grouping based on the development in the IBF industry[1]

Advanced countries (leaders)	*Index values > 41 < 90*	*Developed countries*	*Index values > 18 < 42*	*Developing countries*	*Index values > 2 < 11*	*Emerging markets*	*Index values > 1 < 2*	*Least developed countries*	*Index values < 1*
Saudi Arabia	89.36	United Arab Emirates	41.17	Turkey	10.38	Brunei Darussalam	1.72	India	0.96
Malaysia	82.56	Indonesia	33.11	Bangladesh	9.50	Singapore	1.57	Azerbaijan	0.81
Iran	81.00	Kuwait	31.37	Sudan	9.46	Kazakhstan	1.37	Canada	0.80
		Bahrain	20.67	Egypt	6.78	South Africa	1.32	Australia	0.76
		Qatar	20.41	United Kingdom	5.74	Sri Lanka	1.31	Nigeria	0.74
		Pakistan	18.26	Luxemburg	3.98	Kenya	1.29	Algeria	0.72
				Jordan	3.51	Lebanon	1.25	Germany	0.41
				USA	2.62	Syria	1.15	France	0.40
				Oman	2.29	Thailand	1.15	Senegal	0.36
						Afghanistan	1.02	Gambia	0.29
						Tunisia	1.00	Morocco	0.28
								Mauritius	0.23

[1] Author's own compilation.

almost half of Iran. Hence, UAE has been placed into the next group. Similarly, the last value in the "Developed Countries" group is Pakistan at 18 and the next country is Turkey with almost half the index value of Pakistan at 10; hence, it has been placed in the third group, "Developing Countries", which has an index value between 10 and 2. The countries with a value between 2 and 1 have been placed in the fourth group as "Emerging Countries", while countries with index values less than 1 have been placed in the last and fifth group as "Least Developed Countries". The last three groups have 32 countries, with 9 countries in "Developing Countries", 11 in "Emerging Markets" and 12 in the "Least Developed Countries" group.

For the purpose of proposing enhancements to screening thresholds, only the countries in the first two groups have been selected; "Leaders" and "Developed Countries". The countries in these two groups happen to be based in the GCC and Far East, which is in line with the expectations. As stated above countries in these two groups have well-developed domestic Islamic banking and finance industry and hence Shari'a compliance treatment for companies domiciled in these countries should be more conservative compared to countries in the other three groups where Islamic finance development is rather limited. Furthermore, between the two groups of countries based on the index values; Islamic finance has developed more in the "Leaders" compared to the "Developed Countries" group. As a result Shari'a screening thresholds for organisations in the "Leaders" group should be more conservative than organisations in the "Developed Countries" group.

Further, it is concluded from the univariate as well as the multivariate analysis that countries in other groups still need to develop the domestic Islamic banking and finance industry and hence have not been considered for the purpose of this research. However, it would be worthwhile to undertake the analysis for these countries on a regular basis to see if a particular country's local IBF sector has grown sufficiently to be moved to the "Developed Countries" group. Hence, we propose that for the 32 countries in the last group, the screening thresholds should remain the same as practiced under the current methodologies that are interest-based debt to market capitalisation of up to 33%.

Proposed New Screening Thresholds

As discussed above and in the literature review in Chapter 3, the thresholds for *Shari'a* screening methodologies vary across different methodologies. However, since we are using stocks from DJIMI, we shall use the DJIMI *Shari'a* screening methodology, while for other stocks selected from the stock exchanges of different countries, AAOIFI methodology is used. The difference between the two screens in terms of thresholds is that DJIMI tolerates up to 33% *Shari'a* non-compliant debt while AAOIFI would only restrict to 30%. Yet, for the purpose of our research, it will not make any difference as the thresholds we propose are lower than 30%.

As stated above, with regard to nine countries in the two groups, in consultation with the Shari'a scholars and industry experts, we propose using a 25% threshold for the countries in the "Developed Countries", while further lower thresholds of 20% for the "Leaders". The proposed 25% threshold is based on the recommendations of *Shari'a* scholars and other experts obtained through the interviews process analysed in Chapter 5. The scholars based their opinion on the hadith narrated by Ibn Abbas where he recommend that people reduce the proportion of what they bequeath by will to the fourth (of the whole legacy), for Allah's Apostle (SAW) said, "One-third, yet even one third is too much".

Developed Countries

The developed countries' group includes UAE, Kuwait, Bahrain, Qatar, Indonesia and Pakistan. Since a major focus has been on GCC, Malaysia and Indonesia, and as there were no stocks from Pakistan in DJIMI, it was excluded from research. With regard to the other countries from GCC (apart from Oman), there are 63 *Shari'a-compliant* stocks from these five countries in GCC and 46 *Shari'a-compliant* stocks from Indonesia. Among the stocks of GCC, there are 15 Islamic banks, which are completely *Shari'a* compliant. Other companies are from real estate, Islamic insurance and telecommunications, medical and industrial sectors. It is interesting to note that about 11 companies have clearly stated that all their financial dealings are in line with *Shari'a* (a majority of these companies are from Kuwait), while other companies use a mix of both Islamic and conventional financing. Companies that use both conventional and Islamic financing make the *Shari'a* screening process a bit more sensitive and detailed. Hence, there is a need to have access to the detailed data to ensure that screening is undertaken in the best manner. Furthermore, this also shows that countries in these IBF-developed countries have already started using *Shari'a-compliant* financing for their operations.

Through this research, we propose that stocks of these countries should be screened at lower thresholds, compared to those in countries where Islamic finance has not developed as much. Hence, as based on the recommendation of *Shari'a* scholars, the book used a 25% threshold for stocks in these countries. The research then applied financial screening to this portfolio; it was interesting to note that only seven stocks were deemed to be *Shari'a* non-compliant, while the remaining 56 stocks were classified *Shari'a* compliant. Hence, reducing the financial thresholds from the existing 33% to 25% will not make a significant difference to the *Shari'a-compliant* portfolio in these countries. Table 6.23 shows the *Shari'a-compliant* portfolio based on 25% thresholds.

Further, as stock from Bahrain and UAE are not well represented in DJIMI, we selected all the stocks on the exchanges of Bahrain (46), Abu Dhabi (68) and Dubai (60) and applied AAOIFI *Shari'a* screening methodology. The *Shari'a-compliant* portfolios based on 30% screening thresholds were as follows: Bahrain (17), Abu Dhabi (24) and Dubai (35); this means that more than half of the stocks listed on these stock markets are *Shari'a* non-compliant. When we closely analysed the screened portfolios, it was intriguing to note that all the *Shari'a* non-compliant stocks listed on Bahrain stock exchange were into *Shari'a* non-compliant businesses and hence screened out based on the business screen. Simultaneously, there were 14 stocks from the Abu Dhabi stock exchange that are involved in *Shari'a* non-compliant business and 6 stocks from Dubai stock exchange.

Further, it is interesting to note that based on the proposed thresholds of 25% from the existing 33%, the *Shari'a-compliant* portfolio for Bahrain does not change at all, as is presented in Table 6.24. All 17 stocks remain *Shari'a-compliant* based on the 25% threshold. Furthermore, the *Shari'a-compliant* portfolio for Abu Dhabi reduces by only four stocks to 20, while for Dubai it reduces by only 2. The remaining *Shari'a-compliant* portfolios are presented in Tables 6.25 and 6.26. In total, the effect of reducing the thresholds for these countries based on the *Shari'a-compliant* stocks is losing 7 stocks. To summarise, the difference in portfolio combination between the *Shari'a-compliant* stocks listed on DJIMI for GCC and stocks listed on the exchanges of these three countries based on the newly proposed thresholds is only 13 stocks. This

Table 6.23 GCC *Shari'a-compliant* stocks based on 25% thresholds

	Ticker	*Short Name*		*Ticker*	*Short Name*
1	AACT OM Equity	AL-ANWAR CERAMIC	29	KRE KK Equity	KUWAIT REAL EST
2	ABYAAR KK Equity	ABYAAR REAL EAST	30	LOGISTIC KK Equity	KGL LOGISTICS CO
3	AHCS QD Equity	AAMAL CO	31	MABANEE KK Equity	MABANEE CO SAKC
4	AJMANBAN UH Equity	AJMAN BANK PJSC	32	MARK QD Equity	MASRAFAL RAYAN
5	ALAFCO KK Equity	AVIATION LEASE A	33	MHAS OM Equity	AL MAHA PETROLEU
6	ALBH BI Equity	ALUMINIUM BAHRAI	34	NICBM KK Equity	NATIONAL INDUST
7	ALMADINA KK Equity	AL MADINA FOR FI	35	OCOI OM Equity	OMAN CEMENT CO
8	ALOLA KK Equity	FIRST INVESTMENT	36	OFMI OM Equity	OMAN FLOUR MILLS
9	ALTIJARI KK Equity	COMMERCIAL REAL	37	OOMS OM Equity	OMAN OIL MARKET
10	ARMX UH Equity	ARAMEX PJSC	38	OOREDOO KK Equity	NATIONAL MOBILE
11	AWJ KK Equity	AWJ HOLDING CO K	39	ORCI OM Equity	OMAN REFRESHMENT
12	BARKA BI Equity	ALBARAKA BANKING	40	ORDS OM Equity	OOREDOO
13	BKNZ OM Equity	BANK NIZWA	41	OTEL OM Equity	OMAN TELECOMMUNI
14	BOUBYAN KK Equity	BOUBYAN BANK K.S	42	PSCS OM Equity	PORT SERVICE CRP
15	BPCC KK Equity	BOUBYAN PETROCH	43	QEWS QD Equity	QATAR ELECTRICIT
16	BRES QD Equity	BARWA REAL ESTAT	44	QFLS QD Equity	QATAR FUEL QSC
17	DFM UH Equity	DUBAI FINANCIAL	45	QIBK QD Equity	QATAR ISLAMIC BA
18	DIB UH Equity	DUBAI ISLAMIC	46	QIIK QD Equity	QATAR INTERNATIO
19	EKTTITAB KK Equity	EKTTITAB HOLDING	47	QNCD QD Equity	QATAR NATIONAL
20	ERES QD Equity	EZDAN HOLDING GR	48	RCCI OM Equity	RAYSUT CEMENT CO
21	ERESCO KK Equity	AL-ENMA'A REAL E	49	SALAM BI Equity	AL-SALAM BANK
22	FOOD KK Equity	KUWAIT FOOD CO	50	SENERGY KK Equity	AL SAFAT ENERGY
23	GFH BI Equity	GFH FINANCIAL GR	51	SOKOUK KK Equity	SOKOUK HOLDING C
24	HITSTELE KK Equity	HITS TELECOM HOL	52	SOMS OM Equity	SHELL OMAN MARKE
25	IKARUS KK Equity	IKARUS PETROLEUM	53	VFQS QD Equity	VODAFONE QATAR
26	IQCD QD Equity	INDUSTRIES QATAR	54	VOES OM Equity	VOLTAMP ENERGY S
27	KFIN KK Equity	KUWAIT FINANCE	55	YIACO KK Equity	YIACO MEDICAL CO
28	KIB KK Equity	KUWAIT INTERNATI	56	ZAIN KK Equity	MOBILE TELECOMMU

Table 6.24 Bahrain *Shari'a-compliant* stocks

	Ticket	*Name*
1	ALBH BI Equity	ALUMINIUM BAHRAI
2	BANADER BI Equity	BANADER HOTELS
3	BARKA BI Equity	ALBARAKA BANKING
4	BHOTEL BI Equity	GULF HOTEL GROUP
5	BISB BI Equity	BAHRAIN ISLAMIC
6	CPARK BI Equity	BAHRAIN CAR PARK
7	ESTERAD BI Equity	ESTERAD INVESTME
8	GFH BI Equity	GFH FINANCIAL GR
9	INOVEST BI Equity	INOVEST CO BSC
10	ITHMR BI Equity	ITHMAAR BANK BSC
11	KHCB BI Equity	KHALEEJI COMMERC
12	NHOTEL BI Equity	NATL HOTELS CO
13	POLTRY BI Equity	DELMON POULTRY
14	SALAM BI Equity	AL-SALAM BANK
15	SEEF BI Equity	SEEF PROPERTIES
16	TAIB BI Equity	TAIB BANK -$
17	TAKAFUL BI Equity	TAKAFUL INTL CO

difference is not significant in terms of portfolio construction and hence lower thresholds can be used for the companies in these countries.

With regard to Indonesia, there are 46 stocks listed on DJIMI and as such are *Shari'a-compliant* based on the existing screening methodology. However, when we apply the proposed financial screening thresholds of 25% to the same portfolio, the remaining *Shari'a-compliant* portfolio reduces to 40, hence a loss of only 6 stocks. The remaining *Shari'a-compliant* portfolio is presented in Table 6.27.

To conclude, for the developing countries group it is interesting to note that the loss of stocks from moving the thresholds from 30 and 33% to 25% is only 20 stocks from five countries (86% of the stocks are same). Hence, it will not make much difference to the portfolio combinations if we move to a more conservative financial ratio threshold of 25% for these countries.

Leaders (Advanced Countries)

The "Leaders" group includes Saudi Arabia, Malaysia and Iran; however, as explained above, for the purpose of this research we shall only consider

Table 6.25 Abu Dhabi *Shari'a-compliant* portfolio

	Ticker	*Short Name (Based on 30%)*		*Ticker*	*Short Name (Based on 25%)*
1	1 UAE UH Equity	NBAD ONESHARE MS	1	1 UAE UH Equity	NBAD ONESHARE MS
2	ADIB UH Equity	ABU DHABI ISLAMI	2	ADIB UH Equity	ABU DHABI ISLAMI
3	ADNIC UH Equity	ABU DHABI NATL	3	ADNIC UH Equity	ABU DHABI NATL
4	ADSB UH Equity	ABU DHABI SHIP B	4	ADSB UH Equity	ABU DHABI SHIP B
5	AFNIC UH Equity	AL FUJAIRAH NATI	5	AGTHIA UH Equity	AGTHIA GROUP PJS
6	AGTHIA UH Equity	AGTHIA GROUP PJS	6	ALAIN UH Equity	AL AIN AHLIA INS
7	ALAIN UH Equity	AL AIN AHLIA INS	7	ASMAK UH Equity	INTL FISH FARMIN
8	ASMAK UH Equity	INTL FISH FARMIN	8	ESHRAQ UH Equity	ESHRAQ PROPERTIE
9	ESHRAQ UH Equity	ESHRAQ PROPERTIE	9	ETISALAT UH Equity	ETISALAT
10	ETISALAT UH Equity	ETISALAT	10	GCIC UH Equity	AXA GREEN CRESCE
11	GCIC UH Equity	AXA GREEN CRESCE	11	GMPC UH Equity	GULF MEDICAL PRO
12	GMPC UH Equity	GULF MEDICAL PRO	12	MANAZEL UH Equity	MANAZEL REAL EST
13	MANAZEL UH Equity	MANAZEL REAL EST	13	NBS UH Equity	SHARJAH ISLAMIC
14	METHAQ UH Equity	METHAQ TAKAFUL I	14	NCTH UH Equity	NATL CORP TOU HO
15	NBS UH Equity	SHARJAH ISLAMIC	15	OEIHC UH Equity	OMAN & EMIR(E)50
16	NCTH UH Equity	NATL CORPTOU HO	16	RAKCC UH Equity	RAS AL KHAIMAH C
17	NMDC UH Equity	NATL MARINE DRED	17	RAPCO UH Equity	RAS AL KHAIMA
18	OEIHC UH Equity	OMAN & EMIR(E)50	18	SG UH Equity	SHARJAH GROUP
19	QIC UH Equity	UMM AL QAIWAIN G	19	UCC UH Equity	UNION CEMENT CO
20	RAKCC UH Equity	RAS AL KHAIMAH C	20	WATANIA UH Equity	NATIONAL TAKAFUL
21	RAPCO UH Equity	RAS AL KHAIMA			
22	SG UH Equity	SHARJAH GROUP			
23	UCC UH Equity	UNION CEMENT CO			
24	WATANIA UH Equity	NATIONAL TAKAFUL			

Table 6.26 Dubai stocks *Shari'a-compliant* based on 25% thresholds

	Ticker	*Short Name*		*Ticker*	*Short Name*
1	AGLTY UH Equity	AGILITY	1	AGLTY UH Equity	AGILITY
2	AJMANBAN UH Equity	AJMAN BANK PJSC	2	AJMANBAN UH Equity	AJMAN BANK PJSC
3	ALFIRDOU UH Equity	AL FIRDOUS HOLDI	3	ALFIRDOU UH Equity	AL FIRDOUS HOLDI
4	ALMADINA UH Equity	AL MADINA FOR FI	4	ALMADINA UH Equity	AL MADINA FOR FI
5	ALRAMZ UH Equity	AL RAMZ CORPORAT	5	ALRAMZ UH Equity	AL RAMZ CORPORAT
6	ALSAFWA UH Equity	AL SAFWA ISLAMIC	6	ALSAFWA UH Equity	AL SAFWA ISLAMIC
7	AMAN UH Equity	DUBAI ISLAMIC IN	7	ALSALAMK UH Equity	AL SALAM GROUP H
8	AMLAK UH Equity	AMLAK FINANCE	8	AMAN UH Equity	DUBAI ISLAMIC IN
9	ARMX UH Equity	ARAMEX PJSC	9	AMLAK UH Equity	AMLAK FINANCE
10	ARTC UH Equity	ARABTEC HOLDING	10	ARMX UH Equity	ARAMEX PJSC
11	ASCANA UH Equity	ARABIAN SCANDINA	11	ASNIC UH Equity	AL SAGR NATIONAL
12	ASNIC UH Equity	AL SAGR NATIONAL	12	DARTAKAF UH Equity	TAKAFUL HOUSE
13	DARTAKAF UH Equity	TAKAFUL HOUSE	13	DFM UH Equity	DUBAI FINANCIAL
14	DFM UH Equity	DUBAI FINANCIAL	14	DIB UH Equity	DUBAI ISLAMIC
15	DIB UH Equity	DUBAI ISLAMIC	15	DRC UH Equity	DUBAI REFRESHMEN
16	DRC UH Equity	DUBAI REFRESHMEN	16	DU UH Equity	EMIRATES INTEGRA
17	DU UH Equity	EMIRATES INTEGRA	17	EIB UH Equity	EMIRATES ISLAMIC
18	EIB UH Equity	EMIRATES ISLAMIC	18	EKTTITAB UH Equity	EKTTITAB HOLDING
19	EKTTITAB UH Equity	EKTTITAB HOLDING	19	EMAAR UH Equity	EMAAR PROP PJSC

	Ticker	*Short Name*		*Ticker*	*Short Name*
20	EMAAR UH Equity	EMAAR PROP PJSC	20	EMAARMLS UH Equity	EMAAR MALLS PJSC
21	EMAARMLS UH Equity	EMAAR MALLS PJSC	21	ERC UH Equity	EMIRATES REFRESH
22	ERC UH Equity	EMIRATES REFRESH	22	GFH UH Equity	GFH FINANCIAL GR
23	GFH UH Equity	GFH FINANCIAL GR	23	GULFA UH Equity	GULFA MINERAL WA
24	GULFA UH Equity	GULFA MINERAL WA	24	HITSTELE UH Equity	HITS TELECOM HOL
25	HITSTELE UH Equity	HITS TELECOM HOL	25	MAZAYA UH Equity	AL-MAZAYA HLDG
26	MAZAYA UH Equity	AL-MAZAYA HLDG	26	NGI UH Equity	NATIONAL GENERAL
27	NGI UH Equity	NATIONAL GENERAL	27	SALAMA UH Equity	ISLAMIC ARAB INS
28	SALAMA UH Equity	ISLAMIC ARAB INS	28	SALAMBAH UH Equity	AL-SALAM BANK
29	SALAMBAH UH Equity	AL-SALAM BANK	29	SHUAA UH Equity	SHUAA CAPITAL
30	SHUAA UH Equity	SHUAA CAPITAL	30	TAKAFULE UH Equity	TAKAFUL EMARATI
31	TAKAFULE UH Equity	TAKAFUL EMARATI	31	UAETF UH Equity	UAETF -A
32	UAETF UH Equity	UAETF -A	32	UFC UH Equity	UNITED FOODS CO
33	UFC UH Equity	UNITED FOODS CO	33	UNIKAI UH Equity	UNITED KAIPARA D
34	UNIKAI UH Equity	UNITED KAIPARA D			
35	ALSALAMK UH Equity	AL SALAM GROUP H			

Table 6.27 DJIMI- Indonesia *Shari'a-compliant* stocks based on 25% thresholds

	Short Name		*Short Name*
1	ACE HARDWARE	21	KALBE FARMA
2	AKR CORPORINDO	22	LIPPO CIKARANG
3	ALAM SUTERA REAL	23	MALINDO FEEDMILL
4	ARWANA CITRAMULI	24	MATAHARI PUTRA P
5	ASTRA AGRO LEST	25	MITRA ADIPERKASA
6	BAYAN RESOURCES	26	MNC LAND TBK PT
7	BUMI SERPONG	27	MODERN INTL
8	BUMITAMA AGRI LT	28	PERUSAHAAN GAS N
9	CHAROEN POK INDO	29	PP LONDON SUMATR
10	ERAJAYA SWASEMBA	30	SEMEN INDONESIA
11	HANSON INTERNATI	31	SENTUL CITY TBK
12	HARUM ENERGY	32	SIGMAGOLD INTI P
13	HERO SUPERMARKET	33	SUGIH ENERGY
14	HOLCIM INDONESIA	34	TAMBANG BATUBARA
15	INDO TAMBANGRAYA	35	TELEKOMUNIKASI
16	INDOCEMENT TUNGG	36	TEMPO SCAN PACIF
17	INDOFOOD CBP SUK	37	TRADA MARITIME
18	INOVISI INFRA	38	ULTRAJAYA MILK
19	INTILAND DEVELOP	39	UNILEVER IND TBK
20	JAYA REAL PROPER	40	VALE INDONESIA T

stocks from Saudi Arabia and Malaysia. Hence, we selected all the Malaysian stocks from DJIMI; however, as there are no stocks from Saudi Arabia in DJIMI, for the purpose of this research, we selected all the 175 stocks listed on the Saudi Arabian Tadawul exchange. After selecting the stocks, we applied the AAOIFI screening methodology, which resulted in a list of 79 *Shari'a-compliant* stocks as presented in Table 6.28. The remaining 96 stocks have been deemed *Shari'a* non-compliant and hence not available for *Shari'a-compliant* investments; 19 have been screened out based on the business screen as they were involved in *Shari'a* non-compliant activities, while the remaining 77 did not fulfil the financial screening threshold of AAOIFI. It is striking to note that 55% of the stocks listed on the most developed IBF market are *Shari'a* non-compliant. Additionally, it makes the need for a push from the government and regulators even more vital if they are to develop a strong IBF market globally.

Table 6.28 Tadawul stocks after *Shari'a* screening based on AAOIFI

	Ticker	*Short Name*		*Ticker*	*Short Name*
1	ABDICO AB Equity	AL-BAHA DEVELOPM	41	KEC AB Equity	KNOWLEDGE ECONOM
2	ADCO AB Equity	ARRIYADH DEVELOP	42	MCDCO AB Equity	MAKKAH CONSTRUCT
3	AHFCO AB Equity	FITAIHI HOLDING	43	MEDGULF AB Equity	MEDITERRANEAN &
4	ALALAMIY AB Equity	AL ALAMIYA COOPE	44	MEH AB Equity	MIDDLE EAST HEAL
5	ALANDALU AB Equity	ALANDALUS PROPER	45	MOUWASAT AB Equity	MOUWASAT MEDICAL
6	ALBI AB Equity	BANK ALBILAD	46	NGCO AB Equity	NATIONAL GYPSUM
7	ALHAMMAD AB Equity	AL HAMMADI DEVEL	47	NGIC AB Equity	NATIONAL GAS & I
8	ALINMA AB Equity	ALINMA BANK	48	NMMCC AB Equity	MAADANIYAH
9	ALINMATO AB Equity	ALINMA TOKIO MAR	49	QAACO AB Equity	AL QASSIM AGRICU
10	ALMARAI AB Equity	ALMARAI CO	50	QACCO AB Equity	QASSIM CEMENT
11	ALTAYYAR AB Equity	AL TAYYAR TRAVEL	51	REDSEA AB Equity	RED SEA HOUSING
12	ANAAM AB Equity	ANAAM INTERNATIO	52	RJHI AB Equity	AL RAJHI BANK
13	AOTHAIM AB Equity	ABDULLAH AL OTHA	53	SABBT AB Equity	SABB TAKAFUL
14	APPC AB Equity	ADVANCED PETROCH	54	SABIC AB Equity	SABIC
15	ARCCI AB Equity	AL RAJHI TAKAFUL	55	SACCO AB Equity	SAUDI CEMENT
16	ARCCO AB Equity	ARABIAN CEMENT	56	SADAFCO AB Equity	SADAFCO
17	ASACO AB Equity	ASH-SHARQIYAH DE	57	SAFCO AB Equity	SAUDI ARABIAN FE
18	ASLAK AB Equity	UNITED WIRE FACT	58	SALAMA AB Equity	SALAMA COOPERATI
19	ATC AB Equity	ALAHLI TAKAFUL C	59	SANAD AB Equity	SANAD COOPERATIV
20	BCI AB Equity	BASIC CHEMICAL I	60	SCH AB Equity	SAUDI CO FOR HAR
21	BISACO AB Equity	BISHAH AGRICULTU	61	SFICO AB Equity	SAUDI FISHERIES

(continued)

Table 6.28 (continued)

	Ticker	*Short Name*		*Ticker*	*Short Name*
22	BJAZ AB Equity	BANK AL-JAZIRA	62	SGS AB Equity	SAUDI GROUND SER
23	CARE AB Equity	NATIONAL MEDICAL	63	SIDC AB Equity	SIDC
24	CATERING AB Equity	SAUDI AIRLINES C	64	SIECO AB Equity	SAUDI INDUS EXPO
25	CITYC AB Equity	CITY CEMENT CO	65	SLTCO AB Equity	SAUDI TRANSPORT
26	DALLAH AB Equity	DALLAH HEALTHCAR	66	SOCCO AB Equity	SOUTHERN PROVINC
27	DUR AB Equity	DUR HOSPITALITY	67	SPIMACO AB Equity	SAUDI PHARMACEUT
28	EACCO AB Equity	EASTERN CEMENT	68	STC AB Equity	SAUDI TELECOM CO
29	EAT AB Equity	ETIHAD ATHEEB TE	69	SVCP AB Equity	SAUDI VITRIFIED
30	EXTRA AB Equity	UNITED ELECTRONI	70	TAPRCO AB Equity	TIHAMA
31	FIPCO AB Equity	FILING & PACKING	71	TECO AB Equity	SHAMS
32	FPCO AB Equity	WAFRAH FOR INDUS	72	THIMAR AB Equity	THIMAR
33	GIZACO AB Equity	JAZAN DEVELOPMEN	73	TIRECO AB Equity	TAIBA HOLDING C
34	HB AB Equity	HALWANI BROS CO	74	WEQAYA AB Equity	WEQAYA FOR TAKAF
35	HCC AB Equity	HAIL CEMENT	75	YACCO AB Equity	YAMAMA CEMENT CO
36	HERFY AB Equity	HERFY FOOD SERVI	76	YAMAMAH AB Equity	AL YAMAMAH STEEL
37	JADCO AB Equity	AL JOUF	77	YANSAB AB Equity	YANBU NATIONAL P
38	JARIR AB Equity	JARIR MARKETING	78	YNCCO AB Equity	YANBU CEMENT CO
39	JAZTAKAF AB Equity	ALJAZIRA TAKAFUL	79	ZOUJAJ AB Equity	NATIONAL CO/THE
40	JOMAR AB Equity	JABAL OMAR DEVEL			

When we applied the revised financial screening thresholds of 20% to these 79 stocks from Saudi Arabia, it was interesting to note that 86% of these stocks (68 stocks) were deemed *Shari'a*-compliant, as presented in Table 6.29.

This means that if the screening thresholds for Saudi Arabia are reduced to 20% from the existing 30–33% then the investible portfolio will reduce by only 9 stocks, which is not significant. However, in terms of the benefit to the IBF, if these 9 stocks wish to remain in the *Shari'a-compliant* portfolio, then they will need to convert their existing conventional liabilities to *Shari'a* compliant, thereby indirectly contributing to the growth of the IBF industry. Similarly, DJIMI has 76 *Shari'a-compliant* stocks from Malaysia; when we apply the revised *Shari'a* screening filters of 20%, only 21 stocks fall out of the *Shari'a-compliant* portfolio as presented in Table 6.30.

To conclude, through the creation of an IBF index in this research, it is re-affirmed that IBF industry has developed in a number of countries compared to some others. The IBF developed markets include countries in GCC, Far East (Malaysia and Indonesia), Pakistan and Iran. It was interesting to note that the *Shari'a-compliant* portfolio combination for samples selected did not change much when we applied the revised *Shari'a* screening thresholds of 25% and 20%, respectively. For example, only 20 stocks reduced for developed countries group while 30 stocks from the leaders group, which further support the case of enhancing the screening thresholds. This will be a step in the right direction in aligning the *Shari'a-compliant* equities more with *Shari'a* and thereby a step in removing the *Shari'a* non-compliant activities completely from the *Shari'a-compliant* portfolios. Furthermore, it will also push the local companies to borrow and lend in a *Shari'a-compliant* manner and thereby increasing the size of IBF and assisting in the overall development.

Table 6.29 *Shari'a-compliant* stocks based on 20% thresholds

	Ticker	*Short Name*		*Ticker*	*Short Name*
1	ABDICO AB Equity	AL-BAHA DEVELOPM	36	KEC AB Equity	KNOWLEDGE ECONOM
2	ADCO AB Equity	ARRIYADH DEVELOP	37	MCDCO AB Equity	MAKKAH CONSTRUCT
3	AHFCO AB Equity	FITAIHI HOLDING	38	MEDGULF AB Equity	MEDITERRANEAN &
4	ALALAMIY AB Equity	AL ALAMIYA COOPE	39	MEH AB Equity	MIDDLE EAST HEAL
5	ALANDALU AB Equity	ALANDALUS PROPER	40	MOUWASAT AB Equity	MOUWASAT MEDICAL
6	ALBI AB Equity	BANK ALBILAD	41	NGIC AB Equity	NATIONAL GAS & I
7	ALHAMMAD AB Equity	AL HAMMADI DEVEL	42	NMMCC AB Equity	MAADANIYAH
8	ALINMA AB Equity	ALINMA BANK	43	QAACO AB Equity	AL QASSIM AGRICU
9	ALINMATO AB Equity	ALINMA TOKIO MAR	44	QACCO AB Equity	QASSIM CEMENT
10	ANAAM AB Equity	ANAAM INTERNATIO	45	RJHI AB Equity	AL RAJHI BANK
11	AOTHAIM AB Equity	ABDULLAH AL OTHA	46	SABBT AB Equity	SABB TAKAFUL
12	APPC AB Equity	ADVANCED PETROCH	47	SACCO AB Equity	SAUDI CEMENT
13	ARCCI AB Equity	AL RAJHI TAKAFUL	48	SADAFCO AB Equity	SADAFCO
14	ARCCO AB Equity	ARABIAN CEMENT	49	SAFCO AB Equity	SAUDI ARABIAN FE
15	ASACO AB Equity	ASH-SHARQIYAH DE	50	SALAMA AB Equity	SALAMA COOPERATI
16	ASLAK AB Equity	UNITED WIRE FACT	51	SANAD AB Equity	SANAD COOPERATIV
17	ATC AB Equity	ALAHLI TAKAFUL C	52	SCH AB Equity	SAUDI CO FOR HAR
18	BISACO AB Equity	BISHAH AGRICULTU	53	SFICO AB Equity	SAUDI FISHERIES
19	BJAZ AB Equity	BANK AL-JAZIRA	54	SGS AB Equity	SAUDI GROUND SER
20	CARE AB Equity	NATIONAL MEDICAL	55	SIECO AB Equity	SAUDI INDUS EXPO
21	CATERING AB Equity	SAUDI AIRLINES C	56	SLTCO AB Equity	SAUDI TRANSPORT

	Ticker	Short Name		Ticker	Short Name
22	CITYC AB Equity	CITY CEMENT CO	57	SOCCO AB Equity	SOUTHERN PROVINC
23	DALLAH AB Equity	DALLAH HEALTHCAR	58	STC AB Equity	SAUDI TELECOM CO
24	DUR AB Equity	DUR HOSPITALITY	59	SVCP AB Equity	SAUDI VITRIFIED
25	EACCO AB Equity	EASTERN CEMENT	60	TAPRCO AB Equity	TIHAMA
26	EXTRA AB Equity	UNITED ELECTRONI	61	TECO AB Equity	SHAMS
27	FIPCO AB Equity	FILING & PACKING	62	THIMAR AB Equity	THIMAR
28	FPCO AB Equity	WAFRAH FOR INDUS	63	TIRECO AB Equity	TAIBA HOLDING C
29	GIZACO AB Equity	JAZAN DEVELOPMEN	64	WEQAYA AB Equity	WEQAYA FOR TAKAF
30	HB AB Equity	HALWANI BROS CO	65	YACCO AB Equity	YAMAMA CEMENT CO
31	HERFY AB Equity	HERFY FOOD SERVI	66	YAMAMAH AB Equity	AL YAMAMAH STEEL
32	JADCO AB Equity	ALJOUF	67	YANSAB AB Equity	YANBU NATIONAL P
33	JARIR AB Equity	JARIR MARKETING	68	YNCCO AB Equity	YANBU CEMENT CO
34	JAZTAKAF AB Equity	ALJAZIRA TAKAFUL			
35	JOMAR AB Equity	JABAL OMAR DEVEL			

Table 6.30 Malaysian *Shari'a-compliant* stocks based on 20%

	Short Name	*Ticker*
1	AL-'AQAR REIT	AQAR MK Equity
2	AMWAY MALAYSIA H	AMW MK Equity
3	APM AUTOMOTIVE	APM MK Equity
4	AXIATA GROUP BER	AXIATA MK Equity
5	AXIS REAL ESTATE	AXRB MK Equity
6	BIMB HLDGS BHD	BIMB MK Equity
7	BUMI ARMADA BHD	BAB MK Equity
8	CAPITALAND MALAY	CMMT MK Equity
9	CB INDUSTRIAL	CBP MK Equity
10	COASTAL CONTRACT	COCO MK Equity
11	DAIBOCHI PLASTIC	DPP MK Equity
12	DIALOG GROUP BHD	DLG MK Equity
13	DIGI.COM BHD	DIGI MK Equity
14	DUTCH LADY MILK	DLM MK Equity
15	EKOVEST BHD	EKO MK Equity
16	FELDA GLOBAL VEN	FGV MK Equity
17	FRASER & NEAVE	FNH MK Equity
18	GAMUDA BHD	GAM MK Equity
19	GAS MALAYSIA BHD	GMB MK Equity
20	GLOBETRONICS TEC	GTB MK Equity
21	HAP SENG PLANTAT	HAPL MK Equity
22	HARTALEGA HLDGS	HART MK Equity
23	HIBISCS	HIBI MK Equity
24	IHH HEALTHCARE B	IHH MK Equity
25	JOBSTREET CORP B	JOBS MK Equity
26	KOSSAN RUBBER IN	KRI MK Equity
27	KPJ HEALTHCARE	KPJ MK Equity
28	KRETAM HOLDINGS	KHP MK Equity
29	KUALA LUMPUR KEP	KLK MK Equity
30	KUMPULAN EUROPLU	KEUR MK Equity
31	LAFARGE MALAYSIA	LMC MK Equity
32	MALAYSIA MARINE	MMHE MK Equity
33	MALAYSIAN BULK	MBC MK Equity
34	MAXIS BHD	MAXIS MK Equity
35	MY EG SERVICES	MYEG MK Equity
36	PARKSON RETAIL	PRA SP Equity
37	PCHEM	PCHEM MK Equity
38	PETRONAS DAGANGA	PETD MK Equity
39	PETRONAS GAS BHD	PTG MK Equity

(continued)

Table 6.30 (continued)

	Short Name	*Ticker*
40	QL RESOURCES BHD	QLG MK Equity
41	SARAWAK PLANT	SPLB MK Equity
42	SEG INTERNATIONA	SYS MK Equity
43	SILVERLAKE AXIS	SILV SP Equity
44	STAR MEDIA GROUP	STAR MK Equity
45	TASEK CORP BHD	TC MK Equity
46	TDM BHD	TDM MK Equity
47	TEBRAU TEGUH BHD	TEB MK Equity
48	TH PLANTATIONS	THP MK Equity
49	TIME DOTCOM BHD	TDC MK Equity
50	TOP GLOVE CORP B	TOPG MK Equity
51	TOWER REIT	TRET MK Equity
52	UEM SUNRISE BHD	UEMS MK Equity
53	UNITED MALACCA	UMR MK Equity
54	UNITED PLANTATN	UPL MK Equity
55	ZHULIAN CORP BHD	ZHCB MK Equity

6.4 Conclusion

As analysed from the available literature and confirmed from the interviews with *Shari'a* scholars, the existing practices of screening stocks based on the source of *Shari'a* non-compliant items (like interest-based debt, receivables, cash and securities) are imprecise. However, that is the best manner to capture or estimate the dependence of a company on interest-based variables. This is because the current regulatory practices do not require companies to disclose information on interest income or interest expense on a regular basis. Companies may publish this information on an annual basis but through our analysis we have reached a conclusion that the data on these two items has been missing for most of the sample of stocks selected for this book. This cannot be due to an error in the portfolio selection as we selected about 600 top companies from the US and another 100 companies from the UK based on the market capitalisation. Having said that, screening stocks based on the actual interest income and interest expense are more preferred screening criteria as they directly capture the *Shari'a* non-compliant items. Hence, efforts should be made in ensuring that such data is made available by the companies on a regular basis and at the same time captured by the secondary source provider. Furthermore, it was interesting to observe through our research that some stocks that are *Shari'a-compliant* based on the existing methodology have failed the interest expense to total expenses screen. Hence, we also propose that for the time being, interest expense to total expenses and interest income to total revenue filters should be included in the screening criteria with a threshold similar to that of *Shari'a* non-compliant business revenue of up to 5%. This will ensure that companies remain *Shari'a-compliant* based on all criteria and thereby lower the *Shari'a* governance risk. On the other hand, due to the limitations in the data availability, having screens just based on interest income and interest expense is not practical currently. However, continuous efforts should be made to ensure that screening criteria move from the existing filters to these proposed more precise filters.

Further, Islamic banking and finance has developed in a number of countries; however, based on the IBF index, the clear leaders in IBF are countries in the GCC (excluding Oman), Malaysia, Indonesia and Pakistan based on the top two groups developed in this research. The underlying variables employed in development of the IBF index are with the aim of progressively reducing the financial screening thresholds used in the Shari'a screening methodologies. As such, in line with the aim of the book, all the variables assist in quantifying the development of Islamic finance industry in the country. Hence, other variables such as those based on SRI principles have not been considered as they are not part of financial screening thresholds. Nevertheless, the SRI principles are important to Islamic finance such that an underlying investment cannot be *Shari'a* compliant if it violates the socially responsible principles.

It is clear from the research that Islamic financing availability has enhanced in these countries and hence the equity screening thresholds in these nine countries should be different from other countries; that is, countries in the groups; developing countries, emerging markets and least developed countries. Through this research, we proposed that *Shari'a* screening thresholds for countries in the "developed countries" group should be reduced to 25% and for the "Leaders" to 20%. It was interesting to note that, based on the proposed thresholds, *Shari'a-compliant* portfolio for the former reduced by only 19 stocks out of a total of 185, a 11% decrease while for the latter group it reduced by 32 stocks out of 155; 19%. Hence, in line with the outcome of this research, it was concluded that financial screening thresholds for these two groups can be reduced from current practices of 33% to 25% and 20%. This will have a positive impact on the global IBF industry as well as the domestic IBF market. As companies will now be allowed to borrow up to a lower thresholds then they previously were, this will push these companies to borrow or lend more in a *Shari'a-compliant* manner and thus further develop the size and depth of the IBF industry. Additionally, this will be a positive step in enhancing the *Shari'a* screening methodologies and a move towards making the screening ratios more dynamic and a move away from static filters as the ultimate aim is not to tolerate even a very minimal amount of *Shari'a* non-compliant activity both in business and the capital structure of the company. Concurrently, regulators in the OIC or Muslim-majority countries should play a more proactive role in the development of IBF in domestic markets as well as globally. If regulators are able to do what Malaysia has been doing—that is, supporting the growth of IBF industry at the government level and make the local Islamic IBF market more attractive to the domestic companies—it will make the growth of IBF industry smoother.

References

Field, A. (2005). *Factor Analysis Using SPSS*. [Online] http://users.sussex.ac.uk/~andyf/factor.pdf. Accessed on 8 August 2017.

Field, A. (2011). *Discovering Statistics Using SPSS*. Sage Publications.

CHAPTER 7

Conclusion

7.1 Introduction

After as we approach the conclusion of this book, it is fitting to reflect on the journey we have undertaken together—a journey marked by exploration, discovery and a steadfast commitment to advancing the field of Shari'a-compliant equity investments. Throughout these pages, we have delved deep into the historical roots, current practices and future prospects of Shari'a screening methodologies, seeking to unravel the complexities that define this dynamic and evolving industry.

In this final chapter, we bring our collective efforts to fruition, distilling the key findings, insights and recommendations that have emerged from our exploration. From the historical context of Shari'a screening methodologies to the pressing need for enhanced practices aligned with the principles of Islamic finance, each aspect of our inquiry has contributed to a richer understanding of the challenges and opportunities that lie ahead.

As we embark on the concluding phase of our journey, let us take stock of the ground we have covered, the insights we have gained, and the pathways that lie before us. By synthesising the diverse perspectives, analyses and recommendations presented in this book, we aim to chart a course towards a more robust, equitable and ethically grounded approach to Shari'a-compliant equity investments.

R. Malik, *Shari'a Compliant Equity Investments*,
https://doi.org/10.1007/978-3-031-70822-0_7

7.2 Reflections and Findings of the Book

The book is structured to delve into two fundamental areas: Firstly, it aims to conduct an in-depth examination of the historical evolution of Shari'a screening methodologies. Secondly, it seeks to investigate avenues for enhancing these methodologies to better serve the IBF industry. The genesis of this endeavour stems from the remarkable growth observed in the Islamic equity investments industry, which stands as the largest investment class within the realm of Islamic asset management.

The book sets out to address prominent issues highlighted in existing literature pertaining to the underlying rationale behind the introduction of Shari'a screening methodologies. It also endeavours to explore avenues for their improvement, with the overarching goal of ensuring closer alignment with Shari'a principles while accommodating the evolving landscape of the IBF industry.

Central to the objectives of this book is the undertaking of semi-structured interviews. These interviews are intended to engage with the founding members of the Shari'a board of the DJIMI, renowned for establishing the first globally accepted Shari'a screening methodology back in 1999. Additionally, insights from other experts within the field will be sought. Through these interviews, the book aims to unearth the historical foundations of these methodologies, critically analyse prevailing practices and propose strategic enhancements. These enhancements are envisioned to steer these methodologies towards a more robust alignment with the overarching objectives of Shari'a in contemporary financial landscapes. Shari'a screening methodologies emerged as a stopgap measure to address the pressing need for Islamic financing services in an era of limited availability. Yet, as the IBF industry burgeoned over time, extending its reach across numerous countries, these screening methods remained largely static.

The genesis of this book lies in the desire to glean insights from esteemed scholars on issues highlighted in academic discourse and current practices. Since the advent of the DJIMI screening methodology, a plethora of similar frameworks have emerged from various quarters—index providers, regulatory bodies, Islamic financial institutions and technology providers. While these models bear resemblance to the DJIMI approach, they incorporate subtle yet significant modifications. Of utmost importance, however, is their endorsement by Shari'a boards, cementing their status as Shari'a-compliant.

The adoption of diverse screening methodologies inevitably leads to divergent portfolio compositions, resulting in varied performance outcomes. Notably, while Shari'a proscribes interest income and payments, prevailing screening practices often focus on the source of funds rather than the actual interest transactions. This discrepancy has drawn criticism from scholars like McMillen (2013), who advocate for methodologies rooted in the precise assessment of interest values.

Moreover, static screening thresholds have come under scrutiny, with calls for their transformation into dynamic criteria that mirror the fluid dynamics of the IBF landscape across different jurisdictions. These proposed revisions aim to bolster the accuracy and relevance of screening methodologies, ensuring a closer alignment with Shari'a principles and the evolving tapestry of Islamic finance.

While numerous studies exist comparing the performance of Islamic stocks with conventional or other socially responsible investment (SRI) portfolios, scant attention has been paid in academic literature to the development and enhancement of underlying Shari'a screening methodologies. To address this gap and address criticisms detailed in Chapter 3, this book adopts a unique approach, employing both qualitative and quantitative analytical methods, drawing from both primary and secondary data sources. Notably, this book represents the first known attempt to utilise a mixed-methods approach with the specific aim of proposing enhancements to Shari'a screening methodologies.

The significance of this book lies in its detailed investigation of these issues, engaging directly with scholars who played pivotal roles in crafting these screening methodologies. By facilitating discourse and understanding the imperatives for improving existing practices, this work contributes substantially to expanding knowledge and enriching the literature surrounding Shari'a-compliant equity investments. This academic endeavour is particularly vital given the paucity of extensive research in this domain, despite the remarkable growth of the industry.

It is noteworthy that while criticisms of current practices abound, industry practitioners have not actively sought enhancements to screening methodologies. Instead, the discourse on this matter primarily unfolds between academics and Shari'a scholars. Thus, the findings of this book serve as a springboard for future studies in Shari'a-compliant equity investments, offering valuable insights for industry practitioners. Although the impetus for developing alternative screening methodologies may currently rest with the academic community, these findings provide a solid foundation for such endeavours and pave the way for future research in this field.

The overall scope of this book is delineated into two parts: a qualitative analysis and a quantitative exploration. The qualitative segment delves into the responses and perspectives of Shari'a scholars and other experts regarding the historical underpinnings of screening methodologies, prevailing practices, criticisms in the literature and potential avenues for development. Specifically, it aims to pivot towards a more conservative model characterised by zero tolerance for Shari'a non-compliant activities, while accommodating the evolving landscape of the IBF industry.

In contrast, the quantitative analysis leverages secondary data to complement the qualitative insights and undertake an examination of proposed enhancements to existing practices. This mixed-methods approach imbues the book with an exploratory nature, as it endeavours to unearth and dissect the challenges confronting screening methodologies and elucidate how proposed changes may augment existing practices.

The findings of this book are both intriguing and thought-provoking. It reveals that Shari'a screening methodologies were introduced as a necessity of the time, driven by a "rule of exception" mindset aimed at mitigating tribulations and alleviating hardship for a limited period. Prior to their introduction, Shari'a-sensitive investors faced significant limitations, as investing in companies involved in Shari'a non-compliant activities was prohibited. This restriction hindered access to a majority of stocks listed on conventional stock markets, thereby impeding potential investment opportunities.

Recognising this predicament, Shari'a scholars engaged in extensive discourse and eventually reached a consensus to introduce screening methodologies as an interim solution. While some scholars initially opposed this approach, many eventually acknowledged its necessity, deeming it the optimal solution given the prevailing circumstances. The aim was to continually revise screening thresholds as the Islamic banking and finance industry matured, ultimately achieving a state of zero tolerance for Shari'a non-compliance.

Moreover, the book underscores that waiting for an opportune moment would have left Shari'a-sensitive investors at a disadvantage, depriving them of access to the stock market and hindering their ability to capitalise on technological advancements and global investment opportunities. Thus, the book's findings shed light on the pragmatic evolution of

Shari'a screening methodologies and their instrumental role in facilitating access to the stock market for Shari'a-sensitive investors.

The book's findings shed light on several key issues surrounding Shari'a screening methodologies, providing valuable insights and recommendations for their refinement and evolution.

Firstly, the book identifies widespread disapproval among Shari'a scholars regarding the 5% revenue threshold for Shari'a non-compliant activities. In agreement with Khatkhatay and Nisar (2007), the book suggests eliminating this screen unless it can be demonstrated that such revenue is entirely random. For instance, companies like Costco, which generate revenue from various products including alcohol, tobacco and pork, should not be deemed Shari'a-compliant due to their involvement in non-compliant activities. Conversely, businesses with randomly occurring Shari'a non-compliant revenue may be considered, provided purification is performed.

Similarly, the book advocates for the removal of cash and receivables thresholds in screening methodologies, aligning with recommendations by BinMahfouz and Ahmed (2014) and Khatkhatay and Nisar (2007). It argues that the presence of cash and receivables does not define the nature of a company's business and therefore should not form part of screening criteria.

Moreover, the book highlights a shift in scholars' willingness to move towards more precise measures, such as interest income and expense, for screening methodologies. However, it acknowledges challenges associated with the availability of data for such metrics and advocates for ongoing efforts to ensure data availability and regular analysis to refine screening methodologies accordingly.

Furthermore, the book suggests standardising screening criteria to reduce inconsistencies and confusion among investors. It proposes establishing a Shari'a-compliant stock exchange or developing a globally accepted screening methodology endorsed by key Islamic finance institutions. This would enhance clarity and consistency in Shari'a-compliant investments, fostering confidence among investors.

Additionally, the book emphasises the importance of periodically reviewing and updating screening thresholds to reflect industry developments. It suggests tailoring thresholds based on the level of IBF industry development in different countries, as demonstrated through exploratory analyses. This approach aims to promote IBF industry growth while ensuring Shari'a compliance.

Overall, the book underscores the crucial role of regulators and policymakers in shaping the IBF industry, highlighting the need for proactive measures to foster its development and ensure Shari'a compliance. By addressing these issues and providing actionable recommendations, the book contributes significantly to advancing understanding and practice in Shari'a-compliant equity investments.

7.3 Policy Recommendations

Based on the insights gleaned from this book, several policy recommendations can be proposed to foster the development of the IBF industry and enhance the integration of Shari'a-compliant principles.

Firstly, regulators and government bodies in OIC or Muslim-majority countries should actively support the development and adoption of enhanced Shari'a screening methodologies. This includes aligning screening practices with global standards and encouraging a more conservative approach, as witnessed in Malaysia's recent reforms.

Secondly, governments can introduce tax incentives, similar to Pakistan's 2% tax rebate for fully Shari'a-compliant listed companies, to encourage businesses to adhere to Shari'a principles in both their operations and financial practices. Such incentives would promote the growth of the Islamic equity investments market and attract new investors.

Furthermore, rather than implementing drastic changes to screening thresholds, policymakers should advocate for a gradual reduction to allow companies time to adjust their financial structures. For example, reducing thresholds from 33 to 25% can be a sustainable step towards achieving higher levels of Shari'a compliance.

Moreover, policymakers should explore the implementation of an investment purification method, which removes tainted income from company earnings, regardless of profitability. This would mitigate concerns regarding impure income in Shari'a-compliant portfolios and provide clarity on dividend distribution.

Additionally, there is a need to incorporate social responsibility criteria within Shari'a screening methodologies to ensure portfolios align with ethical considerations. Policymakers can encourage the integration of globally accepted SRI principles, such as the United Nations Global Compact or Principles for Responsible Investments, into Shari'a-compliant investment practices.

Lastly, regulators, policymakers and government bodies should undertake initiatives to raise awareness among Shari'a-sensitive investors about the importance of SRI principles. Investment management companies should be encouraged to embed SRI principles within their Shari'a-compliant screening methodologies, thereby broadening the appeal of Islamic equity investments.

By implementing these policy recommendations, regulators and policymakers can facilitate the growth of the IBF industry while ensuring adherence to Shari'a principles and promoting socially responsible investment practices. This holistic approach will not only enhance the attractiveness of Islamic equity investments but also contribute to sustainable economic development in Muslim-majority countries.

7.4 Conclusion

In conclusion, this book represents a significant milestone in the ongoing evolution of Shari'a-compliant equity investments. Through a meticulous examination of historical antecedents, current industry practices and the invaluable insights of eminent Shari'a scholars and experts, it has shed light on the complexities and challenges facing the field while charting a course towards its future development.

However, it is essential to acknowledge the inherent limitations of this endeavour. While the book's focus on enhancing existing Shari'a screening methodologies provides a solid foundation, it may overlook practical considerations related to their implementation within investment strategies. Additionally, the reliance on the perspectives of supportive Shari'a scholars, while informative, may inadvertently introduce bias into the analysis, highlighting the need for a more comprehensive exploration of dissenting views.

Despite these challenges, the book's originality lies in its pioneering approach to proposing enhancements to Shari'a screening methodologies. By advocating for a more conservative model characterised by zero tolerance for Shari'a non-compliant activities, it offers a fresh perspective on an industry ripe for refinement and innovation.

Looking ahead, there are numerous avenues for future research and exploration. For instance, investigations into the practical feasibility of implementing different screening thresholds within investment portfolios could yield valuable insights for investment managers and policymakers alike. Furthermore, a deeper examination of dissenting perspectives on

Shari'a screening methodologies could enrich the discourse and foster a more inclusive approach to industry development.

Moreover, the integration of socially responsible investment (SRI) principles into Shari'a screening methodologies represents a promising area for exploration. By developing robust rating systems and offering diverse portfolio options, investors can navigate the financial landscape with greater confidence and integrity, aligning their investments with their ethical and religious beliefs.

In closing, this book serves as a catalyst for positive change and innovation in the Islamic finance sector. With steadfast dedication and a spirit of collaboration, the journey towards achieving zero tolerance for Shari'a non-compliant activities becomes not only conceivable but achievable. As the industry continues to evolve, the insights gleaned from this book will undoubtedly inform and inspire future research and practice, shaping the landscape of Islamic finance for generations to come.

References

BinMahfouz, S., & Ahmed, H. (2014). Shariah Investment Screening Criteria: A Critical Review. *Journal of King Abdulaziz University: Islamic Economics, 27*(1), 3–38.

Khatkhatay, M. H., & Nisar, S. (2007). *Shari'ah* Compliant Equity Investments: An Assessment of Current Screening Norms. *Islamic Economic Studies, 15*(1).

McMillen, M. (2013). *Islamic Finance and the Shari'ah.* Riverstone Publishing Group.

References

AAOIFI. (2004). Shariah Standard 21. *Financial Papers*. AAOIFI.

Abdullah, F., Hassan, T., & Mohamad, S. (2000). Investigation of Performance of Malaysian Islamic Unit Trust Funds: Comparison with Conventional Unit Trust Funds. *Journal of Managerial Finance, 3*(2), 142–153.

Abdullah, F., Hassan, T., & Mohamad, S. (2007). Investigation of Performance of Malaysian Islamic Unit Trust Funds: Comparison with Conventional Unit Trust Funds. *Managerial Finance*, *33*(2), 142–153.

Abiad, A., & Mody, A. (2003). *Financial Reform: What Shakes It? What Shapes It* (IMF Working Paper, WP/03/70).

Accounting and Auditing Organisation for Islamic Financial Institutions. (2010). *Shari'a Standards for Islamic Financial Institutions*. AAOIFI.

Adams, G., & Schvaneveldt, J. (1991). Obtaining Data: Documents of the Past. In G. Adams & J. Schvaneveldt (Eds.), *Understanding Research Methods* (2nd ed., pp. 291–314). Longman.

Ahmad, Abū Dāwūd, an-Nasā'ī, Ibn Mājah; Mishkāt al-Masābīh, 2818.

Ahmed, I. (2009). *Incorporating Socially Responsible Investing in Islamic Equity Investments*. Cass Business School, UK.

Ainley, M., Mashayekhi, A., Hicks, R., Rahman, A., & Ravalia, A. (2007). *Islamic Finance in the UK: Regulation and Challenges*. Financial Services Authority.

Akram, M., Rafique, M., & Alam, H. M. (2011). Prospects of Islamic Banking: Reflection from Pakistan. *Australian Journal of Business and Management Research, 1*(2), 125–134.

R. Malik, *Shari'a Compliant Equity Investments*,
https://doi.org/10.1007/978-3-031-70822-0

Al Amine, M. B. M. (2002). *Comments of Muhammad Al Bashir Muhammad Al Amine on Reviewing the Concept of Shares: Towards a Dynamic Legal*. Perspective by Faisal Ahmed Manjoo [online]. http://www.kantakji.com/media/163527/file521.pdf. Accessed on 14 December 2013.

Armstrong, J. S. (1967). Derivation of Theory by Means of Factor Analysis or Tom Swift and His Electric Factor Analysis Machine. *The American Statistician, 21*, 17–21.

Ashkar, A. A. F. (1995). *Towards an Islamic Stock Exchange in a Transitional Stage*. http://www.irti.org/English/Research/Documents/IES/140.pdf. Accessed on 14 December 2013.

BinMahfouz, S., & Ahmed, H. (2014). Shariah Investment Screening Criteria: A Critical Review. *Journal of King Abdulaziz University: Islamic Economics, 27*(1), 3–38.

BOE. (2013). *Financial System*. [Online]. http://www.bankofengland.co.uk/financialstability/Pages/financialsystem/default.aspx. Accessed on 05 October 2013.

Borhan, J. T., & Mohamad, M. T. (2009). Conducts of Partners in al- Sharikah al Mufawadah: An Analysis from Hanafi's Classical Sources presented at *District Level Economy Seminar* [Unpublished].

Brooks, J., & King, N. (2012, April 18–20). Qualitative Psychology in the Real World: The Utility of Template Analysis. *British Psychological Society Annual Conference*. London, UK (Unpublished). http://eprints.hud.ac.uk/13656/

Bryman, A., & Bell, E. (2007). *Business Research Methods* (Rev. ed.). Oxford University Press.

Bryman, A., & Bell, E. (2011). *Business Research Methods*. Oxford University Press.

Central Bank. (2013). *Islamic Finance in Europe*. Occassional Paper Series.

CFA Institute. (2012). *Equity and Fixed Income* (5th ed.). Pearson.

Charofas, D. M. (2005). *The Management of Equity Investments*. Elsevier.

Chorafas, D. N. (2005). Wealth Management. *Elsevier Monographs* (1st ed.). Elsevier.

Clarke, G., et al. (2015). *From the Stockholder to the Stakeholder*. [Online] https://arabesque.com/research/From_the_stockholder_to_the_stakeholder_web.pdf. Accessed on 02 September 2015.

Cognisant. (2012). *Sharia Stock Screening: A Fund Manager's Conundrum*.

Comrey, A. L., & Lee, H. B. (1992). *A First Course in Factor Analysis*. Erlbaum.

Crabtree, B. F., & Miller, W. L. (1999). Using Codes and Code Manuals: A Template Organizing Style of Interpretation. In B. F. Crabtree & W. L. Miller (Eds.), *Doing Qualitative Research* (2nd ed.). Sage.

Creane, G., Goyal, R., Mobarak, M., & Sab, R. (2004). *Financial Sector Development in the Middle East and North Africa* (IMF Working Paper WP/04/201).

Dar Al Istithmar. (2009). *A Universal Platform for Shari'a-Compliant Equity Screening*. Oxford Islamic Finance.

Dar, H., et al. (2011). *Islamic Finance Country Index* (Global Islamic Finance Report 2011). BMB Islamic.

Dar, H., et al. (2013). *Islamic Finance Country Index* (Global Islamic Finance Report 2013). Edbiz Consulting.

Dar, H., et al. (2016). *Islamic Finance Country Index* (Global Islamic Finance Report 2016). Edbiz Consulting.

Deetz, S. (1996). Describing Differences in Approaches to Organisation Science: Rethinking Burrell and Morgan and Their Legacy. *Organisation Science, 7*(2), 191–207.

Delorenzo, Y. (2000). Shariah Supervision of Islamic Mutual Funds. In *Proceedings of the Fourth Harvard University Forum on Islamic Finance*. Harvard University.

Dergis, U., & Marzban, S. (2008). Review and Analysis of Current Shariah-Compliant Equity Screening Practices. *International Journal of Islamic and Middle Eastern Finance and Management, 1*(4), 285–303.

Dergis, U., & Marzban, S. (2009). New Strategies and a New Paradigm for Shariah-Compliant Portfolio Optimization. *Journal of Banking & Finance, 33*(6), 1166.

Domegan, C., & Fleming, D. (2007). *Marketing Research in Ireland, Theory & Practise* (3rd ed.). Gill and Macmillan.

Dudley, N. (1998). Islamic Banks Aim for the Mainstream. *Euromoney, 349*, 113–116.

Dusuki, A. W. (2009). *Challenges of Realizing Maqasid Al Syariah (Objective Shariah) in Islamic Capital Market: Special Focus on Equity Based Sukuk.*

Dusuki, A. W., & Abdullah, N. I. (2007). Maqasid Al Shari'a and Corporate Social Responsibility. *The American Journal of Islamic Social Sciences, 24*(1), 25–45.

Dusuki, A. W., & Abdullah, I. (2014). *Fundamentals of Islamic Banking*. IBFIM.

ECB. (2013). *Islamic Finance in Europe* (Occasional Paper Series No.146).

El Diwany, T. (Eds.). (2010). *Islamic Banking and Finance: What Is It and What It Could Be.* 1st Ethical Charitable Trust.

Elfakhai, S., & Hassan, M. K. (2005). Performance of Islamic Mutual Funds. *Economic Research Forum, 12th Annual Conference*, 1–33.

Elgari, M. (1993). Towards an Islamic Stock Market. *Islamic Economic Studies, 1*(1).

Elgari, M. A. (2000). Purification of Islamic Equity Funds: Methodology and *Shari'a* Foundation. In *Proceedings of the Fourth Harvard University Forum on Islamic Finance.* Harvard University.

Elgari, M. A. (2002, December). Towards an Islamic Stock Market. *Islamic Economic Studies, 1*(1).

Eurosif. (2012). *European SRI Book 2012.* [Online] www.eurosif.org. Accessed on 17 August 2013.

Fabozzi, F., & Modigliani, F. (2009). *Capital Markets: Institutions and Instruments* (4th ed.). Pearson.

Fabrigar, L., Wegner, R., MacCallum, R., & Straham, E. (1999). Evaluating the Use of Exploratory Factor Analysis in Psychological Research. *Psychological Methods, 4*(3), 272–299.

FBR suggest Shariah-compliant criteria for companies. [Online] http://www.brecorder.com/market-data/stocks-a-bonds/0/117957/. Accessed on 30 December 2016.

Field, A. (2000). *Discovering Statistics Using SPSS for Windows.* Sage Publications Ltd.

Field, A. (2005). *Factor Analysis Using SPSS.* [Online] http://users.sussex.ac.uk/~andyf/factor.pdf. Accessed on 8 August 2017.

Field, A. (2009). *Discovering Statistics Using SPSS* (3rd ed.). Sage Publications Ltd.

Field, A. (2011). *Discovering Statistics Using SPSS.* Sage Publications.

Fleuriet, M. (2008). *Investment Banking Explained: An Insider's Guide to the Industry.* McGraw.Hill.

Forte, G., & Miglietta, F. (2007). *Islamic Mutual Funds as Faith-Based Funds in a Socially Responsible Context.* Bocconi University.

Forte, G., & Miglietta, F. (2011). A Comparison of Socially Responsible and Islamic Equity Investments. *Journal of Money, Investment and banking, 21.*

FTSE. (2008). *FTSE Shariah Global Equity Index Series.* [Online] http://www.ftse.com/chinese/Indices/FTSE_Shari'a_Global_Equity_Index_Series/Downloads/FTSE_Shari'a_Global_Equity_Index_Series_Factsheet.pdf. Accessed on 20 April 2014.

FTSE. (2014). *Rules for the FTSE Shariah Global Equity Index Series.* [Online] www.ftse.com/products/ftse_shariah_global_equity_index_series.pdf\. Accessed on 17 February 2014.

Gamaleldin, F. (2015). *Shariah-Compliant Stocks Screening and Purification* (MSc Dissertation). University of Liverpool.

Gelbard, E., & Leite, P. (1999). *Measuring Financial Development in Sub-Saharan Africa* (IMF Working Paper 99/105).

Global Islamic Finance Report (GIFR). (2023). Published by Cambridge Insitute of Islamic Finance. United Kingdom

Government Introduces 2pc tax Rebate for Shariah-Compliant Listed Firms. [Online]. https://www.thenews.com.pk/print/134093-Govt-introduces-2pc-tax-rebate-for-Shariah-compliant-listed-firms. Accessed on 15 August 2016.

Grais, W., & Pellegrini, M. (2006, November 1). *Corporate Governance and Shari'a Compliance in Institutions Offering Islamic Financial Services*. World Bank Policy Research Working Paper No. 4054.

Hansmann, H., Kraakman, R., & Squire, R. (2005). *The New Business Entities in Evolutionary Perspective, Rev. 5.*

Hasan, Z. (2007). *Comments on Mohsin s. Khan and Abbas Mirakhor, the Financial System and Monetary Policy in an Islamic Economy*. (International Islamic University of Malaysia Working Paper No. 3183). Retrieved June 24, 2013, from http://www.iefpedia.com/english/wp-content/uploads/2009/11/Comments-on-Mohsin-S.-Khan-and-Abbas-Mirakhor-The-Financial-System-and-Monetary-Policy-in-an-Islamic-Economy.pdf

Hasan, M. S. (2008). Stock Returns, Inflation and Interest Rates in the United Kingdom. *European Journal of Finance.*

Hassan, M. K., & Mahlknecht, M. (2011). *Islamic Capital Markets, Products and Strategies*. Wiley.

Hayat, U., & Malik, A. (2014). *Islamic Finance: Ethics, Concepts and Practice.* CFA Institute Research Foundation.

Hickson, C. R., & Turner, J. D. (2005). Corporation or Limited Liability Company. *Queens University Belfast.* [Online]. https://profjohnturner.files.wordpress.com/2011/11/corporation.pdf. Accessed on 15 October 2016.

Hickson, C. R., Turner, J. D., & Ye, Q. (2011). The Rate of Return on Equity Across Industrial Sectors on the British Stock Market, 1825–70. *The Economic History Review, 64*(4), 1218–1241. http://www.jstor.org/stable/41262528

Ho, S. F., Rahman, C., Yusuf, N. A. A., & Zaminor, N. H. M. (2011). Comparison of Quantitative *Shari'ah* Compliant Screening Methods. *ISRA International Journal of Islamic Finance, 3*(2), 91–110.

Ho, C., Abd Rahman, N., Yusuf, N., & Zamzamin, Z. (2014). Performance of Global Islamic Versus Conventional Share Indices: International Evidence. *Pacific-Basin Finance Journal, 28*, 110–121.

Htay, S. N. N., et al. (2013). Towards Standardisation of Shariah Screening Norms and Practices. *International Journal of Humanities and Social Sciences Invention, 2*(11), 23–30.

Hussein, K. (2004). Ethical Investment: Empirical Evidence from FTSE Islamic Index. *Islamic Economic Studies, 12*(1), 21–40.

Hutcheson, G., & Sofroniou, N. (1999). *The Multivariate Social Scientist: Introductory Statistics Using Generalized Linear Models*. Sage Publication.

Ibrahim, A. B. (2010). *Islamic Preference Shares: An Analysis in Light of the Principles of Mushārakah and Tanāzul.* Paper Presented at the International Conference on Islamic Banking & Finance: Cross Border Practices & Litigations. http://www.kantakji.com/fiqh/files/finance/m318.pdf

IFSB. (2011). *Financial Policy and Stability.* Constraints on Growth in Islamic Finance.

Iqbal, M., & Moyneu, P. (2005). *Thirty Years of Islamic Banking: History, Performance and Prospects.* Palgrave Macmillan.

Iqbal, Z. (1997). Islamic Financial Systems. *Finance & Development.*

Iqbal, Z. (1999). Financial Engineering in Islamic Finance. *Harvard University Forum on Islamic Finance*, 229–238.

Islamic Finance Gateway. (2013). *Islamic Funds Market Highlights: Q1-2013.* http://www.slideshare.net/Islamic_Finance/islamic-funds-may-2012-2

Islamic Financial Services Board Stability Report. (2023). Published by Islamic Finacial Services Board. Malaysia.

ISRA. (2012). *Islamic Financial System: Principles and Operations*. International *Shari'a*h Research Academy for Islamic Finance.

ISRA. (2015). *Shari'a Stocks, Islamic Capital Markets: Principles and Practices.* Chapter 13, Kuala Lumpur. International *Shari'a*h Research Academy for Islamic Finance.

Jaffer, S. (2004). *Islamic Asset Management: Forming the Future for Shari'a-Compliant Investment Strategies* (pp. 23–30). Euromoney Books.

Jamal, J., Hambali, N., & Hassani, M. A. (2010). Islamic Capital Market and Sharia Screening in Malaysia. *International Research Symposium in Service Management.*

Kahn, R. L., & Cannell, C. F. (1957). *The Dynamics of Interviewing; Theory, Technique, and Cases*. John Wiley & Sons.

Kaiser, H. F. (1960). The Application of Electronic Computers to Factor Analysis. *Educational and Psychological Measurement, 20*, 141–151.

Kaiser, H. F. (1974). An Index of Factorial Simplicity. *Psychometrika, 39*, 31–36.

Kamali, M. H. (2005). *Principles of Islamic Jurisprudence*. Pelanduk Publications.

Khan, F. (2010). How 'Islamic' Is Islamic Banking? *Journal of Economic Behavior and Organisation, 76*(2010), 805–820.

Khatkhatay, M. H., & Nisar, S. (2007). *Shari'a*h Compliant Equity Investments: An Assessment of Current Screening Norms. *Islamic Economic Studies, 15*(1).

King, N. (2004). Using Templates in the Thematic Analysis of Text. In C. Cassels & G. Symon (Eds.), *Essential Guide to Qualitative Methods in Organizational Research* (pp. 256–270). Sage.

King, R., & Levine, R. (1993). Finance and Growth: Schumpeter Might Be Right. *The Quarterly Journal of Economics, 108*(3), 717–737.

Krasicka, O., & Nowak, S. (2012). *What's in It for Me? A Primer on Differences Between Islamic and Conventional Finance in Malaysia* (IMF Working Paper 12/151). IMF. http://www.imf.org/external/pubs/ft/wp/2012/wp12151.pdf

Liaw, K. T. (2012). *The Business of Investment Banking* (3rd ed.). Wiley.

Marzban, S., & Donia, M. (2010). *Shariah-Compliant Equity Investments, Framework.* Harvard University Forum.

McMillen, M. (2013). *Islamic Finance and the Shari'ah*. Riverstone Publishing Group.
Miglietta, F., & Forte, G. (2011, April 22). A Comparison of Socially Responsible and Islamic Equity Investments. *Journal of Money, Investment and Banking*, (21). ISSN 1450-288X.
MSCI. (2011, April 22). *MSCI Islamic Index Series Methodology*. https://www.msci.com/eqb/methodology/meth_docs/MSCI_May11_IslamicMethod.pdf
Naughton, S., & Naughton, T. (2000). Religion, Ethics and Stock Trading: The Case of an Islamic Equities Market. *Journal of Business Ethics, 23*, 145–159.
Norman, T. (2006). *Islamic Investment Funds*. Euromoney Books.
Obaidullah, M. (2005). *Islamic Financial Services*. King Abdulaziz University.
Omar, M. A. (n.d.). *Equity Market Shari'a Stock Screening & Preference*. http://www.ues.ac.ir/files/takmili/islamic_econ./capital_market/equity.pdf
Renneboog, L., Horst, T. J., & Zhang, C. (2008a). Socially Responsible Investments: Institutional Aspects, Performance, and Investor Behaviour. *Journal of Banking and Finance, 32*, 1723–1742.
Renneboog, L., Horst, T. J., & Zhang, C. (2008b). The Price of Ethics and Stakeholder Governance: The Performance of Socially Responsible Mutual Funds. *Journal of Corporate Finance, 14*(3), 302–322.
Russell-IdealRatings Islamic Indexes. https://www.russell.com/documents/indexes/construction-methodology-global-indexes.pdf
Sarakhsi, S. (n.d.). Kitab al- Mabsut, Beirut: Dar al-Ma 'rifah.
Saunders, M., Lewis, P., & Thornhill, A. (2007). *Research Methods for Business Students* (4th ed.). Pearson Education Limited.
Securities Commission Malaysia. (2009). *Resolutions of the Securities Commission Malaysia Shariah Advisory Council*. Securities Commission.
Securities Commission Malaysia. (2014). *Shari'a-Compliant Securities on Bursa Malaysia as at 30 May 2014*. http://www.sc.com.my/post_archive/updated-list-of-shariah-compliant-securities-by-scs-shariah-advisory-council-12/
Securities Commission Malaysia. (n.d.). *Shari'a-Compliant Funds: Investing in a Diversified Portfolio of Shari'a-Compliant Instrument*. http://www.fimm.com.my/pdf/investor/articles/SC_Shari'a%20UT.pdf
Sengupta, B. (2012). *Sharia Stock Screening: A Fund Manager's Conundrum, Cognizant 20-20 Insights*.
Siddiqi, M. N. (2004). *Riba, Bank Interest and the Rationale of Its Prohibition*. Visiting Scholars Research Series No. 2, Islamic Research Training Institute, Islamic Development Bank.
Siddiqi, M. N. (2006). Islamic Banking and Finance in Theory and Practice: A Survey of State of the Art. *Islamic Economic Studies, 13*(2).
Siddiqui, R. (2007). Shari'ah Compliance, Performance, and Conversion: The Case of the Dow Jones Islamic Market Index^{SM}. *Chicago Journal of International Law, 7*(2), 495–519.

S&P Dow Jones Indices, Dow Jones Islamic Market Indices. [Online] http://www.djindexes.com/islamicmarket/. Accessed on 15 January 2014.

S&P Dow Jones Indices. (2012). *Methodology: Dow Jones Islamic Market GCC*. Retrieved June 27, 2013, from Index http://www.djindexes.com/mdsidx/downloads/meth_info/Dow_Jones_Islamic_Market_GCC_Index_Methodology.pdf

Tabachnick, B. G., & Fidell, L. S. (2001). *Using Multivariate Statistics*. Allyn and Bacon.

The Office of Research Integrity. http://ori.hhs.gov/education/products/sdsu/res_des1.htm. Accessed on 15 March 2016

Tryfos, P. (1997). *Methods of Business Analysis and Forecasting: Text and Cases*. John Wiley & Sons.

Usmani, T. (1998). *An introduction to Islamic Finance* (pp. 204–205). Idaratul Ma'arif.

Usmani, T. (2002). *An Introduction to Islamic Finance*. Arab and Islamic Law Series, Brill.

Wachtel, P., & Rousseau, P. L. (1995). Financial Intermediation and Economic Growth: A Historical Comparison of the US, UK and Canada. In M. Bordo & R. Sylla (Eds.), *Anglo-American Finance: Institutions and Markets in the Twentieth Century* (pp. 329–381). Irwin Professional Publishing.

Walsham, G. (1993). *Interpreting Information Systems in Organisations*. Wiley.

Wilson, R. (1997). Islamic Finance and Ethical Investment. *International Journal of Social Economics, 24*(11), 1324–1342.

Wilson, R. (2004). Screening Criteria for Islamic Equity Funds, Islamic Asset Management: Forming the Future for *Shari'a*-Compliant Investment Strategies. In S. Jaffer (Ed.), *Euromoney Institutional Investor*. PLC.

Yaquby, N. (2000). Trading in Equities: A *Shari'a* Perspective. In *Proceedings of the Fourth Harvard University Forum on Islamic Finance: Islamic Finance: The Task Ahead Cambridge, Massachusetts* (pp. 119–128). Center for Middle Eastern Studies, Harvard University

York, J. G., & De Colle, S. (2008). Why Wine Is Not Glue? The Unresolved Problem of Negative Screening in Socially Responsible Investing. *Journal of Business Ethics, 85*(1), 83–95.

Zaheer, K. *What Is Islamic and What Is Not?* http://www.khalidzaheer.com/essays/kzaheer/islamic%20shariah/what_is_islamic_and_what_is_not.html

Zaher, T. S., & Hassan, K. M. (2001). A Comparative Literature Survey of Islamic Finance and Banking. *Financial Markets, Institutions and Instruments, 10*(4), 155–199.

Zhuang, S., Shao, H., Guo, F., Trimble, R., Pearce, E., & Abmayr, S. M. (2009). Sns and Kirre, the Drosophila Orthologs of Nephrin and Neph1, Direct Adhesion, Fusion and Formation of a Slit Diaphragm-Like Structure in Insect Nephrocytes. *Development, 136*(14), 2335–2344.

Zuriyati, Z. A., Yusoff, M., & Azrae, A. N. (2009). Separate Legal Entity under Syariah Law and Its Application on Islamic Banking in Malaysia. *International Journal of Banking and Finance, 6*(2).

Index

A

AAOIFI, 42, 51, 54–56, 58, 61, 62, 64, 67–69, 195, 235, 236, 242, 243

B

Business screening, 49

D

Debt contract, 124, 134, 135, 137, 140
Debt-to-market cap, 124, 135
Dow Jones, 3
Dow Jones Islamic Market Index (DJIMI), 83, 85, 86, 88, 89, 95, 108, 109

E

Equity investments, 1, 2, 5–9, 11

F

Factor analysis, 109, 110, 114
Financial screening, 53, 55, 68

I

Interest-bearing Securities, 57
Interviews, 121, 175, 188, 189, 191
Islamic banking and finance (IBF), 1, 6, 9, 13, 14, 18, 24–26, 29
Islamic equity investments, 33, 34
Islamic finance, 13, 15, 17–20, 24, 29

L

Level of debt, 56
Liquidity ratio, 124, 135, 137, 141
Liquidity screen, 55, 56

M

Maqasid *Shari'a*, 124, 145, 148, 178, 179
Market capitalisation, 61, 62, 69
Musharaka, 43

R. Malik, *Shari'a Compliant Equity Investments*,
https://doi.org/10.1007/978-3-031-70822-0

N
Nasdaq, 195
Non-permissible income screen, 57

O
OIC Fiqh Academy, 38, 45

P
Purification, 46, 62

R
Research, 81–91, 94, 95, 97, 99, 102–104, 107, 109–117
Research methodology, 81, 82, 117

S
Shares, 35, 43, 44
Shari'a, 1–11, 15, 17–22, 24, 29, 30, 33–35, 37–46, 48–58, 61–76, 83, 85, 88, 92, 95–98, 100, 107, 117
Shari'a board, 83, 88
Shari'a-compliant, 1–11, 33, 41, 45, 46, 48, 49, 51–54, 56–59, 62, 64, 65, 67, 69–71, 76
Shari'a scholars, 83, 85–89, 92, 93, 95, 97–99
Shari'a screening, 1, 3–11, 81, 84–86, 88, 95–100, 109, 117
Socially Responsible Investment (SRI), 34, 65, 71–75
Standardisation, 65

T
Template analysis, 89, 90
Total assets, 69

The manufacturer's authorised representative in the EU is Springer Nature Customer Service Centre GmbH, Europaplatz 3, 69115 Heidelberg, Germany. If you have any concerns regarding our products, please contact ProductSafety@springernature.com

Printed and bound by CPI Group (UK) Ltd, Croydon, CR0 4YY

01/10/2026

02225953-0011